Narrating the Storm

Narrating the Storm:
Sociological Stories of Hurricane Katrina

Edited by

Danielle A. Hidalgo and Kristen Barber

Cambridge Scholars Publishing

Narrating the Storm: Sociological Stories of Hurricane Katrina, Edited by Danielle A. Hidalgo and Kristen Barber

This book first published 2007 by

Cambridge Scholars Publishing

15 Angerton Gardens, Newcastle, NE5 2JA, UK

British Library Cataloguing in Publication Data
A catalogue record for this book is available from the British Library

Copyright © 2007 by Danielle A. Hidalgo and Kristen Barber
and contributors

All rights for this book reserved. No part of this book may be reproduced, stored in a retrieval system, or transmitted, in any form or by any means, electronic, mechanical, photocopying, recording or otherwise, without the prior permission of the copyright owner.

ISBN (10): 1-84718-362-X, ISBN (13): 9781847183620

This book is dedicated to the people of the Gulf Coast whose lives were forever changed by Hurricane Katrina and its aftermath.

TABLE OF CONTENTS

List of Images x

Acknowledgements xi

Introduction: Storytelling Sociology
Danielle Antoinette Hidalgo 1

Part I:
Experiencing Race and Class In and Through Disaster

Filler Up Please: Coping With Racial Stigmas after Hurricane Katrina
Andrea Wilbon Hartman 10

How I Spent My Hurricane Vacation
Carl L. Bankston III 19

Cataclysm in New Orleans: Story of a Black Single Mother
Ruth S. Idakula 33

Volunteering on Galveston Island: How Poverty Shaped My Response to Hurricanes Katrina and Rita
Deanna Meyler 47

Subverting Social Vulnerabilities and Inequality in Disaster Survival
R. L. Stockard, Russell L. Stockard, Jr., and M. Belinda Tucker 62

Part II:
The Managed Self: Identities, Emotions, and the Treatment of the Hurricane "Other"

The Emotional Management of a Stranger: Negotiating Class Privilege and Masculine Academics as a Hurricane Katrina Evacuee
Kristen Barber 80

On Managing Spoiled Identity: The Escape from Hurricanes Katrina and Rita
Stan C. Weeber 92

Volunteer Voices: Making Sense of Our Trip to the Mississippi Gulf Coast After Katrina
Jeffrey T. Jackson and Kirsten A. Dellinger 106

Part III:
(Ir)Rationality as a Tool for Making Disaster-Related Decisions

Disaster and the Irrationality of "Rational" Bureaucracy: Daily Life and the Continuing Struggles in the Aftermath of Hurricane Katrina
Timothy J. Haney 130

My Aunt Po: Collective Memories Shaping Collective Responses
Sarah Stohlman 141

Using Simmel to Survive: The Blasé Attitude as a Disaster Reaction and Response
Jessica W. Pardee 153

The First Major U.S. Urban Evacuation: Houston and the Social Construction of Risk
Pamela Behan 171

Part IV:
After the Storm: Navigating New Meanings of Self and City

Trauma Written in Flesh: Tattoos as Memorials and Stories
Glenn W. Gentry and Derek H. Alderman 186

A Bricolage of Loss
Donna Maria Bonner 200

Hurricane Katrina: A Turning Point for Families
Nicole Buras 212

Isn't New Orleans Back to Normal? A Dramaturgical Analysis of Post-Katrina New Orleans
Carolyn Corrado and Tamara L. Smith 223

Contributors 238

Index 246

List of Images

4-1	Author sorts donations at The Jesse Tree
5-1	R.L. Stockard on his 80th birthday
13-1	Andrea Garland displays her tattoo that reads "9th Ward RIP Lower 9"
13-2	Steve Soule gets a tattoo shaped like a hurricane graphic
13-3	Tom's memorial "rescue X" tattoo
13-4	House in the 9th Ward bearing the ubiquitous "X"
13-5	Brock's crawfish and fleur-de-lis evacuation tattoo
14-1	Author returns to her New Orleans home after the floods
14-2	A New Orleans Art Car
14-3	Carnival costume built on a bicycle
14-4	Post-disaster view of the Haney backyard
15-1	Boothville-Venice following Hurricane Katrina
16-1	"It's OK to drink on the streets"
16-2	St. Louis Cathedral
16-3	Complete destruction seen seventeen months after Katrina

ACKNOWLEDGEMENTS

These are the stories of people directly affected by Hurricane Katrina. We owe a great amount of gratitude to them for being open and honest about their experiences, and for completing their stories no matter how difficult and emotional the process was. While these stories represent only a fraction of those caught up in Hurricane Katrina and its aftermath, this book is dedicated to all of those who suffered as a result of a government whose priorities laid elsewhere. There are a plethora of unsung heroes and victims to which we dedicate this book.

We would like to thank a number of people for their interest in and support for this project, particularly Carl Bankston, Mike Messner, and Beth Schneider who helped us navigate the publication process, were always willing to share their expertise, and who are, without a doubt, fabulous mentors. Also, we would like to acknowledge April Brayfield for her early interest in and support for this project. Many thanks are due to all those who participated in and supported the Southern Sociological Society panel from which the idea for this book first emerged. Following the presentation, a number of scholars encouraged us to turn our storytelling into a book project so that they would have the opportunity to share our sociological stories with their students and colleagues. Gratitude is due to Dr. Bob, who graciously donated his time and talent to provide the hardcover edition of this book with beautiful and politically charged cover art. Also, we thank Cambridge Scholars Publishing for believing in our book and for providing us with the space to tell our stories. We would especially like to thank Amanda Millar for her patience and guidance throughout this process.

We also thank our families and close friends for their unwavering support, which has been invaluable throughout the editing of this book. Danielle would like to thank Denise Baggiani, Philip Hidalgo, June Baggiani, Rich Hidalgo, Ray Parres, Laureen Heinz/Hidalgo, Rocky and Buzz Hidalgo, and, especially, Daniel Gutiérrez for always pushing her to do work that resonates with those outside of the academy. If our friends and family can pick up our book and find meaning and new ideas in it, then we have accomplished our goal. Kristen thanks Elaine Barber, Bill Barber, and Tommy O'Connell for their unwavering love and encouragement as she moves forward with her life in academics. Finally, we owe a special thanks to our partners who lived with this project more than anyone else; they are the ones who lived with us through both exciting and frustrating moments, who listened to us as we worked through ideas and concepts, who gave us invaluable feedback regarding every step of the process, and who loved and supported us: to Damien Ricklis and Teresa, thank you.

Introduction

Storytelling Sociology

Danielle Antoinette Hidalgo
University of California, Santa Barbara

"Society runs through our blood. We are not separate from it"
—Ronald J. Berger and Richard Quinney, 2005.

We were alone. During the immediate aftermath of Hurricane Katrina, many of us were alone—some literally and others figuratively. We were separated from our homes and forced to reflect on our current situations and potential futures. While I sat in my family's kitchen, frantically watching every news channel covering the disaster, Kristen spent hours on the road, eventually finding a temporary home in Corpus Christi, Texas. Months, and now years, after the storm, the contributors to this book, Kristen, and I continue to deal with the after-effects of Katrina. Whether we were directly impacted by the storm, conducted research on the impact, engaged in volunteer work on the Gulf Coast, or had loved ones missing in the chaos of the aftermath, we all have been deeply affected by the events that took place in late August of 2005. For many of us, our lives have suffered irreparable damage. Yet, a great lesson emerged from our experiences: our stories and the telling of our stories are important sources of data that allow us and our audience to better understand how our "personal" troubles are shaped by larger public issues (Mills 1967 [1959]).

In the fall of 2005, New Orleans was in a state of disrepair. Many New Orleanians were not allowed to return until months after the storm. As a resident of New Orleans and a graduate student, I remained out of the city conducting fieldwork in Thailand. Nonetheless, I was keenly aware of and frightened for the complicated future of the city in which I lived. I mourned for my city. In order to get through the more difficult days, I read a lot. One day, I read Ronald J. Berger and Richard Quinney's (2005) *Storytelling Sociology: Narrative as Social Inquiry* and was drawn to their "new" methodological approach for understanding how our personal experiences are not so personal, but are, in fact, reflections of larger social patterns of race, class, gender, sexuality, age, and so on. They discuss the healing process of storytelling and its undeniable connection to sociology. What could we learn by taking this approach seriously in sociology? What could we gain from pushing some methodological boundaries through creative storytelling? I pondered these questions as I reflected on my own complicated and frustrating story with Katrina, and as I reflected on the story of the city of New Orleans. I also pondered these questions as I remained in contact with friends from New Orleans; I remember telling a good friend of mine to keep a journal as she was having so many new, daunting, and unique experiences as she returned to New Orleans. We remained in contact throughout the diaspora, and as I thought about her story as well as the stories of other friends and colleagues, I decided they should be shared with others.

In the spring following Katrina, I worked as the Chair of Local Arrangements for the Southern Sociological Society's (SSS) Annual Conference, which was scheduled in New Orleans. Immediately after Katrina, Judith Blau, then president of the society, and I discussed whether or not it was feasible to remain in New Orleans for the upcoming conference. Although I had many doubts, she thought we could do it. After much planning, we made it happen—although not without the occasional roadblock along the way. One of the conference events that I was determined to organize was a special session titled *After Hurricane Katrina: Storytelling Sociology*. In order to prepare the panelists for the session, I sent my own short story to them, describing my experiences during Hurricane Katrina, and asked them to think about and write their own. I wanted them to use their sociological imaginations (Mills 1967 [1959]) to make sense of their experiences, and to simultaneously tell their stories and reflect on the sociological implications of their hurricane experiences. Using one's sociological imagination entails understanding how one's "personal" experiences are shaped by and reflect larger social phenomena. I knew that using storytelling sociology could be an important part of the healing process for all of us; however, I had no idea that the panel would be as well received as it was. Our stories had all of the ingredients of a compelling narrative, yet they were also sufficiently sociological. The next step seemed obvious; I had to make this a book project and I had to use my sociological imagination to see it through.

Using Our Sociological Imaginations

In C. Wright Mills' (1967 [1959]) pivotal book, *The Sociological Imagination*, he cogently outlines his approach to "doing sociology." How, he asks, does one effectively begin, work through, and complete a sociological study? How do we go about our daily lives as sociologists? How do those in the everyday world act as sociologists? And, how can we begin to understand how and why people act as they do? Mills insists that the sociological imagination allows sociologists to understand and see both the enabling and constraining aspects of sociological phenomena. The sociological imagination:

> enables its possessor to understand the larger historical scene in terms of its meaning for the inner life and external career of a variety of individuals. It enables him *[sic]* to take into account how individuals, in the welter of their daily experience, often become falsely conscious of their social positions. Within that welter, the framework of modern society is sought, and within that framework the psychologies of a variety of men and women are formulated. By such means the personal uneasiness of individuals is focused upon explicit troubles and indifference of publics into involvement with public issues (Mills 1967 [1959], 5).

Mills continues by asserting, as we have seen in the work of Anthony Giddens (1984), that we as individuals are influenced by social structures at the same time we create these structures:

> By the fact of his living he contributes, however minutely, to the shaping of this society and to the course of its history, *even as he is made by society and by its historical push and shove* (6; emphasis added).

With a sociological imagination, one analyzes and theorizes about the whole of society, and acknowledges and accepts the inevitability that "everything" is not explained within *one* study. Rather, the sociological imagination "consists of the capacity to shift from one perspective to another, and in the process to build an adequate view of a total society and of its components" (Mills 1967 [1959], 211). In this book, the contributors, Kristen, and I put our sociological imaginations to the test as we analyze critically and sociologically how our personal troubles with Hurricane Katrina were and continue to be connected to larger public issues. Further, we tease out how those connections between personal troubles and public issues emerged in a particular time and place, and with a particular set of actors.

In order to make our own contributions to the debates surrounding Katrina, each contributor analyzes and discusses their own sociological story. The telling of one's experience with loss and disaster is an extremely emotional process and, as Kristen notes in her sociological story, all of the contributors to this book managed their emotions (as sociologists) at the same time that they aimed to share and expose their emotions (as human beings). While this process seems obvious and quite simple, it was extremely difficult in its practical deployment. Further, all of the contributors to this volume *do* sociology, whether they identify as sociologists or not. As people read our stories, they will see that many of us are located in positions of relative privilege. However, we believe it is important to reflect on the workings of privilege as well as disadvantage in order to better understand how inequality shaped options, choices, and experiences of Hurricane Katrina.

Becoming Storytelling Sociologists

I began the very early stages of this project with Tulane University sociologist April Brayfield. However, another graduate student and close friend, Kristen Barber, and I decided that together we had the energy and the emotional strength to see the project through. After our panel discussion at the SSS Conference, Kristen and I put out a call for papers on a wide range of listservs. We were interested in working with contributors who were comfortable writing about their narratives in a personal *and* sociological way. As we worked on the book's various stages, we experienced both the rewarding and the difficult effects of storytelling. For many of our contributors, storytelling came naturally. While the subject of Hurricane Katrina is not immediately lively or fun, our writers managed to deliver their stories with humor *and* honesty, exposing the good and the bad of their experiences. For other contributors, the act of writing their personal stories and simultaneously reflecting on those stories in a measured and sociological way was extremely difficult. For some who dropped out of the project, the process of healing is many months or years away.

By using Sociological Storytelling as a methodological approach to understand our experiences with Hurricanes Katrina, Kristen and I have some main goals for this book: 1) in the Mills tradition, each contributor connects their "personal" experiences to larger public issues in a compelling and sociologically significant way; 2) building upon feminist methodology, instead of privileging the researcher's often disconnected, "authoritative voice of reason," we aim to tell our "own" stories with emotion and honesty; 3) we go beyond Berger and Quinney's storytelling sociology approach by relying on social theory more heavily to make sense of our experiences. Instead of simply telling their stories or presenting their "data," the contributors to this book step back and reflect on why their stories are important, and they use theory to better illuminate how their "personal" stories are not entirely personal, as they are *always* connected to larger social phenomena. Although the contributors come from a variety of different backgrounds, in this book they are all storytelling sociologists. Each story illuminates another aspect of the social phenomenon that is Hurricane Katrina, the largest (not so) natural disaster to impact the United States to date. Storytelling "humanizes" the disaster, and helps us answer the questions: Why should we care about Hurricane Katrina? And, what can the stories of those who experienced Katrina teach us about our social world?

Emerging Themes: Doing Sociology

This book is divided into four parts: Part I) Experiencing Race and Class In and Through Disaster; Part II) The Managed Self: Identities, Emotions, and the Treatment of the Hurricane "Other;" Part III) (Ir)Rationality as a Tool for Making Disaster-Related Decisions; and Part IV) After the Storm: Navigating New Meanings of Self and City. Instead of recounting similar experiences of evacuation, diaspora, and new normality (see Barber et al. 2007), or of the process of dealing with the after-effects of Hurricane Katrina, each author offers unique theoretical perspectives that are weaved throughout their varied stories. For example, in Part I Andrea Wilbon Hartman and Carl Bankston both discuss their experiences with evacuation, but approach their narratives from different sociological perspectives; while Wilbon Hartman queries how racialization impacted her experience, Bankston critically analyzes how his privileged class position shaped his evacuation options and positioned him as an evacuee "on vacation." In the next chapter, Ruth Idakula tells her emotional narrative of being a Black single mother in New Orleans before, during, and after Hurricane Katrina. In this piece, we are faced with a very different story: one in which race, class, and gender undeniably intersect as Idakula maneuvers from her flooded home to the Superdome, out of the city, and then back again. Deanna Meyler illuminates the emotional experiences of volunteering and evacuating during Hurricanes Katrina and Rita—a smaller, but no less destructive storm that followed immediately on the heels of Katrina. Part I end's with

R. L. Stockard's harrowing experiences during Katrina and his untimely transition out of New Orleans.

Part II begins with Kristen Barber's managed emotions as she tells us how she negotiated her emotional and academic selves, as well as her class privilege as both a Michigander and a New Orleanian graduate student. Building upon the work of Georg Simmel and Arlie Hochschild, Barber shows us how social theory illuminates experiences that are often difficult to recount and understand. Stan Weeber addresses identity as it is tied up with attachment to place. Weeber discusses how he came to better understand the shifting identities of New Orleans Katrina evacuees when he, himself, was forced to evacuate his hometown during Hurricane Rita. Part II ends with a socio-psychological portrait of the experiences of two Gulf Coast volunteers. In their essay, Jeffrey Jackson and Kirsten Dellinger tell an incredibly honest narrative of how their particular social positions impacted, both positively and negatively, the people they assisted after Katrina. Their portrayal of the complicated practice of volunteer work opens up space for future discussions regarding how to best respond to similar disasters.

In Part III, contributors recount their experiences with Hurricane Katrina while remaining focused on the rational and irrational consequences of Katrina, and on the "logic" that shaped their actions and experiences. Tim Haney locates how rationality and irrationality played out in his various interactions with Post-Katrina bureaucracy. In the next chapter, Sarah Stohlman shows us how past experiences with hurricanes shaped the decisions and experiences of her Aunt Po. Stohlman reflects on and complicates her Aunt's assumed "irrational" decision to remain in New Orleans, reminding us that while there is no easy explanation for her Aunt's attachment to New Orleans, there is a stark and sad explanation for the poor government response to Katrina. Jessica Pardee's deeply moving piece utilizes Georg Simmel's blasé attitude to analyze how her experiences were shaped by social processes that were often out of her control. She shows us how she maneuvered through and attempted to both challenge and resist the inequalities that she experienced as an evacuee. Pamela Behan ends Part III with a reflection on how she and her students assessed risk during Hurricane Rita. Reflecting on the frustrating process of actually evacuating, she challenges us to rethink how evacuation is actually accomplished and to consider how to make it more effective.

In our concluding section, Part IV, Glenn Gentry and Derek Alderman share the narratives of tattoo artists and clients who were deeply impacted by Katrina. They show how these actors used their bodies to convey their deep emotions regarding their attachment to New Orleans and their personal experiences with Katrina. Next, Donna Bonner reflects on the unique culture of New Orleans, and how the symbolic and material milieu of the city has shifted post-Katrina. Nicole Buras shares four deeply moving narratives, showing how family, gender, and age shaped both the experiences of women who were impacted by Katrina and these women's decision-making power post-storm. We end our book with a dramaturgical analysis of Post-Katrina New Orleans from the uncompromising yet complex perspective of two New Orleans tourists, Carolyn Corrado and Tamara Smith. Their story gives us a glimpse into how non-New Orleanians who visit Post-Katrina New Orleans might see the city and understand its need for help in the rebuilding process.

Conclusion

We began this project with one goal in mind: to provide people who were impacted by Hurricane Katrina with a space where they could share their voice and, we hope, educate all of us on what it means to have experienced disaster. We aimed to create a space for debating the issues, and for challenging assumed notions of how and why events unfolded as they did. I hope we accomplished this goal.

References

Barber, Kristen, Danielle A. Hidalgo, Timothy J. Haney, Stan C. Weeber, Jessica Pardee, and Jennifer Day. 2007. Narrating the storm: Storytelling sociology as a methodological approach to understanding Hurricane Katrina. *Journal of Public Management & Social Policy, Special Issue: Voices of Katrina* 13(2): 99-120.

Berger, J. Ronald and Richard Quinney. 2005. *Storytelling sociology: Narrative as social inquiry.* Boulder: Lynne Rienner Publishers, Inc.

Clawson, Dan, Robert Zussman, Joya Misra, Naomi Gerstel, Randall Stokes, Douglas L. Anderson, and Michael Burawoy, eds. 2007. *Public sociology: Fifteen eminent sociologists debate politics and the profession in the twenty-first century.* Berkeley: University of California Press.

Giddens, Anthony. 1984. *The constitution of society: Outline of the theory of structuration.* Berkeley: University of California Press.

Mills, C. Wright. 1967 [1959]. *The sociological imagination.* New York: Oxford University Press.

Part I

Experiencing Race and Class
In and Through Disaster

FILLER UP PLEASE: COPING WITH RACIAL STIGMAS AFTER HURRICANE KATRINA

ANDREA WILBON HARTMAN
UNIVERSITY OF ILLINOIS AT URBANA-CHAMPAIGN

Waking early Sunday morning from a restless sleep, I looked to my left to see the time. Straining to decipher the clock's dim green numbers, I realized it was 4:30am. The ghostly darkness of my apartment was met with the flickering light of a small television set, which gave the corner of my bedroom a slight glow. To my right, on the nightstand, were my glasses. I quickly slid them on, but waited to look at the television for a few moments while my eyes adjusted to the darkness. I directed my attention to the meteorology report being broadcasted on the screen. From the weather report, it was evident that Hurricane Katrina was strengthening and my precious city, New Orleans, was in harm's way. I had decided to evacuate the Saturday night before, but had held out in case the hurricane made a drastic turn that would spare New Orleans altogether. However, I soon realized that in order to dodge this bullet an evacuation was pertinent. By 6:00am that morning, August 28, 2005, my friend, Douglas, and I were on the road. The two of us headed for safety to my Aunt Cleo and Uncle JC's farm in Marion County, Mississippi. My car's headlights cut through the darkness of the city surrounding us, eerily foreshadowing the events that were about to unfold: events that would leave the city in total darkness for many weeks.

Both the trunk and the backseat of my car were crammed with our belongings for the 2½ hour trip to the family farm. Being a graduate student, my most precious belongings included not only photo albums and important documents like my driver's license and passport, but also my computer, a hard copy of my thesis I wrote for completion of my Master's Degree, and several out-of-print books I had accumulated over the years. Douglas and I nervously listened to weather updates on FM 88.9, and alternated the news updates with tunes from the CD player. Memories have somewhat faded as to what CD's were in my player, but I believe Johnny Cash's sorrowful yet redemptive tunes filled the air as we headed east on I-10. The sun began to rise and the light that it provided was a welcome contrast to the darkness we had left behind. Optimistic that Hurricane Katrina would weaken, we anticipated a quick return home. I was under the assumption that we would be homeward bound by the end of the week. Two hours into our drive, the Louisiana landscape already far behind us, we exited the freeway in Mississippi and, as a precaution, pulled into a Shell Station to fill up my gas tank—we were scared that we would run out of gas after leaving the farm once the hurricane passed.

The farm has been in my family's possession since my great-grandmother Molly Watts was alive. Molly raised seventeen children including my grandmother, Lucille Jackson—who raised four children of her own, my mother, Vertia, included. Cotton has grown in the fields since my grandmother was a young girl. The land is spacious, and long dirt roads connect distant neighbors. On our property, there are two homes side by side. One home is the original house that my great-grandmother Molly owned and Grandmother Lucille grew up in with all of her brothers and sisters. It was the home in which my mother had spent the earliest years of her life before moving to California. Uncle JC and his son, my cousin Tony, both care for the property where they raise cows, hogs, and chickens, and grow sugar cane, greens, black-eyed peas, and green beans. Knowing that prior hurricanes had left the farm untouched, it was to this rural community that Douglas and I evacuated. We arrived on the farm just after 9:00am and immediately felt a sense of safety. Aunt Cleo and Uncle JC welcomed us with open arms and encouraged us to make ourselves at home. It was here that we waited.

The next morning, August 29, Hurricane Katrina crept in. We awoke to radio reports advising listeners that Hurricane Katrina had unexpectedly "bobbled" approximately twenty miles east; they advised people along the Gulf of Mississippi to begin taking cover. Although eastward movements meant a lesser chance that the eye of the storm would hit New Orleans, it also meant that the storm was moving closer and closer to us in Mississippi, something we did not expect when planning our evacuation. Prior to the eastward bobble, we had expected Hurricane Katrina's outer bands to impact Mississippi, but only slightly. Knowing that with each passing moment the hurricane was quickly approaching landfall, the knot in my stomach grew tighter. I feared the worst for my great-grandmother's home as the roughly 100mph winds thrashed into the old farm house.

I stood at the window in my pajamas, watching the wind and rain rip through the farm. Roofing pieces tore away and were tossed into the fields; I watched as some roofing shreds blew clear across the yard, coming to a rest near the barn. In the distance, I could see that the support beams holding up the barn had already given out and completely collapsed. Despite knowing that I should stay away from windows, I could not help but stare out of them, watching Mother Nature batter my family's farm. The sky was gray and dark, and the trees thrashed violently around in the wind. The rough winds picked up my uncle's Ford F-150 on two wheels so that all of the weight of the truck rested on the passenger side; I thought for sure that the truck would topple over. The windows around us rattled, and it reminded me of the 1989 earthquake I had experienced while living in Northern California, where I was born. My aunt, uncle, Douglas, and I sat together awaiting Katrina's passing. For hours, the wind and rain ripped through the farm with a vengeance.

As the eye of Katrina passed over us, an eerie calm fell over the farm. My uncle seized this opportunity to go outside and clean up articles of debris such as small pieces of wood that could soon turn into projectiles. I stepped outside for a moment and stood in Katrina's stillness. I looked over my shoulder to see that a white plastic swing-set designed for small children had collapsed onto a silver sedan. Yet, the sky was bluer than it had been all day—as if a hurricane had not passed over us at all. It was as blue as any other southern spring day. I had heard stories about how an eye of a hurricane is still as it passes over you, but it was eerie to watch birds flying through the still air. The cows slowly come out to graze, but were not out long before blackened clouds crept over our heads and the winds began to pick up, again. Knowing that it was time to retreat, the cows formed a single file line and walked calmly off into the distance. I looked to my uncle with a confused grin, shocked at the sense of danger the cows were predicting. JC turned to me and said, "The cows know when it's time to go. They know when it's bad weather." Part two of Hurricane Katrina was beginning to approach.

After the Storm: Race Relations in Small-town Mississippi

Katrina finished her assault, leaving us without electricity or running water. I would have given anything to make some dark roast coffee, maybe some scrambled eggs fried soft and maple thick-cut bacon for breakfast, and to turn on the television to see the images of the storm's aftermath. Some of our neighbors had generators and were able to watch the news immediately following the storm. One neighbor had borrowed our generator, so we were left with only a battery-operated radio—and the batteries were running low. The radio transmitted tales of devastation, but wanting to see the damage for ourselves, my cousin Tony and I toured the community via 4-wheelers.

We drove over downed power lines and dodged fallen branches. Along the way, we stopped and talked with people who were standing dazed on their porches, assessing the damage to their homes. Surprisingly, many of the people were smiling. Large mature trees had crashed into their homes and branches were blocking their driveways, yet they were smiling. I saw residents in the community working together—chainsaws in hand—to clear debris from roads and from their homes. My family picked up their own chainsaws and cleared roads and bridges of tree debris. As a 4-wheeling sociologist, I noticed racially mixed groups conversing, coming together, and sharing their first-hand experiences of the sights and sounds of the storm. However, such interactions were few and far between. My knowledge of historical race relations encourages me to pay attention to how mechanisms of informal social control shape people's interactions, or the lack thereof. I noticed such interactions as I quickly rode by on the 4-wheeler, and I thought about bell hooks' historical accounts of race relations since slavery in *Ain't I a Woman* (1999). Likewise, I thought about W.E.B Du Bois' *Souls of Black Folk* (1995 [1903]) and what it means to be a "problem race" as he cautions readers that, "The problem of the twentieth century is the problem of the color-line" (54). I was a long way from the urban environment of New Orleans and was not prepared for the hurricane's impact on Black and white race relations in this small rural community.

Some days later, Tony left on the 4-wheeler to go to the only gas station in the area that had not been sucked dry because of the panic surrounding the storm. It was a very small gas station with only one pump. Initially, Douglas and I stayed behind on the farm while Tony drove off to the station. Tony did not have far to travel to get to the station, but when he returned nearly two hours later we assumed he had purchased gas. Considering the station is no more than a fifteen minute drive, he quickly told us that he had not bought any gas because the line was incredibly long—two hours long. Tony returned from the station to get more money after thinking of other items he needed to purchase. "Someone is saving my spot," he told us. I asked if I could join him on his trip back to the gas station; I thought that another ride on the 4-wheeler would be a fun break from the monotony of post-storm life on the farm.

We arrived at the station and pulled into line. Friends and relatives from New Orleans who had also evacuated to our family farm had saved Tony's spot, so we were able to get right back into the approximately 150-person line. Tony resumed conversation with the strangers in the car ahead of us and with those in cars behind us. Since Tony was in line for several hours prior to his return, the strangers waiting for gas had quickly become acquaintances. I was nervous about the two of us re-entering the line, but noticed others, who happened to be white, re-enter the line at various points. My fears were allayed as everyone welcomed us back into the line with open arms and smiles. The people around us commented on how the heat made the wait for gas seem much longer than it was. After shutting off the engine, my cousin and I went inside the store. The electricity was out, so the only light in the store was the natural sunlight streaming through the dusty, foggy windows. Without air conditioning, the stuffy heat of the store was suffocating. The shelves were almost bare, so we purchased the few items that were left, including chips and pretzels. After paying for the items, we returned to the gas line outside.

Another thirty minutes passed—a hot thirty minutes. As we sat there sweating profusely in the heat, waiting for the line to move, a middle-aged white gas station attendant, not more than 5'9" tall, approached us. He said that someone had reported us, telling him Tony had cut in line. My cousin calmly explained that he had not cut in line, but that he had been in line for hours prior. Other customers waiting in front of and behind us quickly substantiated our story and explained that my cousin had been patiently waiting to purchase gas for the past few hours. Despite customers corroborating our story, the gas station attendant went back into the store to request assistance from his brother and father, as this was a small, family-owned business. He wanted his family's assistance, presumably to intimidate us into voluntarily removing ourselves from the line. But in his absence, my cousin and I remained. "I will not get out of this line. This is ridiculous. I've been here waiting just like everyone else," Tony exclaimed to those around us, but loud enough so that the attendant could hear him.

Within minutes, the attendant returned with his brother and father, and demanded that we get out of line. The father added that if we didn't, he would call the police. Despite threats, we remained in line and continued to explain that we had not taken cuts. I began to feel nervous; I felt butterflies in my stomach as tempers began to boil over. Before we knew it, we were all engaged in a shouting match. We accused the attendant of not listening to our story and not listening to the truth. "We've been told that you cut in line," one of the sons shouted. "No I did not!" Tony exclaimed. They accused us of cutting in line and declared that they did not have to listen to our side of the story. It became more heated as my cousin rightfully accused the owners of discrimination. Tony kept his distance from the father and two sons at which point Tony yelled, "You let those white people get in and out of line, and they still got their gas." Tony was pointing in the direction of other white customers ahead of us who were not refused service, had gotten gas, and were in the process of leaving. "I didn't get any complaints about them. I have to go off of what my source told me," the owner responded as he pointed to his chest. Tony and I were aware that our race was apparently discrediting our account of the events. People ahead of and behind us looked confused. One unknown person commented, "This is ridiculous…I don't know man. You should get your gas." It was as if people around us wished they could help us more, but were simultaneously afraid to jeopardize their only chance at getting gas.

Erving Goffman (1959) argues that the information we possess prior to meeting others is extremely crucial in shaping how we interact with people once we meet them:

> We can appreciate the crucial importance of the information the individual initially possesses or acquires concerning his fellow participants, for it is on the basis of this initial information that the individual states to define the situation and starts to build up lines of responsive action (10).

What the gas station attendant was supposedly told by his "informant" overshadowed all other information Tony and I gave him. The attendant had no reason to believe us, although he should have. Further, as Goffman notes, in the event that we have no information prior to the meeting, it is common to look for clues to identify the person's personality. These clues determine our interactions and are commonly based on previous experiences with others bearing similar qualities. These first impressions are very important in everyday life, but judging by my experience they can be distorted and misused.

The gas station attendant never pointed out who had reported us for supposedly cutting in line; I suspect that this informant did not actually exist. Although neither Tony nor I thought to ask to speak with this "informant," it is interesting that the attendant ignored several patrons who supported our account of the events. The nearly ten patrons in front and behind us were mostly black, but white patrons also came to our aid. Each and every one of them discredited the informant's account of the situation. As the patrons came to our aid, the attendant and his brother and father kept their backs to them, staring at us. When it was evident that we were not going to get out of line, the attendant's only recourse was to call the police.

Pierre Bourdieu's (1977) concept of habitus helps us make sense of what happened between the white gas station attendant and the two of us. Bourdieu suggests that people's practices and habits are a result of their cultural history, making up their habitus. Habitus integrates "past experiences, [it] functions at every moment as a *matrix of perceptions, appreciations, and actions* and makes possible the achievement of infinitely diversified tasks" (Bourdieu 1977, 83: italics in original). Using this concept, we can understand the attendant's actions to be the result of his own internationalization of historic race relations. He perhaps internalized racist stereotypes of African Americans, believing Tony and I to be only liars and deceivers, and reacted to us as such. Relying on these stereotypes, he could not take our account of the situation as reliable. The only "credible" people at the station then, were the attendant, his brother, his father, and the "informant" with whom he potentially shared a habitus. Our anger stemmed from our feelings of being targeted by the attendant because of our race. Our position and frustration were primarily due to having witnessed white patrons getting in and out of line with impunity. After the attendant walked away, our tempers calmed but we still refused to get out of line—we were not to be moved. Well, I take that back; we didn't move until the sheriff arrived on the scene.

The sheriff arrived; he was a black man in his mid-thirties to early forties, was about 6' tall, and had a slender build. I initially expected that there would be some sort of racial loyalty: I was fairly certain that as a black man living in the south, the sheriff would understand that what was happening was unfair as it was racially charged and motivated. However, he immediately ordered us to leave, "You need to get out of line or I'll have to arrest you." My jaw dropped and I felt a sinking feeling in my stomach. I was prepared to deal with the aftermath of Hurricane Katrina, but completely unprepared to be taken to jail in Mississippi. We told the sheriff our side of the story; he nodded along and acted disinterested in what we were saying. We pleaded with the sheriff, telling him we did nothing wrong and we needed the gas—as there was no gas for miles around—but he just shrugged his shoulders. He could not let us stay in line, and if we did he would have to forcibly remove us. Defeated and deflated, Tony and I got back onto the 4-wheeler and left the line. As we sped away, without our gas, the words *the customer is always right* sounded in my head. The attendant, his brother, his father, and the sheriff watched with keen eyes and aggressive stances as Tony parked across the street. The officer and the attendants looked to us with their heads raised; they had obviously won the battle. Refusing to be denied service, Tony again, approached them offering to solve the problem by getting at the end of the line and re-waiting for gas over the next several hours, taking the risk that there would be no gas by the time he got to the front of the line. With hands on hips, the gas station attendant still refused Tony service. A mile from the gas station, our 4-wheeler ran out of gas.

It was not until about four days after the storm that our neighbor returned our generator to the farm. For those four days, we had only limited electricity in the house. Finally, at night break we were able to sit down and turn on the television to watch the news. The rest of the house was pitch black as Douglas, my aunt and uncle, and I huddled around the small television set. For the first time, we saw the extent of the devastation both Mississippi and Louisiana had accrued: floodwaters reaching up at least 6', but higher in some neighborhoods such as the lower 9th ward; houses that, like our barn, crumbled to the ground under the pressure of wind and water; and the city was completely deserted. I realized I would not return home anytime soon.

Packing Up and Shipping Out of Mississippi

After seeing the images of destruction on television, I knew it was time to leave Mississippi. Desperate to continue with my schoolwork, I moved temporarily to New York City to attend graduate classes in Sociology at Columbia University. During exile, I watched the news fervently and saw race as a salient aspect shaping people's hurricane and post-hurricane experiences. Already existing racial tensions in the south were unveiled and racialized relationships between Blacks and whites were reinforced. There were images of black New Orleans residents stranded in the Superdome, images of dozens upon dozens of black residents stranded at the Convention Center, and reports of black residents walking across the Crescent City Connection to dry land where they were denied entry into Algiers by armed police officers. These reports claimed that police officers used belittling and racist language and gunfire to force black evacuees back into New Orleans to take their chances with the floodwaters. Race can illicit empowerment for some, like the gas station attendant who was allowed to deny service to black patrons. Race can also illicit disenfranchisement for others, as we saw when the Superdome filled with a disproportionate number of black residents.

Four months after the storm, I returned to New Orleans and immediately noticed the change in the racial composition of the city. In what used to be a predominately black city, New Orleans was now predominately white and Latino, as a number of immigrant laborers from South and Central America were recruited to rebuild the city. In the time since my return, I can say that the city has undergone much recovery and rebuilding, although this has been a begrudgingly slow process. Everyday is a battle, everyday is a fight. However, there are many aspects of life in New Orleans that are in need of much more recovery, including interpersonal relationships across racial lines. The predominately black residents of the Lower 9th Ward have yet to see drastic improvements to their destroyed neighborhood. Additionally, you cannot read the local newspaper or watch the local evening news without being bombarded by crime-related stories that overwhelmingly show black faces as perpetrators. The news neglects to show how black youth are helping to rebuild the city, and instead depicts them as the criminals of New Orleans and responsible for the city's continuing demise. Katrina may have ripped through the Gulf Coast and torn away the facades of homes and shredded family and friendship networks, but it has also effectively unveiled the hidden racial tensions that have historically permeated the city of New Orleans and shaped people's experiences of everyday life, both before and after Katrina.

References

Bourdieu, Pierre. 1977. *Outline of a theory of practice.* Cambridge: Cambridge University Press.
Du Bois, W.E.B. 1995 [1903]. *Souls of Black folk.* New York: Penguin Books.
Goffman, Erving. 1959. *The presentation of self in everyday life.* Garden City: Doubleday Anchor Books.
—. 1974. *Frame analysis: An essay on the organization of experience.* New York: Harper & Row Publishers.
hooks, bell. 1999. *Ain't I a woman.* Boston: South End Press.
Jensen, Leif. 2006. At the razor's edge: Building hope for America's rural poor. *Rural Realities* 1. http://ruralsociology.org/pubs/RuralRealities/Issue1.html (accessed February 1, 2007).
Link, Bruce G., and Jo C. Phelan. 2001. Conceptualizing stigma. *Annual Review of Sociology* 27:363-85.
Simmel, Georg. 1908. The stranger. In *On individuality and social forms*, ed. Donald N. Levine, 143-49. Chicago: University of Chicago Press.
Wilson, James Q., and George L. Kelling. 1996. Broken windows. In *The city reader*, ed. Richard T. LeGates and Frederic Stout, 267-76. New York: Routledge.

HOW I SPENT MY HURRICANE VACATION

CARL L. BANKSTON III
TULANE UNIVERSITY

On Friday, August 26, 2005, I was moving my daughter into her new dormitory at Tulane University. I had heard news of a hurricane approaching Florida, but it seemed at the time far away and, anyway, hurricanes are a regular feature of life in southern Louisiana. We had coffee at the little shop across from the dorm and took the moving at a leisurely pace. In the coffee shop, one of the other young women moving into the dorm told my daughter that she had heard the university was announcing that new students should evacuate as soon as they completed the arrangement of their rooms. Returning to the dorm, we saw handwritten signs announcing that there was indeed to be an evacuation. This was still no cause for alarm. When I was a child growing up in the New Orleans area, it would have been unthinkable to flee every time there was a hurricane. In recent years, though, with the growth of the area's population, increased awareness of the danger of hurricanes, and an increased real danger as a result of the shrinking of Louisiana's protective coastal wetlands, it has become more common to flee with each threat of an approaching whirlwind. This has more the character of caution than of real fear, though, and the decision to leave was a matter of watching the neighbors. The most nervous booked their hotel rooms at the first indication of an approaching storm. The stalwarts would not leave until officially told to do so, and, even then, some would insist on waiting out the winds. Most people followed the wisdom of the trend and left when they saw others leaving. My own weathervane was my mother. If she said that she wanted to leave, I'd pack up my children and take off as well. That way, I could not only make use of the benefit of Mom's experience, I could also avoid any accusations of being alarmist or cowardly, since I could always claim to be only humoring her.

It was also easy for me to leave the New Orleans area for a couple of days. My extended family still owned some land and a small farmhouse in Washington Parish, a couple of hours north of New Orleans. Evacuation meant only a few relaxing days in the country house where my grandfather and great-grandfather were born. Getting there was an easy drive on the causeway across Lake Ponchartrain and then north into the big toe part of the leg and foot part of the state, near Mississippi. The traffic on this route would be relatively light because the majority of evacuees would head north on the I-12 toward Baton Rouge, and because we were leaving at an early stage.

We expected that we would spend a day or two in the country and then return to life as usual, once the storm had passed. The small hurricane excursion had become a yearly routine, traumatic only for our cat who hated her pet carrier and the car trip. On Saturday morning, we threw a few changes of clothes into our bags, packed the cat, and took off before the rush. If I had been less casual, I might have checked on the preparation of my younger son, a 12 year-old. He had gotten into the car barefoot and, I would find later in the journey, had neglected to pack any shoes.

Before we left, I called my mother again and she said that she would meet us in the country. She wanted to pick up a couple of her friends who could no longer drive because of problems with their vision. She also said that she'd heard news that the hurricane had begun to turn toward Louisiana.

The causeway is a boring drive. Twenty-four miles of straight bridge, it connects Jefferson and Orleans Parishes south of Lake Ponchartrain, with St. Tammany Parish on the north. Commuters make this long drive every day since the north shore has become a booming bedroom community for the Greater New Orleans area over the past thirty-five years. The largest part of middle-class growth in the area has taken place in these spreading suburbs, contributing to the transformation of New Orleans itself into a polarized city of the rich and the poor. The availability of homes on the north shore has also helped to change the city's racial demographics. The rapidly expanding commuting population of St. Tammany is mostly white, although middle-class black movement out of New Orleans to the north shore has been slowly increasing in the late twentieth and early twentieth century. The city had a majority white population from the early nineteenth century until 1970. By 2000, two-thirds of its residents were black.

Causeway Boulevard, the multi-lane thoroughfare to the bridge through Jefferson Parish is now known as the Metairie Central Business District, with several tall buildings and a major shopping mall along its sides. When I was a child, no one would have expected that we would ever speak of a CBD in Metairie, a suburban appendage of New Orleans with substantial greenspace and a scattering of surviving small farms. Along with the demographic changes of the region, many of the economic activities formerly associated with the city have moved out into the surrounding fringe.

The water of the lake was smooth as we drove over. The bridge has personal associations for me. My father, growing up in Louisiana, had studied engineering at Vanderbilt and then moved back to the state because one of my great uncles had helped him get his first job in Baton Rouge, working for the state government. My parents had moved to the New Orleans area because this first job led to another one, helping to design the roads and bridges around the city in the 1950's. My father was one of the engineers who worked on the design of the first span of the causeway.

The trip was uneventful as we made it, but it had replaced more arduous journeys. When my grandfather was a boy in the early twentieth century, growing up on the farm where we were headed, going to or from New Orleans was a matter of two or three days. He and his family would ride in an ox cart to the southern narrows of the lake, take a ferry across, and then catch a train up to New Orleans. A van ride across a long flat bridge is less picturesque than an ox cart and a ferry, but much easier, especially if you're carrying a querulous cat demanding to be let out of her container and immediately returned to her comfortable mattress. It is a lot quicker, though, and an hour and a half after leaving home we pulled up into the small white farmhouse. I planned on a pleasant weekend in the country followed by a return to routine. A cousin, who usually stays with his wife and small child in a little caretaker's house next to the old home, had left with his family for Mobile for the weekend, but the keys were in a lockbox.

Exodus: Networking in Dallas

My mother called that evening to say that she and her friends would not be in until the following morning. Before they arrived, though, I was awakened by a phone call from my cousin, the caretaker, at about 5:30am. He told me that the hurricane had changed course and was headed straight for the Louisiana coast. Washington Parish was now right in the path of the storm. "If I were you," he said, "I'd get out of there as quick as I can." This was beginning to be a little different from the usual hurricane holiday.

I could not, of course, leave until my mother showed up. She and her friends made it in fairly late in the morning, about 11:00am. Before she left, some reports that there might be a mandatory evacuation of New Orleans began to spread, and she had e-mailed or phoned various people about where we might go if forced to leave Washington Parish. I have a stepmother in Monroe, and my mother tried to call her, but was unable to make contact. One of her friends had a daughter in Jackson, Mississippi who said that she might be able to find places for two or three people, but would be unable to accommodate a large caravan. As a last resort, my mother e-mailed the grown daughter of one of my older sister's friends, in Dallas. The daughter had said that her own mother was vacationing in Europe, but that any "refugees" who appeared in Dallas would be welcome in her mother's house.

After lunch, my mother, her friends, and my family set out in two cars toward I-55, which would either take us north to Jackson or to I-20, which led west to both Monroe and Dallas. The holiday feeling was dissipating. Traffic was unusually heavy on the country roads and many of the gas stations were already out of gas. When our tanks fell below half-full, we would pull over to fill up with gas in order to avoid running empty.

The interstate was the first sign we saw of a full-scale disaster in progress. The south-bound lanes had been switched to north-bound, according to the "contraflow" plan, and all vehicles were headed away from the coast. Even with all lanes leading the same way, though, there was so much traffic that everyone was reduced to creeping along at a few miles per hour, with frequent stops. Reports on the radio told us that the entire Gulf Coast along Mississippi and Louisiana was being evacuated. I remember thinking: When you tell an entire region of people to leave, where do they go?

With no shortage of time for contemplation, I realized that even this automotive Völkerwanderung didn't constitute the whole of the Coastal area. The people in the vehicles around me were a cross-section of nuclear households, like neighborhoods of single-family dwellings folded in Transformer-fashion into cars and minivans and set on wheels. Empty nest older couples, families with children of various ages, and single people with dogs on the seats beside them or in their laps, were all around. But there were no buses. This was a mobile metropolis that included no high density housing, no urban pedestrians, and no daily bicyclists. The mandatory evacuation order, translated into action, meant: get out *if* you can. This wasn't a mandate, this was advice.

After a few hours of inching along the interstate, we pulled into an overfilled rest stop, with long lines leading up to each bathroom. Some friends that we saw there told us that they were heading to Houston, where they had relatives. My mother's friend called her daughter in Jackson on a cell phone. The daughter said that she had room for my mother and the two friends for a few days. We agreed that we would split up at the I-20 juncture. I would head west to Monroe first and try to call my stepmother and, if that didn't work, continue on to Dallas. It was already clear that hotel rooms would be scarce, with most people within a hundred miles or so of the coast heading inland and looking for places to stay. Interstate 20 was no better than I-55. Long stretches of the former seemed to be under repair, narrowing to one lane at points carefully calculated to create traffic jams even under normal circumstances. It is a good thing we live in the age of soft car seats and the compact disc.

We made it to Monroe well into the night and I called my stepmother hoping that she would be home. She was, but wanted to know, "Why didn't you call me earlier? I've already filled up my house with people from New Orleans." I thought of houses all across the South filling up with people from New Orleans. There was nothing to do but to continue on to Dallas, on the strength of my sister's friend's daughter having told *my* mother that *her* absent mother would be happy to play host to unspecified evacuees. If that didn't work, at least Dallas would be far enough away to have a good shot at a hotel room.

We did stop at a couple of motels along the way to see if we could get a place to rest, and at least show up as self-invited guests at a decent hour of the morning. No luck, until we were almost to the Texas border. There we found a motel with one room left. Unfortunately, the air-conditioning was out in this room, which was probably the reason it was still vacant. But it wasn't bad for an unventilated room in Louisiana in late August, and the cat liked it better than riding for hours in a pet carrier; she has her share of snobberies, but she's never objected to sharing a bed with humans.

In the morning, we crossed into the Lone Star state and introduced a cosmopolitan note into our travels by breakfasting at the International House of Pancakes. Then, on to Dallas. I reached my sister's friend's daughter on the cell phone and she not only welcomed us, she gave us directions to the house and told us where to find the key. An hour or so later, we were parking in front of a nice red brick house in an upscale Dallas suburb.

I knew Dallas pretty well; I had attended SMU as an undergraduate in the early 70's. The city hadn't changed, as far as I could tell; there was just more of the same, more expressways and more shopping malls. It hadn't developed, but spread. The barefoot kid and I stopped in a discount shoe place.

The sister's friend's daughter (SFD) came by in the evening to show us where the food was and to tell us that she had managed to speak with her mother (SF), who was already on a flight back. SF reportedly said that she was delighted we could drop by and was looking forward to having a barbecue with us by the pool. She hoped we had brought our swim trunks. SFD also gave us the password to log on to SF's computer. This was my first attempt to contact Tulane since fleeing. No luck. The Tulane website, email system, and all electronic links to the university were out. I created a Yahoo email account and used it to send a message to a former colleague, now at a university in Florida, to see if he had any news from others at Tulane. Then my daughter and I went to visit the local museum.

When SF came home, she told us that she was indeed happy that we'd come to Dallas and that we should plan on staying as long as we liked. Her son (SFS) was studying at a college not far away, and he came over to help with the barbecue. Between cooking and swimming in the pool, I watched television in the sunroom. Events in New Orleans were playing out on the screen.

The first reports indicated that the storm had passed to the less dangerous eastern side of the city, and that New Orleans had missed the historic apocalyptic storm everyone has always feared. Ah, good, I thought, the hurricane holiday has turned out to be a little longer and more adventuresome than I had planned, but we'll be headed back soon. Then, there was news of floodwaters rising. The television cameras projected desperate people, most of them poor and black, inside the Superdome. It was becoming more unclear just what was happening.

If my memory serves me correctly, Max Ernst once defined surrealist collage as the coupling of two realities, irreconcilable in appearance, on a plane that does not suit them. By this definition, sitting near a pool in the suburbs, watching the Louisiana apocalypse on television was jarring evidence of how surreal the real can be in the modern world. As the drama went on, reports made claims of murders and rapes in the Superdome, of looting and anarchy breaking out in the city, and of snipers opening fire on rescuers. Some of these claims later appeared to have been true, but exaggerated in numbers and in scale. The looting, it seemed, was sometimes looting and sometimes just incidents of people securing the food and water they needed. At the time, though, I felt like I was watching the complete collapse of the physical and social world, while eating a hot dog and drinking a beer.

A day or so later, SF said that a friend who worked at SMU had called to say that the university had agreed to accept New Orleans-area college students, provided they enrolled right away. Since it had become clear that Tulane would not be immediately open for business, this possibility was worth investigating, so we drove down to SMU and went to the building where SF's friend had said the unusual admissions would be taking place.

A circular hall was filled with young people and parents who were waiting to see advisors. I put my daughter's name on a waiting list and we settled in to see what would come.

I recognized one of my own students from Tulane. Her family lived in Dallas, so she had evacuated there on first word of the hurricane. Just that morning, she had also heard by word of mouth that SMU would be admitting New Orleans students. Her main concern, she confided, was that staying with her parents would put a crimp in her social life, "They just don't get it when I stay out all night to party." As I recalled, she did look a little sleepy sometimes in my class. When our turn came, we went back into a suite of offices, where we filled out paperwork, went to an advisor, and then had my daughter's picture taken for an ID card. I thought that everything was surprisingly well-organized and efficient for a last minute ad hoc enterprise. I was also impressed by how hard all of SMU's staff and advisors were working to enroll these unexpected students.

When I asked the individual in charge of taking the paperwork how tuition charges would be handled, she told me, "Oh, don't worry about that. Just go ahead and pay the tuition you owed to Tulane. We want the New Orleans universities to have that money to get going again." Since, as a faculty member at Tulane, I paid no tuition, this seemed like a pretty reasonable arrangement to me.

My uncle had a pleasant vacation home in the hills. We stayed there about a week. Searching on my uncle's computer, I managed to contact several of the faculty members and graduate students in my department, all of whom had set up non-university email accounts, as I had. One of the graduate students had created an ad hoc departmental website, and my colleagues said that they were all checking in at this site and leaving news about themselves and their contact information. Within a few days, this departmental website had a link to an unofficial university site that was putting the departments in contact with the upper administration. The institution was re-forming itself from the bottom up, in a fashion that would have been unthinkable only a decade earlier, making it possible to hold the dispersed faculty and staff together and to make plans to re-start in the spring. Ironically, the staff member who had created the unofficial website was one of the victims of Tulane's first round of staff layoffs when the university did reopen.

I asked about dorm rooms and was told that space was limited, but that we should go to the residential housing office to find out what could be worked out. The staff member at residential housing confirmed that they had little available space, but said that they were committed to finding a room for any New Orleans student who needed one. By the end of that day, my daughter had a schedule of classes, a dorm room, and I'd opened an account for her at a local bank. One down. Returning to SF's house, I managed to contact my mother. Cell phones with New Orleans area codes were only working sporadically, so I hadn't heard from her since she split off from us to go to Jackson. Winds from the hurricane had made it all the way up there and she and her friends had been without electricity much of the time; she was thinking about moving on. My mother's younger brother is a retired federal judge with a part-time law practice in Birmingham. He and my aunt spend many of their days at their vacation home by the lakes to the north of the city. The newest plan was that we would regroup at my uncle's vacation home in Alabama. So, leaving my daughter in Dallas, we waved goodbye to SF and headed northeast. Maybe I can deposit one kid at each stop, I thought.

Leviticus: Family Rituals of a Bourgeois Refugee

My uncle took us on tours of the lake in his boat, which he let my sons steer. We went swimming a lot, something that was becoming a constant theme during this disaster. But it was clear that this could not be a long-term place of refuge, since my uncle and aunt made regular use of their lake home, and they didn't have enough room to continue sharing it with a family of displaced Louisianans. My younger sister and her husband called to offer a solution. My brother-in-law and my second sister are avid golfers, who live north of Chicago. Northern Illinois has many charms, but it falls short of a golfer's paradise during the winter months. So, they keep a condominium on a golf resort in Naples, Florida. My generous relations were offering to let my brood and me sponge off of them as long as we needed. My thoughtful sister had even called the Naples school district to find out about enrollments. It made me regret tying her to a tree when we were playing cowboys and Indians as children.

So, we headed out on another long road trip. The interstate system has made it much more convenient, if less scenic, to rip around the country than it was in Jack Kerouac/Route 66 days. Across Alabama, through Georgia, into Florida, and down the long tongue of the nation that hangs out into the ocean. For the next three months, my sons and I lived in Florida. I should have taken up golf. Unfortunately, I lack the patience for the game and I usually lack the time. My Fall 2005 wanderings may not give the impression of a busy man, but I actually do work seven days a week when massive destruction doesn't give me a respite.

Naples is a beautiful town with good beaches, nice parks, fine restaurants, and streets lined with palm trees. One does often have to wait in line at stores because there is a severe shortage of service workers. The cost of living, especially the cost of housing, is so expensive that only the well heeled can afford to stay there. There was no waiting in line for organizational resources, though. School registration was easy. Everyone was attuned to the New Orleans diaspora and ready to oil the bureaucratic works. We also received special library cards and memberships to the local YMCA.

In October, I had to attend a meeting of the Mid-South Sociological Association in Atlanta. As it happened, a new hurricane appeared off the coast of Florida the very week of the meeting. I was able to change my Atlanta hotel reservations to show up a few days early, and the boys and I took off for another road trip. I had learned that hurricanes are best experienced on television. My older son, who turned seventeen at about the time of our new Georgia excursion, had a friend whose family had relocated to Atlanta in the wake of Katrina. Computers made it possible for my son to stay in touch with his scattered friends, just as they had made possible the online re-assembly of Tulane. This connectivity spared him from having to spend the whole of his time in Atlanta with his father and brother, and to explore local opportunities for skateboarding.

By the time we returned to Naples, the electricity had returned and the grounds crews had cleaned up every sign of weather disturbance in the resort. The New Orleans area had not fared as well in recovering from its hurricane, though. Through trips back and forth between Florida and Louisiana, I began discussions with insurance adjusters and FEMA (Federal Emergency Management Agency) representatives. My house had suffered about a foot of flooding downstairs, destroying much of the furniture and making it necessary to rip out the molding sheetrock. Upstairs, the wind and rain had come in through a vent, causing the ceiling to collapse. The siding had come off the back of the house. Some of the shingles had come off and a new roof would be needed. Most of the large trees had fallen, but, fortunately, not on the house. All in all, not too bad, comparatively speaking.

Numbers: Taking Account in the FEMA Wilderness

At the end of the Fall semester, we left Florida and returned to spend four or five months living in a small FEMA trailer in our front yard, while contractors worked on the house. My daughter returned from Dallas to her dorm room at Tulane. I have little to say about the trailer, since I've tried to purge every trace of it from my memory. I will say that it was far preferable to sleeping on the street or camping out in a tent city for a similar period of time.

Well, so what? I escaped a hurricane, spent some time wandering and mooching off of friends and relations, and then stayed in a tin can for a few months. Why would this be of the least interest to anyone else? I think I'm doing more than putting a plug in for my own discipline if I suggest that the work of sociologists may hold the answer to this question. In his well-known book on the sociological imagination, C. Wright Mills (1967 [1959]) argued that people could think about a society by connecting their personal issues to abstract social structures and forces, by imagining the social reverberating through the individual.

The first larger social theme that I can see illustrated in my small and ephemeral story is that of social class. There was a clear distinction between those of us who enjoyed the luxury of watching the events of the hurricane on television and those who made up the majority being watched. In addition, maybe the narrative can say something about the nature of social class. Americans often think of themselves as a mostly middle-class society, or as a society in which class divisions are fairly permeable. But the televised scenes from New Orleans pose serious challenges to this self-image.

The difference between the people on the two sides of the television screen was not simply a matter of having more or less income. Income certainly played a role: my own income enabled me to have a credit card, which made it possible for me to take off around the country and eat pancakes with strawberry syrup in Texas on a moment's notice. Social class is also a matter of interpersonal connections across time and space. The class backgrounds that Annette Lareau (2003) considers in her work gave me a head start in life, as well as in running away from hurricanes. Having grown up in a middle-class family, I had received a heritage that contributed to my obtaining the education that placed me in the professorate. This background gave me a material heritage: a family-owned farmhouse that would serve as a first stop on the wanderings.

The interpersonal connections across time created useful interpersonal connections across space. At every point in my flight, I touched down on a fabric woven out of family relations. Since my mother, my sisters, and I had grown up in a family that occupied a relatively advantaged place in history, we all tended to have resources and friends with resources that we could use to help each other. My older sister had a generous friend with a nice home in Dallas because my sister's own background had led her to a position in American society where she met and made friends with people with nice homes. My mother had a brother who was an attorney and a judge in part because my maternal grandfather had been an attorney and a judge; and my uncle's professional level enabled him to own a vacation home where he could entertain ne'er-do-well nephews and their families fleeing from disasters. My younger sister and her husband belonged to a social set in which resort homes in Florida were, if not universal, at least not out of the ordinary.

Apart from the farmhouse, I had no ownership of any of the places we stayed, nor was it necessary to have ownership. My opportunities did not come solely from what I had or solely from my family relations, but from having family relations with people *who had things*. To my mind, this touches on the idea of social capital, in the sense discussed by James S. Coleman (1988), and on what social capital has to do with social class. Sometimes understood as relationships with other people that can be turned into assets, social capital is an important part of class. Coming out of a family in a relatively advantaged situation means that one has family members who have things to offer: a house to occupy temporarily, information about the chance of a college enrollment, or the telephone numbers of reliable contractors.

Not every member of the contemporary middle-class has exactly the same network that paid off so well for me. Nor is family in itself always an exclusively middle-class phenomenon. I have often heard it said that the New Orleans tragedy would have been much worse if it were not for the fact that so many people from New Orleans had relatives in Baton Rouge, creating an overnight population explosion in the latter city that was almost impossible to track, since many of the new residents of the Louisiana capitol moved into the living rooms and extra bedrooms of their cousins and siblings. The networks are also not limited to family, although family is frequently central to a personal network. The evacuees in my stepmother's house in Monroe were her friends, members of her book club or members of her church. Those we know in various capacities and the benefits that those we know can offer us, and are willing to offer us, can be seen as assets that shape our possibilities. The fact that these possibilities are rooted in historically-based connections to other people indicates the depth and complexity of social class.

Observers have noted that many of the worst hit parts of New Orleans were overwhelmingly African American, and that those who took refuge in the televised locations of the Superdome or the Convention Center were African American. The one-hundred and forty-years since the formal end of slavery do not constitute a very long time if we think about social possibilities as accumulated and passed over generations, and the less than half a century since the end of legally imposed segregation in Louisiana is well within the memory of living people (including young guys like me). A pattern of contemporary racial inequality rests on a history of racial inequality, and inequality results in clusters of possibilities that are closely associated with race.

Themes of transportation and communication can also be seen reflected in this story. When the local authorities announced mandatory evacuation, those with cars got out, and much of the Gulf Coast became a vehicular translation of itself. The automobile has played a critical part in re-shaping the modern American city. Suburbs have spread out from urban centers in response to cars and the roads that carry cars. Our cities have themselves become more densely interconnected by the interstate system.

The automobile has also helped to shape modern American class. As internal combustion has moved many out of central cities, the poorest people, those with the least access to cars, have tended to be concentrated inside of cities. In a laissez faire evacuation, it is precisely those without vehicles, as well as those without social connections that can offer places of refuge, who are left behind. The work of urban sociologists such as Mark Gottdiener and Ray Hutchinson (2006) has attempted to describe how urban spaces are interlinked with social class, political power, and lifestyle, giving theoretical views of events behind stories such as mine.

Modern communication is a key part of this story. As I mentioned above, only a few years ago Tulane University would not have been able to regroup the way that it did and it would have taken much longer for the university to begin running again. Radio and television made possible the evacuation and it gave evacuees information, however partial and distorted, about what was happening in the storm-hit area.

The topic of communication brings up still another matter of social class, though. Modern social science is sometimes criticized as a kind of voyeurism, with privileged classes of people watching, investigating, and analyzing less privileged classes of people. The former are the subjects of perception and the latter the objects. With that in mind, I think it is interesting and disturbing that those of us who were able to leave the city were also mainly on the watching side of the televisions during this disaster, while those who were unable to leave were on the side as the watched.

The computers that enabled us to link up with scattered colleagues were an aspect of the class structure that defined the whole situation. Everywhere I stopped there were computers because the same categories of people who own cars that enable them to drive away from metropolitan areas on the brink of destruction, or who own homes to accommodate evacuees or who know people who own those homes, also own computers.

Very often, the new information technologies make much more rapid flows of communication along pre-existing, socially structured lines. Institutions such as my own university could electronically re-form themselves with unprecedented quickness in the wake of the disaster. Many of those who lacked the wheels to leave the city also lacked the information to rebuild their lives.

Deuteronomy: Still Waiting to Get Back to the Promised Land

When I met with the representative from FEMA who was examining the damage to my house, I remarked on how depressing all of the surroundings were. "Oh, the real depression won't hit people for another year or so," he said, "when they start to realize that the re-building will go on and on and just doesn't seem to end, then the depression is gonna really sink in." Well, now it is nearly two years later and large parts of the city are still struggling to return. The university has recovered, in outward appearance, and we even have near-record enrollments. But it is a different place now, with entry to many graduate programs suspended and all important decisions descending from the central administration with little faculty influence.

Few doubt now that the city of New Orleans has a future ahead of it. But just what that future may be is unclear and a subject of debate. Many of the citizens, especially those lower income citizens that I saw on the television screen, have yet to return after their belated resettlements in places like Houston. The city's initial decision not to rebuild much of its public housing met with vehement objections from those who felt that the denial of housing would be one more injustice heaped on those who had suffered the worst of the storm. Public housing advocates also pointed out that a rebuilding city had a desperate need for workers and therefore for affordable housing for workers. On the other side, some believed that New Orleans had become a dense concentration of poverty before the hurricane, with high rates of joblessness and one of the highest crime rates in the nation. It was not yet, they argued, in a situation to support a massive return of the poor. Still, even without the restoration of public housing, the city's rate of murder and other violent crimes appeared to be going beyond pre-hurricane levels in many neighborhoods.

New Orleans is struggling to provide schools to many of its students. Its public school system was one of the nation's worst before the storm. Now, many of its schools have re-opened as charter schools. Its rump Recovery School District, operating under direction from the Louisiana

Department of Education, faces the task of preparing some of the least prepared students for an uncertain future.

For the present, the rebuilding itself creates much of the city's economic activity. Workers, especially newly arrived Latino workers, find jobs in construction, and construction pours money into businesses that supply hardware and materials. But to what economic end is the city being rebuilt? Tourism and gambling are the most common answers. Tourism, though, provides mainly low-income jobs, while gambling not only provides low wages to most workers, it has the potential to siphon off money from residents to the owners of casinos.

As I sit in my comfortably restored home and think about the problems the city now faces, I wonder about my own part in all of this. Does living in this area mean that as a part of this community I have the obligation to throw myself into its reconstruction and to work for the resolution of its problems? If so, why not move to a place that would make fewer demands on me? Or, do I have the right to go about my own private life ignoring public woes? Sociologists know that individuals live in communities, and we can explore the connections between individuals and their communities. But there is always this inescapable, but ultimately irresolvable moral dimension to membership in a community for which no amount of research or specialized knowledge can provide final answers. I am still wondering about what life will be like when we all really get back home.

References

Coleman, J. S. 1988. Social capital in the creation of human capital. *American Journal of Sociology* 94 (supplement): S95-S120.

Gottdiener, Mark, and Ray Hutchinson. 2003. *The new urban sociology*. Boulder: Westview Press.

Lareau, Annette. 2003. *Unequal childhoods: Class, race, and family life*. Berkeley: University of California Press.

Mills, C. Wright. 1967 [1959]. *The sociological imagination*. New York: Oxford University Press.

CATACLYSM IN NEW ORLEANS: STORY OF A BLACK SINGLE MOTHER

RUTH S. IDAKULA
NEW ORLEANS, LOUISIANA

New Orleans is a city full of spirit, full of soul. It's the sumptuous food, the music that seems to give you the superhuman energy to dance for days. It's the mystique of the Mississippi River that slowly snakes through the city. It's your neighbors sitting on the front porch all night eating crawfish, gossiping, and drinking. It's the affection in the "good evenin'" that is exchanged between strangers as they saunter down the hot grey sidewalk. But New Orleans also has a dark sordid side: the stench of racism and poverty accompanies the aroma of gumbo and magnolias. Hurricane Katrina exposed these deep-seeded racial and economic inequalities. New Orleans' inner-city poor have relied on social support systems for generations because of political and economic issues that date back to slavery. The poor public school system and the lack of living-wage jobs have kept the city's African American population in poverty with little or no opportunity to escape.

I struggled with poverty for seven years before Hurricane Katrina. I couldn't afford a lawyer to adequately represent me when I divorced my husband; and while I was awarded custody of our two children, I did not receive child support or alimony. As a result, my children and I lived in a series of shelters without sufficient resources or support to help me find stable and adequate employment. Down to my last dime, and with no job or transportation, I eventually moved back in with my ex-husband. After a year and a half, and another child, his abuse forced me to leave once again. I was a first grade teacher, and my ex-husband stalked and harassed me at work—the school let me go a month later.

My mother moved to New Orleans to support me; she helped me pay for a small apartment while I looked for work. Then, one weekend my ex-husband picked up our two older sons for his visitation and never brought them back. I spent days at the district attorney's office trying to find someone who would help me, but I only received shrugs and blank stares.

Every lawyer I visited refused to take the case pro bono. Eventually, I located my ex-husband and found the kids at home alone. When I called the police, they threatened to arrest me for trespassing. I asked myself: How does an intelligent, educated, and resourceful person find herself in this position? I was emotionally and spiritually exhausted, and on the brink of a mental breakdown. Finally, I dedicated myself to giving my one remaining child a stable home. For the next three years, my son and I continued to live below the poverty level. My job paid for food, clothing, and shelter, but just barely.

The Storm

When Hurricane Katrina hit, we were living in a Black New Orleans' neighborhood called Zion City. We lived on the second story of a large lavender-colored apartment building that had six units in it. That day, I had two dollars in my purse; my meager salary was too high to qualify us for food stamps, so all of my money had gone toward that week's groceries. The city had been watching the storm for a few days as the hurricane made its way up through the Gulf. I did not have a car, and so I would catch a ride home from work with a coworker. Just a couple of days before the storm, I was on my way home with one coworker when she received a phone call from her father asking her to evacuate. She turned to me and said, "I don't think I'll leave." An eerie feeling came over me and I told her, "You need to leave for this one, it's going to be bad."

Before the storm made landfall, friends tried to convince me to evacuate. I was too prideful to ask for help or to reveal that things were too hard for us; after all, I couldn't contribute money for gas and didn't want to financially burden anyone. I told my friends that we would be just fine. That night, I fell asleep on the couch while watching television. When I awoke in the middle of the night, the electricity was out and my four year-old son was calling for me. I felt my way to his room through the dark and carried him to bed with me. The next morning, I awoke to the hammering of the wind and the rain on the window. My cell phone rang, and a good friend of mine was on the other end of the line. He had left the city with his family and was calling to check in on me. According to the news, we wouldn't get hit too hard by the storm and he planned to return in just a few days. I felt relieved at the news. I received three more phone calls and assured everyone that I was fine—there was no damage to the apartment, we had food and water, and I could still cook because I had a gas stove. I have always loved storms, but the truth was this one made me a little nervous. I had never experienced a storm of this magnitude, the sound of the wind and rain was almost deafening. The possibility that something could go horribly wrong constantly nagged at me. I ate breakfast with my son and we played Go Fish, read books, and put a few puzzles together. Then, we laid down on the couch together to listen to the storm. The noise was horrendous, it sounded as if someone was groaning in pain. I had heard stories about hurricanes sounding like freight trains and found that's not far from the truth. I just prayed that none of the windows would blow in and shatter.

We had just begun to fall asleep when we heard the sound of running water. I looked up and saw that a foot-long crack had formed in the ceiling. Water began pouring into the living room. I ran to grab a bucket, but before I could get back to the leak part of the ceiling caved in, leaving a large hole in the plaster. We could now see all the way to the roof of the apartment building. I grabbed bowls and buckets, whatever I could find that would catch the rain that was streaming into our little apartment. Finally, at two o'clock that afternoon, the rain stopped. Half of my living room ceiling lay in wet pieces on the floor, but I thought to myself that I was lucky not to have to deal with flooding.

The Breach

I dumped the remains of my ceiling on the landing outside of my door. My downstairs neighbor was evaluating the damage around the neighborhood. He spotted me, asked if I was okay, and helped me clean up my living room. By this time, the battery to my cell phone was dead, but I wasn't worried because I was sure we wouldn't have to wait too long for the electricity to return. There had been a little flooding, but that would subside by nightfall, I was sure of it. After all, Tropical Storm Cindy, which had hit just a few weeks earlier, did more damage to the neighborhood. When I finished cleaning the apartment, things were almost like normal, except for the gaping hole in the ceiling. I fried some chicken and made smothered potatoes for dinner, and my son and I ate while we listened to the news on the radio. Apparently, the Superdome and other various parts of the city had suffered serious damage, but there were other areas with nothing but a few fallen branches.

Tuesday morning I woke up hot and sticky. I looked out of my bedroom window and was dismayed to see that the water hadn't receded at all, but had actually risen about three feet! What in the world was happening?! I turned on the radio and heard that no water was being pumped out of the city because all of the pump workers had been evacuated. I was amazed at how calm I felt; after all, I had learned from life experiences to never panic in the face of danger. As the day wore on, the water continued to rise. I saw people wading down the street through waist-high water, looking for higher ground. They carried bags of clothes and food with them, and some lunged children on their backs and shoulders. I watched them go by, some were crying while others laughed. Neighbors yelled out to each other from the water, and I laughed at a man with a huge grin on his face as he peddled beer and liquor—I guess he thought the situation was ripe for economic gain and if anything would drive people to drink, this was certainly it. The couple who lived downstairs from me had to move into the two-story building across the street because their apartment was flooded. An elderly woman who lived a few doors down had her house flooded, so she was brought to my apartment by the neighbors—my son was delighted to have more company. We talked about the rising water and about how the floodgates had been opened during Hurricane Betsy, sacrificing the lower-lying Black neighborhoods in order to save the Central Business District.

According to the radio, one of the canals was overflowing and people called into the radio panicked because they were trapped on their rooftops without food or clean water. The radio commentator interrogated people about *why* they had decided to stay and reported on the "looting" in the city. I rolled my eyes as I listened to the debate over people taking things from flooded stores. In a city where so many people live below the poverty line, what else could they do to survive? From the landing outside of my apartment, I saw streams of smoke rising from around the city. The high water levels had caused gas leaks that caught on fire. People were screaming for help and dogs were howling. The radio announced body counts and urged citizens to scramble to the Superdome, which was deemed the temporary shelter for the city. I threw away food as it started to rot in the heat and sprayed myself and my son with water to keep us cool—I used tap water to cool our sticky bodies because our drinking and cooking supply was running low. We heard helicopters chopping by every few minutes. The floodwaters began to cause real damage and structures around the city collapsed; the number of people in danger rose. The conditions surrounding us were dire and it looked as if the water wasn't going anywhere. We were trapped.

Getting Out

The next morning, I awoke to the sound of saws grinding through lumber as my neighbor built a boat. The water was now only a few feet below my apartment and I had just finished giving my son a bath when the water stopped running. Yes, it was time to go. I wasn't sure about my neighbor's makeshift boat, but it looked like our only hope. We couldn't rely on the city to save us. In the distance, I saw other little boats and people coming together to try to save themselves. A family not too far from my apartment was rescued from their roof by their neighbors, and another boat went back and forth to pick up people who were stranded on a bridge just a few blocks away. Self-reliance and determination kicked in; we decided that together we would save ourselves. We planned to head toward the Superdome in the makeshift boat my neighbor had built, but as soon as the boat was placed in the water it began to leak. As a last resort, two men from our group swam off in the dark murky water, through debris, hoping to find another boat. I threw what I could grab into a bag, said a prayer, and looked around my apartment one last time before my son and I stepped out to wait.

The boat was old, its motor was broken, and it too leaked. While four of us paddled with scraps of lumber, others bailed water out so that we wouldn't sink. We had no choice but to head for the Superdome. There we hoped to find dry space, water, and support. On our way, we stopped to pick up people who were stranded and floating on mattresses. When we finally made it to the Superdome, we had sixteen people in the boat. All the faces around me were Black, and I thought of the extraordinary odds these people had overcome just to be on this boat: flood, fire, and death. In this post-Katrina space, the racialization of New Orleans was too stark to deny. We were reflections of the raced and classed mappings of the city. We broke the tension by trying to remain positive, laughing, and cracking jokes; and from out of nowhere, a lady pulled out a bucket of barbecued chicken and passed it around. We had become family as we huddled together on this small boat. We had no choice but to trust each other with our lives and nothing brings you closer to another human being than that.

We came across a smaller boat that was just as packed as ours yet half full of children. As we paddled closer, we saw it begin to sink and then capsize. We all screamed in horror. Two men jumped off our boat to try to rescue whomever they could, but they urged us to go on. I still don't know what became of those men. My son began to cry and I turned back to comfort him, but an elderly woman had him on her lap and she motioned for me to keep rowing as she rocked and sang to him. I was unfamiliar with the song, although it sounded like a spiritual verse with full-throated moaning and humming. As we approached the Superdome, I began to smell sewage in the water and when I opened my mouth to make a joke about it, I saw a man's dead body floating face in the water. And then another body floated by, and another. There was a body tied to a pole just a few yards to my left. People in the boat muttered prayers and cried out, "Jesus!"

The Superdome

A few yards from the Superdome, the water became shallow enough for us to get out and walk. Police directed us toward buses that were evacuating people out of the city. Tired and wet, we hiked up a staircase packed with stunned and confused people. Everybody looked lost, nobody had any information, and they were all unsure of where to go. We made our way up the steps, wading not through water but through fallen dead bodies that lay strewn and uncovered. A paramedic screamed for people to get out of the way and rushed past us with a baby in his arms; her little face was gray and she looked like she had gone into convulsions.

We heard we needed IDs to get onto the buses, and then we heard we didn't need IDs; we heard the buses were loading immediately, then we heard they weren't; we heard we needed to wait in line and register inside the Superdome before anyone could go anywhere. It was pandemonium. We were packed like sardines on the stairs, waiting to get into the Superdome. Everyone was pushing and shoving each other, and fights broke out. People picked up their children so that they wouldn't be trampled. The heat was stifling and I was dripping in sweat. I looked around me: There was a young mother with three little daughters trying who was trying to push her way through the crowd and hold on to her girls at the same time. In her way, there was a young man pushing a wheelchair with an elderly woman in it. The woman's eyes were closed and she was leaning slumped over. The man screamed for help as he tried to push the chair through the crowd and several people called out to the police to help him. People began to scramble as we saw a police officer passing out water. Until we got inside of the Superdome some six or seven hours later, I had only one bottle of water to share with my son.

Most of the group I came with stood near me in line. My elderly neighbor from across the street leaned over and said to me, "You know, I'm doing pretty well." I looked up into his ebony face and gray eyes and smiled, "How's that?" "I'm claustrophobic," he told me. But, as soon as he said that, his eyes closed and he toppled over. Someone caught him before he landed on me. His body began to shiver and shake, and we all yelled for a paramedic. A few men helped to carry him away and I haven't seen him since. The situation was desperate and hopeless, and the lady next to me, who was there with her young children, burst into tears. Children all around me passed out from the heat and dehydration, and parents struggled through the crowd with their small children in their arms, desperate to find paramedics. I nudged my son every few minutes to ask if he was okay. If I could just keep his eyes open, I thought to myself, he'd be okay.

A little after midnight, we finally made it into the Superdome. The police searched my bag, which had torn so that I lost half of the things I had packed. A police officer pointed my son and me toward one part of the stadium. People were lying everywhere and the stadium seating area was already packed. You had to find space anywhere you could. We found a spot against the wall of a long, dim corridor that wound around the dome. The smell of waste was atrocious; you could smell it and see it. Luckily, I had a towel and a sarong in my bag that I was able to spread out on the floor, my son went to sleep immediately. I laid down beside him and dozed off for about a half hour.

I awoke and immediately felt revulsion rising up in my throat as I took in the sights and smells around me. I grabbed a headscarf to cover my mouth and nose. A woman ran past us screaming about how children didn't deserve to be dying. I stopped a man who was walking by and he told me a little girl had been raped and killed in the bathroom, and that she wasn't the only person killed in the past few days. I couldn't believe how much danger we were in, and the scariest thing was that there was nowhere to which we could escape. At one point, I heard what sounded like gunshots. I scooted closer to my sleeping son. People began streaming past me; I guessed that they were running to a spot as far from the gunshots as possible, which was not far at all. A couple with four teenage children came to occupy the space next to us; they shared their water with us and the men in the family searched for and brought back more.

There was a rumor that the Superdome officer's would load people onto the buses at five o'clock, so we proceeded to the closest gate at four just to be shooed away by National Guardsmen. It was impossible to tell who was really in charge: the police, the National Guard, or the military. Nobody had any information. We were shooed away at each gate until we reached the last one, then they finally let us outside to the plaza where thousands of people were already crowded. It reminded me of photos I had seen of war-stricken "Third World" cities or of the devastation in Somalia. There were people in wheelchairs and on stretchers crying, shouting, and screaming. I saw only two or three white faces in the entire crowd. Everyone looked dirty and tired with torn clothing and messy hair, and some were bleeding from cuts and bruises. There was no one around to inform us of what was happening, and the National Guardsmen patrolled without answering any questions. There was no mention of FEMA for hours. My son and I were hungry and there was no food to be had, so one little girl shared a piece of gum with us. We chewed hard on that gum—it was the best piece of gum I've had to date.

As the sun came up, we saw dozens upon dozens of buses approaching the Superdome from a distance. People rose up and cheered; some grabbed and hugged each other. We sat on the ground and all I could do was look around because the magnitude of what was before me was incredible. I looked down at my filthy jeans and t-shirt, and I knew that one of the first things I would do after we got out was throw them away. I felt relieved, but I knew that it would be hours before we could leave—if they would let us leave at all. One woman told us that someone had shot a guard and his gun had been confiscated. Someone else said that a number of people had already died from disease or had been killed, and that their bodies had been taken to the Convention Center.

My son and I walked around the area and came across another long line of people who turned out to be waiting for army rations. Very eager at this point for any morsel of food, I joined the line. It took an hour to get to the front, but it was worth it. My son and I were given a meal of rice pilaf with a chicken sauce that to us tasted like gourmet.

A man who looked like Army climbed up on a structure with a bullhorn; we gathered anxiously to hear him. He announced that the buses were there to take us to Houston, we would load up soon and from Houston we could go to various cities around the country. He added that whoever wanted to go back into the city could do so, but that anyone who wanted to evacuate would be in Houston that night. I wondered why they would suggest people could return to the city. What city? I believe those in charge of the thousands of lives at the Superdome were not sincerely concerned, not for a crowd of Black people. I looked around, it was going on noon and I was doubtful that every single person would get on a bus by that night. Hundreds were already waiting at the New Orleans Center doors to leave.

Finally, a National Guardsman appeared and ordered everyone standing by the doors to move twelve yards back so that the loading process could begin. Barricades were erected to control the crowd and keep them from the doors until they were ready to start loading the buses. The guards told us that women and children would board first, so I headed toward the barricade with my son. I was able to push through to the middle of the crowd, but I immediately wanted to go back: it was blazing hot, people were pushing and shoving, and it was hard to breathe. I looked down and told my son to grab my shirt and to not let go. He nodded. I continued to push through the crowd. I felt dizzy and weak, and I could hardly hold myself up. At the front of the crowd, a group of men refused to move out of the way, they said they were human too and they weren't stepping aside for anyone, not for women or for children. Women screamed at them in frustration and other men pleaded for them to move aside. The guards just stood there expressionless and watched the pandemonium. All the guards seemed to do was bark orders and threaten you if you didn't jump to obey. I squinted up at the helicopters flying overhead and wondered why this wasn't better organized; they could have streamlined the crowd before loading the buses. It seemed as if they wanted chaos.

The guards ordered all of us to "Move back! Move back!" while they held their guns close to their sides. At times they would point their guns at the crowd, seemingly unaware that we were the victims not the enemy. They treated us like criminals, harsh and callous. It felt as if they thought this entire catastrophe was our fault. We tried to move back, but those far back in the crowd weren't moving and many of them were more willing to die trying to get out of the city than to go back into the hot, stinky, and rank hell of the Superdome. When a guard threatened, "We're going to open fire!" people fell over themselves trying to move back. I picked up my son and my bag of belongings and moved as far back as I could. This happened over and over again at the Superdome; instead of being seen as disaster survivors, we were being treated like out-of-control criminals and our human rights were disregarded. Although I was confused and scared at the time, I can now reflect on how my marginalized position as a single Black mother was further heightened in this space. Like so many experiences I had while living in New Orleans, I felt trapped and marginalized. However, this space was much more dangerous than anything I had experienced before and, unlike other more subtle ways race, class, and gender have played out in my life, inequality was oppressively blatant at the Superdome.

We were ordered to move back a few yards every couple of minutes, and then two or three people at a time were allowed to pass through the barricades. At one point shots were fired through the crowd. I didn't know where the shots had come from, but the guards at the barricades yelled for everyone to get down. As hours passed, the heat and desperation grew worse, and it dawned on people that they might have to spend the night in this hellhole. People fell down and were crushed by the crowd while others fainted and went into convulsions. Dead bodies were carried overhead to the front. I was so scared, and had to shake my son every few minutes to make sure he was still coherent. His little face was flush and he was beginning to nod off; so, I put him up on my shoulders in the hopes he could get some air.

My son was heavy on my back. I couldn't breathe and I thought I was going to collapse. Finally, I couldn't stand it any more and so I turned to go back to the edge of the crowd. The two men standing behind me stopped me, "Where are you going?" I started to cry, "I can't do it." "You'll regret it. You can do this, you gotta!" "I can't hold him anymore," I said. One of the men reached over, lifted my son and put him on his own shoulders. Tears rolled down my face as I thanked him. He and his companion took turns holding my son in order to share the weight; I'm sure they were as exhausted as I was.

Parents, afraid for their children's lives, passed them overhead to the front just so they could get them out of the crowd. I considered sending my own son to the front of the crowd, but I thank the Creator today that I didn't because so many children were separated from their parents in the aftermath of the storm. At one point, the National Guard announced that they would not accept any more unaccompanied children.

A couple next to us had two sons with asthma and I saw how they suffered, it was like being trapped in a cage two feet wide and there was nothing they could do to get out. Their father was filled with rage because he couldn't help his kids. He shouted to no one in particular. He yelled about the fact that we had been herded like cattle and couldn't get out. His hands were balled up in fists, but all he could do was yell. We were all sitting ducks. The boys' mother kept them awake by feeding them candy. She generously handed me a whole bag for my son who actually smiled—he loves candy. We poured rationed water onto our bodies to keep us from collapsing in the heat; my son and I had been wet since we escaped our apartment the day before.

"Next time they let some folks out, what you do is push with all your might and you'll get out," said one of the men behind me. I nodded while he handed me my son. I had to wait only a few minutes before it was time. "Push! Make it all the way to the front!" I felt their hands on my back and shoulders as they helped me push forward. Miraculously, I made it the next two yards to the barricade. The call for women and children had changed to "entire families." I think this was an attempt to try and keep family members together, but it was also a prejudiced patriarchal view of what constituted a family. I worried that my son and I would not be considered a family because there was no adult man attached to us (Baca Zinn 1994; Collins 2000). A man next to me was getting on board and pointing to members of his family so that the National Guard knew who to let him bring. He looked at me. Desperate, I gave him a pleading look. He pointed to me and my son, and just like that we were on the bus. We all had been so eager to get on the bus that we didn't ask anyone where it was going; we had just assumed we were all going to Houston. I found out later that the buses went all over the country and, consequently, many family members were separated from each other. Once we were in Houston we found ourselves sheltered at the Astrodome, which was filled with people looking for family members. People walked around for hours confused, tired, and overwhelmed, and they cried as they held up cardboard signs with the names of lost loved-ones written on them.

America's Wake-Up Call

A few days after we left the Superdome, a god-sister bought my son and me bus tickets to her home in Shreveport, Louisiana. There, I watched CNN for days, trying to see and understand everything that had happened during those last few days in New Orleans. One sound bite sticks in my head because it finally broke me down after weeks of numbness: a Black woman looking out over the city said, "There must be a heaven for us, because we've just been through hell." For me, this statement captures all the fear, desperation, and loneliness surrounding Katrina, and the feeling of being at death's door. I think it made me cry not only because it captures my own experience of Katrina, but also because it captures my entire existence as a single Black mother living in poverty.

Just like me, thousands of Blacks in New Orleans went through hell before the storm. The insult and injustice of having been left, stranded by the government to fend for ourselves, were compounded by the criminalization of New Orleanians after the storm. The television and radio waves bombarded us with stories about Black New Orleanians committing fraud, theft, and murder. Underneath the outpouring of empathy and support from the nation, the stereotype of Blacks as lacking work ethics and responsibility always managed to permeate the news. Take, for example, Barbara Bush's callous comment regarding those suffering in relief centers: "And so many of the people in the arena here, you know, were underprivileged anyway, so this, this is working very well for them."

After living in Shreveport for four months, and having no luck finding employment, I finally secured a part-time job in Atlanta. I worked in the rental office of the apartment complex my son and I moved into. There, a woman asked me, "Why can't all those people from New Orleans get off their behinds and find a job like you have?" I didn't explain to her that it took me eight months to find employment and that the job I had when I met her was not meeting our needs. Although I worked full time, I never made enough to pay for our basic needs (see Ehrenreich 2001). FEMA was making me jump through hoops just to get a little assistance and, honestly, I was just exhausted with the back-and-forth phone calls. At the same time, I was barely making ends meet with the little I was earning through work. I was fired after only a few weeks and was never told why. Life as an evacuee just wasn't working, so I decided to take a chance and move back to New Orleans, where I found work after only a month.

It amazes me that so few people understand how traumatized the displaced New Orleanians were and continue to be. Getting up to look for work every day was not easy, and doing so after having been shipped off to start my life over again in an unknown place made it even harder. Since Katrina, there have been documented increases in depression, addiction, and violence among those who were affected. People want to come home, just like I finally did, but federal, state, and local bureaucracy continue to roadblock the way home. FEMA denied housing aid to thousands of people and the New Orleans Department of Housing and Urban Development not only evicted families from public housing, but decided to demolish habitable apartments to make room for mixed-income housing which only a small percentage of low-income families could afford. In the meantime, rent rose at least fifty-percent and homeowners are still unable to afford repairs to their homes. According to an article published in the Washington Post, 40,000 people have received "Road Home" grant money to rebuild, yet more than 180,000 have applied (Goldfarb 2007). And so, the devastation of Katrina continues. However, it is important to remember that this devastation is not the fault of Mother Nature, but a result of the nation's inability to place value on this region and its people.

New Orleans has a legacy of 246 years of slavery and 100 years of Jim Crow discrimination. The number of Black New Orleanians who live in poverty is a direct function of this historical racial oppression. Racism has long blockaded Blacks from advancing economically and socially by denying them financial and educational support (Shapiro 2004). Social patterns persist in this country that stem from old conscious and unconscious racial discrimination, and that determine factors such as where people live. This racialization of space is evident in the way pre-Katrina New Orleans neighborhoods were segregated. According to the U.S. Census Bureau (2000), the population of New Orleans was 468,453, approximately three-fourths of whom were Black. Also, of the 142,000 New Orleanians who lived below the poverty line, 110,000 of these people were Black. These statistics alone tell a very sobering tale.

Most Americans would like to believe that a Black child who lives in an inner city has the same opportunities as a white child who lives in a gated community and attends a private school. Americans are deeply wedded to the notion of meritocracy, which suggests that anyone who works hard enough will "make it." However, there is a great discrepancy between what Americans think and the way systems actually work, between cultural ideology and the reality of social life in America (McNamee and Miller 2004). In her work on responses to Hurricane Katrina, Kathryn A. Sweeney (2006) points out that the hurricane made race salient, revealing to the world that those who are generally left behind are poor and of color. Despite the obvious racial inequality illuminated by media images of victims such as those of us at the Superdome, people continue to rely on the ideology of meritocracy to make sense of the devastation. This means that people rationalize and marginalize inequality, and suggest that those who were left behind did not make enough of an effort to evacuate. Meritocracy supports the notion that if those at the Superdome really wanted to leave, they could have. Sweeney suggests that people are willing to disregard the fact that many of these same people were without the financial capabilities to leave. Unlike a white-collar worker, those living below the poverty line could not afford to leave work for what many thought would be just another hurricane; and, even if they had wanted to evacuate, many lacked the information, the transportation, and the monetary funds necessary to pay for gas, hotel, and food. So, we must ask ourselves: How can a country have the audacity to suggest it leads the world in human rights, yet allow groups of people within its borders to continue to suffer without any hope for empowerment? I believe in a spiritual tradition that says the environmental climate is an indication of a society's spiritual energy. If that is true, then maybe attempting to actually fix some of society's historically-rooted ills will calm the fury of Mother Nature.

References

Baca Zinn, Maxine 1994. Feminist rethinking from racial ethnic families. In *Women of color in U.S. society*, ed. Maxine Baca Zinn and Bonnie Thornton Dill, 303-314. Philadelphia: Temple University Press.

Collins, Patricia Hill. 2000. *Black feminist thought: Knowledge, consciousness, and the politics of empowerment.* Routledge: New York.

Goldfarb, Zachary A. August 2007. Va. Firm grows fast, but Katrina aid lags. *Washington post.* http://www.washingtonpost.com/wp-dyn/content/article/2007/08/28/AR2007082801782_pf.html (accessed August 2007).

Ehrenreich, Barbara. 2001. *Nickel and dimed: On (not) getting by in America.* New York: Metropolitan Books.

McNamee, Stephen J., and Robert K. Miller Jr. 2004. The meritocracy myth. *Sociation Today* 2.

Shapiro, Thomas M. 2004. *The hidden cost of being African American: How wealth perpetuates inequality.* New York: Oxford University Press.

Sweeney, Kathryn A. 2006. The blame game: Racialized responses to Hurricane Katrina. *Du Bois Review: Social Science Research on Race* 3: 161-174.

Volunteering on Galveston Island: How Poverty Shaped My Response to Hurricanes Katrina and Rita

Deanna Meyler
Higher Ed Holdings, LLC

Galveston Island is a barrier island in the Gulf of Mexico. No more than 33 miles long and three miles deep, everything is close to water. Pelicans, seagulls, and sandpipers, along with multiple migrating birds, shriek and dance in the air all year while people work, play, and live on the beaches. I loved living on Galveston. I was a Post-doctoral Fellow at the University of Texas Medical Branch in Preventive Medicine and Community Health from 2004 to 2006. I frequented the beach, and island living agreed with me. I enjoyed how everything seemed to go at a slower pace compared to other cities I had lived in. For example, everyone drove under the speed limit along Seawall, the road that runs along the Gulf beach. Watching the waves and ships was always more interesting than the speedometer. Although originally from Dallas, Texas, I moved to Galveston from Nebraska and was happy to find I made friends faster and felt deeper relationships with everyone compared to my previous home. I had read about small town living, where everyone knows everyone else's business, and Galveston felt like that. Since I had never lived in a small town, it was great fun to watch and listen to the gossip of my new island friends, some of whose families had lived on the island for generations.

Living on an island sounds ideal to many people. However, Galveston has experienced high levels of poverty; homeless have been constantly drawn to the temperate weather and industry has dwindled since the 1980s, leaving many blue-collar workers underemployed or unemployed. Consequently, there are several housing projects, food pantries, and shelters on this island of approximately 58,000 residents.

The island is separated into east and west. The west end is populated by vacation homes and condos, while more permanent residents live on the east end. Due to economic downturn, a number of buildings on the east end of the island have long been empty. Certain areas on the east end were also once segregated by race. When the economy suffered in the 1980s, the poorer areas of town with higher concentrations of African Americans suffered the most. Now, ancient storefront signs and marquees beckon customers who no longer arrive. Dust and salty air grime cover the boarded up the windows of storefronts that have been closed for decades. These areas are considered "high crime" due to slightly higher levels of mugging, shooting, and burglary, and to their history of segregation. Island conversations rarely directly revolve around these less appealing parts of the island. Instead, residents advise where to park or where to walk. The "bad" parts are conspicuously absent.

The east-west mentality has even seeped into the consciousness of non-islanders. For example, when I told my father that I was moving to Galveston, he said, "Make sure you don't live on the east end; that is where the gangs are." What he was trying to convey, in his protective fatherly way, was that crime was higher on certain parts of the island and that he had read about gang activity. The local media has helped to reinforce this idea: the Galveston County Daily News constantly runs articles about crime on the east end and rarely discusses unflattering issues on the west end, with the exception of flooding. News channels out of Houston rarely run stories about Galveston; therefore, it is local newspapers and gossip that have shaped public opinion about crime on the island.

Defining island space as safe or unsafe benefits certain people. By subtly encouraging residents and tourists to avoid certain areas, supposed "safe" areas receive a higher concentration of attention and commerce. For example, shop owners in the "safe" Historic District on the east end receive a greater number of customers. Despite this, stores in these safe spaces are not guaranteed success because the island does not receive enough tourism to keep the commerce economy afloat. Stores are constantly opening and closing, and in my two years on the island, one storefront turned over four times and sat empty for several months between each change.

Despite the poverty on the island, tourists have continued to support the local economy, myself included. As a Texan, I had vacationed on Galveston many times before I moved there. The beaches and warm water have always welcomed me with warm Gulf winds, the sound of waves hitting the beach, and the smell of salty, fishy water.

Galveston Island's Hurricane Mentality

In line with sociohistorical approaches to analysis (Habermas 1979), Galveston Island's hurricane history and mentality influenced how I and others responded to both Hurricanes Katrina and Rita. As a Texan, I knew that hurricanes were a concern for the island, even if the last one to cause major damage was in the 1980s, over twenty-years earlier. Once I moved there, I was socialized to follow the weather closely from June through November: the hurricane season. My first hurricane season on the island was uneventful with only the threat of a tropical storm.

Overall, Galvestonians are keenly aware of hurricanes for two reasons. First, hurricanes remain a constant threat to the livelihood of those on the island. If even a category 1 storm hits the island, the city will experience structural and environmental damage, and the constant threat of floods makes hurricane damage salient. It is normal to hear about flooding from neighbors and co-workers, or to read about it in the Galveston County Daily News. Seasonal storms and daily high tides cause streets to flood and residents to park their cars on higher ground, often in a front yard. Here, parking a car in a front yard is not a sign of poverty but a sign of island living. However, on the east end, mansions and dilapidated houses sit side by side. As time between hurricanes has continued to expand, investment in island property has increased with many areas experiencing gentrification. The current path of city development has and will continue to displace poor residents.

The second reason Galvestonians are always aware of hurricanes is a consequence of "The Great Storm" that had hit the island on September 8, 1900. That night, the island was washed away: approximately 6,000 women, men, and children were engulfed by and lost their lives to the waters. Only a few buildings had remained intact, including the University of Texas Medical Branch building, "Old Red." UTMB was the first medical school west of the Mississippi and had only opened in 1891 (UTMB Facts and Figures 2006). "Old Red," as well as any other buildings that had survived the storm, was marked with a plaque in remembrance of the storm and of the rebuilding that followed. At the time, Galveston had been the largest city in Texas and a major shipping port for cotton and other local supplies. After the storm, Galveston spent the next two decades recovering and never reached the same popularity. Further inland, Houston grew to take over the former status of Galveston. To recover, prominent wealthy families gave their money to quite literally raise the height of the east end of the island and to build a protective seawall (Lutz 2006). Similar to New Orleans, residents of Galveston wait for "the big one" that will inevitably come and once again wipe the island clean.

Standpoint

Sandra Harding (1991) suggests that research begins with and is inspired by the standpoint of the researcher. People's standpoints are the lens through which they see the world, shaping both their past and future experiences and actions. My particular standpoint influenced how I responded to Hurricanes Katrina and Rita in the fall of 2005. Much of my childhood was spent in poverty in poor Dallas neighborhoods, and the experience taught me that neighbors are the stopgap of poverty in the United States. If we needed a ride to the grocery store, because we did not have a car, a neighbor was often willing to take us along. In return, neighbors would ask us to help with a chore that needed more than one person, like moving furniture or clearing a yard. For years, I kept a broken jewelry box I had received for helping with a neighbor's yard sale. Without such a neighborly give and take, many Americans would face even greater difficulty surviving both economically and socially. These early experiences shaped my standpoint and ultimately the way I experienced and reacted in the devastating wake of Hurricane Katrina.

August 29, 2005

Leading up to Labor Day weekend, I knew people from Louisiana would be visiting the island as Galveston has long been a playground for vacationers seeking an inexpensive holiday close to home. The island sees Louisiana license plates all summer, and the tourism is welcomed. There is an assumption that anyone heading to the island will have resources to pay for hotels and entertainment, helping keep the island's tourist economy afloat. The day Katrina hit, I was glued to the news and was relieved to find the storm had not turned our way and New Orleans seemed to have weathered the storm fairly well. As the day and week wore on, I began to realize there was a much bigger problem than initially reported. Slow in coming, news outlets began to show flooding in New Orleans. Stories about breached levees became more frequent, and then came the images of people on roofs begging for help with makeshift signs: "Please Help," "Help Me," or waving white flags. I am not an emotional person, but these images, especially of small children struggling for their lives, struck me and I cried. I could not imagine being in that situation. Since phone towers were destroyed and news outlets were focused on

New Orleans, I did not yet realize the extensive damage that much of the Gulf Cost had endured.

Thinking back, I did not place the news scenes into a context of poverty. The television showed people attempting to escape from their flooded homes, and my own experience of poverty had taught me that homelessness is the ultimate poverty. If one has a home, there are relative degrees of poverty after that. Of course, neighbors in New Orleans were finding boats and trying to help each other—that would have been the response of my childhood neighbors. We would not have waited for police or other authority figures (who may never come) to rescue us. We would have taken the first opportunity to help ourselves, just like those in New Orleans did. What frustrated me most was when news outlets flew by stranded people yet did nothing to help them. Media fly-bys were for getting good images for ratings, not for helping people. Anderson Cooper from CNN and local New Orleans reporters from the Times-Picayune, on the other hand, were helping in addition to shooting footage of the devastation. Because of this, their stories were more real to me, and the Times-Picayune won several awards for its coverage of the storm and its aftermath.

Piers Blaikie et al. (1997) suggest that there are no natural disasters, only human disasters driven by economic need. I was once one of those people with great economic need and I knew I needed to do something, anything, for the hurricane evacuees who had already sought refuge on Galveston Island. I called a friend of mine that runs The Jesse Tree, an organization on the island that seeks to fill social service gaps poor people experience. The Jesse Tree works with other community members and organizations to help those who sometimes need a little extra help each month, week, or even each day. They have programs like the Friday Food Fair, where a truckload of fresh produce is made available to patrons for free. Disadvantaged community members can choose what they want and take what their families can eat. This weekly event brings so many people to the center that The Jesse Tree uses it as an opportunity to screen people for high blood pressure and subsequently refer them to physicians. They also run a diabetes screening and education class before the food arrives. Those who participate in the diabetes class are rewarded by getting to "shop" first at the free Food Fair. This is only one of several programs at The Jesse Tree. I called my friend and asked if I could help out with anything that coming Saturday.

Although my father had warned me against living on the east end, all of the parades and island events are held in the east end's "Historic District." My husband and I found an apartment that overlooked the only open square with benches and shade. It draws weary walkers and multiple peddlers of art and chachkas. Watching the square, I noticed little change at first. As the week wore on, more people began to gather in the square and mull about at all hours of day and night. My Jesse Tree friend informed me that bus loads of evacuees were arriving on the island, makeshift shelters were full, the hospital was receiving higher numbers of patients that could not pay for health care, and lots of help was needed everywhere. Since I worked full-time, I first donated supplies to the shelters. By Thursday morning, the square outside my window was full of people. As I walked the block to my bus stop, I became keenly aware that the normally empty steps of the building were full of people. The building at the bus stop holds Texas social service offices, as well as a museum, UTMB offices, and other businesses. The rainbow of unfamiliar people, including several children, was quiet and many people were starring at the ground with long faces. Normally, new faces at this building are jovial because they are heading in or out of the museum. Staring at the ground was not a normal occurrence and I certainly did not understand what was happening. Looking back, many of these new faces were probably asking for help from social service workers for the first time and were uncomfortable with their new need.

That afternoon, I took the bus home for lunch and encountered many of the same faces. After lunch, I had to wait for the bus and sat on the steps with everyone else. I decided to ask one of the people I had seen that same morning what was happening, "Hi, do you know why so many people are here?" The James Dean look-alike explained that he and everyone else were waiting for food stamps. He looked away from me and starred at the ground, "I got nothin'. I need a job and a home, and now I got nothin'." I was quiet and followed his queue to avoid eye contact. I remembered needing food stamps as a kid. My past experience with poverty flooded back and I felt guilty for having just eaten. I had been perfectly comfortable asking this young man what was happening, but once I knew, I could only be still. We were quiet until my bus came and I said goodbye.

Physical Work at The Jesse Tree

At least one bus from the Superdome in New Orleans had arrived on the island, and those who had brought themselves were beginning to feel an emotional and financial crunch. Saturday arrived quickly and I walked by the empty storefronts on the east end to The Jesse Tree. I had no idea what I was in for. Chaos only begins to describe the state of the center. I could barely cross the foyer between racks and stacks of donated clothes that rose above my head. Boxes of food were stacked from floor to ceiling along the hallway and every office had at least one full wall of boxes holding donations. The previous night, 13,000 plus pounds of food had arrived from the Houston Food Bank. This food needed sorting, re-boxing, and distributing, and there was a large donation of clothing that needed sorting and labeling for easy access.

I was immediately led to the room that would be the staging area for food sorting and a metaphor for the strain on services available to evacuees. A large table stood in the middle of the room and was piled with individually wrapped snack foods that quickly slipped to the ground as more were added on top. A long table along the back of the room contained stacked canned food six and seven rows deep; stacks tall enough that everyone was watching to make sure the cans did not fall, again. Another table contained all of the other food that could not be easily categorized. I learned quickly that donated food is not always helpful as we were not sure where to place jars of capers among instant potatoes, dried milk, cereal, and cans of tuna and vegetables. The staging room was not big enough for all three tables, yet five people were crammed into the room and diligently working to open boxes, sort food, and refill boxes. I was asked to help organize this room and keep it moving. The center table of snacks was intended for creating "snack packs" of water or juice, fruit, and crackers—or at least as close to this as we could get. These snack packs were to be quickly handed to anyone who knocked on the door. I found baskets in The Jesse Tree's small kitchen and filled them with food. Once the table no longer looked as if everything would tumble off, I headed to the canned goods table and began to organize the table by the content of the can. I showed other volunteers who trickled how to build nutritionally balanced boxes of food (See Image 4-1). As sorting progressed, one man would load a new stack of unopened food boxes at the center of the room and take away repacked boxes from the entrance door. The pace of sorting the food, and the never-ending stacks of boxes, was exhausting.

I remember going to food pantries for help as a child. My dad would go in and volunteers would hand my brother and me something fun to eat at the door like a candy or a popsicle. Later, Dad would reappear with a box of food. I always enjoyed these adventures because I knew I would get to eat that night. As an adult, I now understand that it must have been difficult emotionally for my dad to acquire food in this manner. Our society teaches us the value of meritocracy where we believe that people can be successful if they just try hard enough, if they just pull themselves up by their own bootstraps. Unfortunately, no matter how hard some people work, they are often unable to achieve the markers of success that we are all judged by: new cars, whole healthy foods, and more clothes than we can wear in one year.

Image 4-1: Author sorts donations at The Jesse Tree after Hurricane Katrina. September 2005. Photographer: Director of The Jesse Tree.

Normally, The Jesse Tree is open weekday mornings only, but if an employee is there patrons are not turned away. This weekend, the local radio stations were announcing where hurricane Katrina evacuees could receive various forms of help. The Jesse Tree had approximately 25 free gas certificates that they kept on hand, and the radio stations had listed these vouchers as available. Many evacuees arrived in hopes of procuring a gas voucher, and, happily, the center was able to give more than just gas vouchers. Even with a closed and locked front door, The Jesse Tree helped at least 200 evacuees that weekend alone and worked with over 2,000 evacuees that first week. All kinds of people visited The Jesse Tree that weekend: short, tall, Black, white, old, young, Spanish-speaking, well dressed, and poorly dressed in tattered clothes.

Emotional Work at The Jesse Tree

Besides helping with sorting everything, I was often asked to help up front by answering the door and assisting patrons in finding what they needed. The first family I helped was a heavy set Black woman, who appeared to be in her late sixties, and her very thin daughter of about forty years-old. I stayed with the woman and found her a place to sit while her daughter worked with Jesse Tree caseworkers. The woman explained how she was very sick and was running out of medicine. She felt lucky that she had evacuated with 25 members of her family, but others were missing. She smiled when she mentioned that that she was happy to get out of the hotel where all of her family members were crammed into three rooms with only six beds; she was especially happy because some of the smaller children (kids who ranged in age from six to sixteen) were hyper and needed more room to play. Then, her smile faded and she began to cry. She told me that everyone in her family was running out of money. I moved closer and held her hand. She explained that her family planned to head back to New Orleans the next day to try and find missing family members. I asked her where they would go, since New Orleans was not yet open. She said they hoped to land in a town close to New Orleans and find houses to rent while all family members old enough secured jobs.

This woman realized she could not yet return home, but felt a real need to get closer and start earning money. Once her daughter returned, I helped her find two business suits for her pending job search. She tried to be stoic, but I saw tears well-up in her eyes as we sorted through the used clothing. She kept asking me if it was okay to take advantage of all the services The Jesse Tree was offering; it seemed she was not accustomed to seeking and receiving the kind of help we offered. Unfortunately, I was unable to find the women new underwear. One of the reoccurring themes for the weekend was a need for underwear and the inability to provide them. The Jesse Tree, along with a number of makeshift shelters, sent out a call for new underwear, yet large donations continued to arrive full of winter clothes—while the generosity was amazing, so was the lack of understanding. After unsuccessfully looking everywhere for underwear, I helped the woman and her daughter carry five boxes of food to their car, a old cream-colored Cadillac. I was happy that I was able to help, and when they left, I received the first of many hugs and kisses.

The next day, I noticed that a white couple in their forties came to The Jesse Tree seeking a gas certificate. The wife was wearing a silk blouse, tan shorts, and a large diamond ring while her husband wore a golf shirt and tan shorts with a big lump in his back pocket from his wallet. The husband went to talk with a caseworker while the wife picked through the rack of clothes and selected a silk dress. The Jesse Tree has several computers with internet access for patrons; and so the wife sat down to check her e-mail. It turned out that her neighbor had not evacuated. After the storm, he had taken several photographs of his neighbors' homes and e-mailed them out to everyone he knew. She saw her house for the first time and learned the first floor of her home was under water; she began to cry. She looked at me and said, "Class doesn't matter. It didn't protect us." I asked if she had insurance and she said, "Yes." She explained that she had been vacationing in Europe for three weeks and had arrived back in New Orleans in time to only collect her mother and evacuate. She had not seen her home in over a month. Her comments implied that she felt betrayed by her class; she obviously thought that she would be protected in a way others were not. But class *was* protecting her: she had insurance, a second floor that was untouched, a house to return to, a neighbor that was trying to keep her and others updated, and she knew where all of her family members were.

I remained busy with sorting, but when the husband with the bulging wallet returned, the wife came to me, said thank you, and gave me a hug. The entire time I was volunteering I was happy to give hugs or listen, and many people seemed to want one or the other. I was surprised by this woman's hug. She seemed out of place by her style of dress and "bee line" for a computer—the computers were always available, but few people used them. This suggested that while some people were familiar with and literate in technology, many others devastated by Katrina were not. I was also surprised that she picked anything at all from the free clothes, even if it was a somewhat impractical article. But the hug was the strangest. The Jesse Tree is similar in many ways to other centers that try to help the poor, and the middle-class people in my life would not have sought a gas card. If they did go to The Jesse Tree, they would leave as soon as possible in order to disassociate themselves from need. In addition, physical contact, particularly a hug, would have been an awkward acknowledgement of having received aid. This woman's deliberate move to hug me felt as if she were crossing a class-based border of etiquette.

I was lucky to have met and helped several families this first weekend. The two families above represent different ways people were impacted by Katrina and its aftermath. The differences in their style of dress, what they sought from The Jesse Tree, and how they interacted with others were clearly informed by their class position.

During my post-Katrina work at the Jesse Tree, I was surprised by how much people wanted to help one another. Individuals would come in knowing that they had little to nothing left; I could tell by how they were dressed and by how much aid they needed and took with them. Despite their need, many of these people offered to help sort clothes and food for other evacuees. They seemed to want to be busy and feel helpful. We were clearly overwhelmed with our tasks and always accepted their contributions. While dress and need indicated the class positions of people seeking aid, these class lines were blurred when people came together to help their fellow evacuees. At one point, to my right, a child without shoes and with a dirty face pulled on the tattered shorts of his Spanish-speaking mother who had come in seeking aid and was instead helping me sort donated clothes. To my left was another island volunteer who was retired. To walk into this situation and assume the class of each person would have been difficult, yet class was certainly impacting what people sought and how they interacted.

The Astrodome

Working at a medical school, all employees were solicited to help serve Katrina evacuees: doctors and nurses were asked to see extra patients and attend to clinics at shelters. The staff, on the other hand, was asked to collect and distribute clothes and toiletries. As a person working in the public health program, I was asked to help with identifying infectious disease at the local shelters, including the Astrodome in Houston. Groups took trips to the Astrodome to help and although I wanted to go, I was nervous about encountering all the grief I imagined everyone was feeling. I had already witnessed the deep emotional turmoil of those evacuees who sought aid at The Jesse Tree, and I was certain the need and grief at the Astrodome would be much more concentrated.

Thousands of Katrina evacuees were sheltered in the Astrodome and the surrounding Reliant event area (Reliant, a local energy company, is the corporate sponsor of the event area complex). Media flocked to the site and reported several times on the cramped conditions of evacuees and the loud noise-level created by so many people living in a covered sports arena. In order to help prevent the spread of disease, public health workers interviewed everyone in the shelters each day and identified those with possible infectious disease symptoms such as rash, diarrhea, coughing, and vomiting—this was my task. Upon arrival, I could choose which area to work in, the Astrodome or a Reliant building. I wanted to see the Astrodome specifically because I knew that families were housed there; I was curious to see how families were creating and sharing space in the dome.

Although I was intrigued by the history that was taking place inside of the dome, I was not ready for what I saw. There was no creating and sharing of space, just space filled with cots and disheveled bedding. In addition, there was an incessant loud hum of noise from hundreds of conversations that made talking to people difficult. Being a sports arena, the lighting was bright and on 24 hours a day. Along all of the walls were stations of services: a medical station, a flight station to get free one-way tickets through Continental Airlines, a clothing station, a toiletry station, a snack food station, a computer station for internet access, and, the most depressing station of all, the message station. At the message station, push boards were hung and filled with photos and notes pleading for help to find mothers, fathers, sisters, brothers, children, grandparents, aunts, uncles, cousins, best friends, and family pets. Some people tried to make their plea stand out with bold letters on colored paper while others scribbled in crayon looking for Mommy or Daddy. The jumble of notes might have looked like a pretty mosaic from a distance, but close up it made my heart break. People shuffled around the arena, their shoulders hunched over and staring at the ground, again avoiding eye contact. Possessions were stored under and on top of cots with security personnel watching everything. However, nothing was secure and the situation was amplified when I heard, "I did not steal your stuff" ring out through the dome. Two women argued until security came by and helped quell the situation.

I spoke with approximately fifty evacuees who took refuge at the Astrodome. One middle-aged white man I spoke with was trying to get medicine for his HIV and was running into problems. Mistaken as a doctor (I was asking questions about health and wearing a UTMB shirt), he asked me for help. All I could do was direct him to the medical area. An older Black woman with a cane wanted someone to listen to her. I sat quietly on the edge of her cot as she shared with me how she had lost everything, including her dog. Tears streamed down her face as she told me that although I couldn't help her replace anything, my listening was "wonderful." When she finished, she gave me a big hug. I hugged her back, even though we were told not to touch the evacuees as they could have infectious diseases. Of the few things I could provide, a hug was one of them. I was outraged when Barbara Bush publicly claimed that evacuees at the Astrodome had it pretty good, "Everyone is so overwhelmed by the hospitality. And so many of the people in the arena here, you know, were underprivileged anyway, so this, this is working very well for them" (Yahoo! News 2005). Her comment was ignorant; I would never have described how people were living in the Astrodome as "working very well." It was certainly better than staying in the Superdome after Katrina, but by no means appropriate, safe, or even humane. Her class privilege and lack of personal experience with the disaster allowed her to be insensitive to the hardship experienced by evacuees in the Astrodome.

And Then Came Hurricane Rita

After Hurricane Katrina, everyone on the island was even more aware of the weather; friends and coworkers asked me daily if I had seen the status of hurricanes in the Atlantic. Every May, Galveston runs stories in the local newspaper about evacuation routes and the damage storms can inflict on people's homes and lives. The only route off the island, and out of many mainland communities near the coast, is Interstate 45, which runs through Houston. Luckily, by late September, the makeshift shelters on Galveston were empty. When Hurricane Rita, which promptly followed Katrina, grew in intensity in the Gulf of Mexico and threatened Galveston, the island came under voluntary evacuation. Tuesday afternoon, the Mayor announced that the next morning our new community center would have free buses available for evacuation of all the residents, and their caged pets, who could not transport themselves—something unfortunately not initiated by the city leaders of New Orleans. The mayor also asked residents to look in on their neighbors to make sure they planned to leave. By five o'clock Tuesday evening, UTMB closed for all non-essential personnel and patients were asked to leave. Many patients did not have the resources to leave and had to be flown off the island in helicopters. That evening, the Mayor of Galveston announced a mandatory evacuation that would take effect Wednesday morning. My husband and I prepared as best we could Tuesday night, and took our cat to my brother's house in Dallas. We were lucky because we had a working car and a safe place to go. Our evacuation was uneventful, but we left with the understanding that we may never return. Others with fewer resources had a much more difficult time evacuating. By Thursday night, news stations reported that everyone had taken the evacuation seriously and Galveston was effectively empty.

Because of Galveston's high poverty rate, many people who did not have access to a working car stood in lines for hours in the hot sun to board free busses that would transport them off of the island. A friend said that he had managed to get a floor seat on a yellow school bus. Anyone who left after Wednesday morning got stuck in parking lot traffic for the entire day. My friend on the bus floor was miserable with no air conditioning, no food or water, and no wind relief as the bus ran out of gas. His bus did eventually make it to a shelter in Huntsville, just north of Houston. He told me that he had been very uncomfortable sleeping in a shared room with all of the other evacuees, and as soon as the storm passed he had hitchhiked his way back to the island. He could have waited for another free bus that was promised once the island officially reopened, but decided not to. Others waited and the island felt empty for a long time.

Ironically, my friend has a PhD in physics, yet he was in a situation where his own class status was undermined by the severity of the situation. He had been out of work and was making ends meet through odd jobs, such as carriage driver. Without the free bus he might not have made it out of Rita's predicted path, and so it would not have been his fault for staying. He and I knew the danger of staying and we did what we could to protect ourselves. There is no "shelter of last resort" on Galveston, such as New Orleans' Superdome, so there was no place to go other than off of the island.

Galveston's poor were very similar to those New Orleanians who had been in the city when Katrina hit. Many had lived on the island for generations and held great pride in that identity. A major damage-causing storm had not struck the island for decades, and so those who stayed at home and waited for whatever was to happen were not ignorant, but rather lacked resources and options. Many others who stayed made calculated decisions given their situation. The day I evacuated, I ran into a shop-owning friend who said he had decided to stay because he was terribly worried about possible looting after the evacuation. His decision was calculated, weighing the pros and the cons of each option, and he did what he thought was best for him and his property. It is not fair to say that all people who are faced with danger make good or bad decisions. Rather, many decisions are shaped by accumulated social capital and, thus, opportunities. Choosing to stay in the path of danger is not an ignorant decision, but the one many people feel is best based on their previous experiences, cultural socialization, their understanding of the possibilities, and class resources.

Galveston was lucky. Hurricane Rita caused little damage and almost everyone evacuated. If Rita had hit the island directly, as predicted, very few lives would have been lost, but an entire island of residents would have been homeless. Some would have fared better than others. Those like me, who could stay with loved ones until finding new jobs and building new lives, had an advantage over those who would land in a shelter after a long ride in a school bus. My standpoint, shaped by my experiences with poverty, would have led me to continue volunteering no matter what position I held; whether I was unaffected by disaster or a displaced evacuee. We live in a society were social class shapes people's opportunities, choices, and experiences. People are prepared for the trials of life to varying degrees and, therefore, as a society that claims to value equality, we all have a responsibility to offer aid to everyone, especially in the face of disaster.

References

Blaikie, Piers, Terry Cannon, Ian Davis, and Ben Wisner. 1997. *At risk: Natural hazards, people's vulnerability, and disasters.* New York: Routledge.

Habermas, Jurgen. 1979. *Communication and the evolution of society.* Boston: Beacon Press.

Harding, Sandra. 1991. *Whose science whose knowledge? Thinking from women's lives.* Ithaca: Cornell University Press.

Lofland, John, and Lyn H. Lofland. 1995. *Analyzing social settings: A guide to qualitative observation and analysis* (3rd Edition). Davis: Wadsworth Publishing Company.

Lutz, Heidi. 2006. One night of terror became a lasting part of Galveston's history. Galveston Daily News.
http://www.1900storm.com/storm/index.lasso.

UTMB Facts and Figures. UTMB Office of Institutional Effectiveness.
http://www.utmb.edu/ia/facts.asp?which=history.

Yahoo! News. Associated Press. 2005.
http://news.yahoo.com/s/thenation/20050906/cm_thenation/120080 (accessed September 6, 2005).

SUBVERTING SOCIAL VULNERABILITIES AND INEQUALITY IN DISASTER SURVIVAL

R. L. STOCKARD
BATON ROUGE, LOUISIANA
RUSSELL L. STOCKARD, JR.
CALIFORNIA LUTHERAN UNIVERSITY
M. BELINDA TUCKER
UNIVERSITY OF CALIFORNIA, LOS ANGELES

We constantly prepare ourselves, perhaps subconsciously, for our encounters with disease, death, crime, job loss, a relationship's end, and other calamities. This mental preparedness allows us to plot our responses, giving us a sense of control over the perpetually looming travails of ordinary life. Though social planners would have us believe otherwise, natural disasters really do catch us by surprise, since the average person has so little direct experience with them and can hardly imagine such events in their totality. Planning for tornadoes, earthquakes, floods, hurricanes, fires, and numerous other social disasters requires an extraordinary degree of abstraction, imagination, and faith, since we rarely have a conscious memory to guide us. Catching us as they do—off guard and exposed—our vulnerabilities frame our reactions and our resiliencies.

We tell this story as family, surrounding Russell Stockard Sr.'s account of his harrowing but fortifying experience with Hurricane Katrina and his remarkable ability to endure, resist, escape, and recover. Having survived war, southern segregation, two pioneering careers (held simultaneously), and the daily vulnerabilities of being an African American man in the United States (whether today or yesterday), provided Russell Sr. with a set of survival skills and tools that propelled his resilience and assured his survival.

As the most expensive "natural" disaster in U.S. history, as the largest relocation ever of masses of Americans, and, perhaps, the greatest assault suffered by an American city in modern times, Hurricane Katrina will have continued historical significance. Yet, it is the masses of African

Americans cast adrift and abandoned that has stamped the most indelible impression on many. Russell Sr. was embedded in that mass of suffering humanity that seared our television screens, newspapers, and, we hope, our souls. The unparalleled significance of Hurricane Katrina in the collective consciousness of not only Americans but countless others around the world imbues narratives of that event with a special value. For Russell Sr., whose life span is distinguished not only by the fullness of his accomplishments, but also by his hybrid role as academic-journalist, the intersection of narrative, self, and society in a time of disaster is vivid and compelling. We will tell the story of Russell Sr. in collective terms, as though we are the chorus and he is the leading man—rational, but sensitive—in the complex drama that reflected the tragic underside of New Orleans' signature carnivalesque culture. He confronted and overcame vulnerabilities in part because he simply had those special characteristics that enable certain people to "anticipate, cope with, resist, and recover from the impact of a natural hazard" (Blaikie 1994, 9). Russell Sr. was also able to draw on the unique and specialized knowledge base and experience derived from his professional training as a geographer, a journalist, and a military veteran.

The Katrina disaster narrative of Russell Sr., his son, and daughter-in-law offers the opportunity to tell a story not only of an individual who experienced Hurricane Katrina first-hand, but of the impact on and involvement of his extended family before, during, and after the event. Besides the narrative in question, the terms of the discourse may also prove useful. It is helpful to focus on the discursive resources involved in the narrative since previous studies on the language employed by disaster survivors do not often reflect their diversity let alone consider the role of race and ethnicity in the experience. Our story is contexualized by the complex intersections of race, age, and class, yet grounded in the unique strengths that each survivor discovered and nurtured within.

The View from New Orleans

As August's end drew near, Russell Sr. looked forward to the long Labor Day weekend. Before he knew it, Thanksgiving would be upon him and his family ties would manifest themselves: his daughter, Janice, from North Carolina and her younger son would visit for the holiday. They would take in the Bayou Classic, the annual football contest between Southern University in Baton Rouge and Grambling State University. This was one of the biggest dates of the tourist calendar for New Orleans, drawing tens of thousands of partisans from the two largest Historically

Black Colleges and Universities (HBCUs) in Louisiana. The fans would not only attend the game; they would extend the festivities into a full week of shopping, dining, and partying. The gratitude expressed by thousands of families in Louisiana over the long holiday weekend would be shared by the city's Convention and Visitors Bureau.

For Russell Sr., who had helped found the Bayou Classic, the holiday would fill his heart with pride while giving him the chance to renew old acquaintances and spend time with children and grandchildren. But all that was nearly three months down the road. Before he could put on his hat as progenitor of a hallowed football tradition, he had to don his other hat—that of an active college professor, despite his earlier "retirement" and the fact that only six months earlier he had celebrated his 80th birthday. The birthday had been a very happy occasion, though diminished by the loss two years earlier of his wife of 57 years, Helen. Importantly, despite his years, he jogged several times a week and was (and remains) remarkably fit for a man of any age. His unique physical condition would play a key role in his surviving Hurricane Katrina.

Image 5-1: R.L. Stockard on his 80th birthday, New Orleans. February 2007. Photographer: Russell L. Stockard, Jr.

By the time the storm roared into the Gulf Coast, Russell Sr. had been retired from full-time college teaching for fifteen years. As a geographer, he was able to turn a trained eye to the progression of tropical storms and hurricanes from his home in Pontchartrain Park, the signature all-Black subdivision that opened in the Gentilly area in the late 1950s, and later from Academy Park, a few miles further east.

Among those loved ones living outside of New Orleans were Russell Sr.'s oldest child, Russell Jr., who, with his wife Belinda, had come to the birthday festivities in late February. Both daughters, Sharon and Janice, had also made the trip, along with two grandchildren: Stephanie (Sharon's middle daughter and a graduate student) and Paul (Janice's fifteen year-old son). All of these kin would join the chorus imploring their father to evacuate the city as the cloudy mass that was Hurricane Katrina filled the Gulf of Mexico.

Anxious Anticipation

In California, we watched with growing anxiety and dread as reports covered Hurricane Katrina, which was racing closer and closer to New Orleans. We kept the television tuned constantly to the Weather Channel and could barely get on with our normal professorial duties given what seemed to be a primal need to gather more and more information about the rapidly expanding storm. We were especially alarmed by the ghastly forecasts on the National Weather Service website which warned of a life-threatening catastrophic storm of unprecedented strength. We, along with every member of Russell Sr.'s large extended family—his sisters, daughters, grandchildren, and friends—used every argument we could muster to entice him to leave what appeared to be a doomed city. Yet he had responded with a carefully reasoned rebuttal; after all, he had survived Betsy, a Category 5 hurricane in 1965, and had more direct experience with storms and horrifying circumstances (including war) than all of us put together. He was angered in particular by his sisters' implication that they had a better understanding of the risks of riding out the storm. How could they? We also acknowledged his long-standing avoidance of air travel—virtually the only feasible mode of escape at this late date. Reluctantly, we eased off—particularly as realistic options for evacuation disappeared.

On Sunday, August 28, the eve of the Hurricane's descent on the Crescent City, we, along with sister Sharon and her daughter Stephanie had a fête of sorts to celebrate Stephanie's admission to the Asian Languages program at Harvard. Stephanie had not had the best couple of years and this acceptance seemed like the dawn of a new and wonderful era for her. We met at a vegetarian Indian restaurant in a somewhat tarnished section of mid-town Los Angeles. Despite our excitement, we could scarcely think about anything other than the approaching storm. Of course evacuation was now out of the question. So we telephoned Russell Sr. during the celebration (on his land line since he refused to even

7entertain using a cell phone) and exhorted him to at least take certain precautions: pull down the disappearing stairs to the attic, make sure to put a hatchet in the attic (you might need it for escape), bring food, a potty, etc. As we went through this exercise, gaining assurances from Russell Sr. that he would indeed do as advised, deep inside we could not accept that these admonitions were anything more than protests from overly concerned children. Was this any different from the advice we routinely issued to our own offspring to prepare for bad times, but all the while never truly believing it would actually be needed? So, we bade farewell to Stephanie and Sharon and drove the forty odd miles to our home in Ventura County, filled with an odd admixture of dread and hope.

Of course, if we had been familiar with the scientific disaster literature, the distinction between the views of Russell Sr.'s largely female-based kin network (that he ought to go) and his own staunch resistance would not have been surprising. There is evidence that women are more likely than men to evacuate when faced with disaster (Bateman and Edwards 2002; Fothergill 1996; Whitehead et al. 2000). Julie M. Bateman and Bob Edwards (2002) actually tested a series of hypotheses related to this effect with a survey of North Carolinians who had survived Hurricane Bonnie in 1998. They found that women (compared to men) are more likely to be in socially constructed roles, such as caregivers, that compel greater attention to risk and greater perception of themselves as more vulnerable in a number of respects (e.g., more likely to believe their homes will be flooded). Predictors of evacuation favoring women included single parenthood, number of children, special medical needs, living in a mobile home, and perceived risk of flooding. On every one of these indicators, Russell Sr. would not be on the exit side of the equation. By contrast, the women in his family could relate to these situations.

We kept the television on all night as we awaited news from New Orleans. Ironically, we had spent quite a bit of time in New Orleans that year, first celebrating Russell Sr.'s 80th birthday in February. Then, in June, a summer institute for an academic group that Belinda directed was held at the luxurious Windsor Court Hotel just across Canal Street and the French Quarter. We had spent a week at the Windsor Court marveling at the extraordinary welcome we had received from the members in our group who resided in New Orleans as well as from the remarkable hotel staff. It truly felt like home. Scarcely two months later, during the height of the storm, right on our television, were reporters broadcasting from the area next to the pool at the Windsor Court. At the very spot where we had relaxed and entertained stood news crews fighting to keep their footing in the face of the winds. They seemed to be marveling at the city's survival and expressing relief that the storm had dropped to a category 3 at landfall. We breathed a sigh of relief, but became a bit concerned when we were unable to reach Russell Sr. by phone. Of course, the phones were out. After all, a category 3 storm is still a mighty phenomenon, so a temporary loss of electricity was to be expected.

Dread Becomes Nightmare

We were, as they say, glued to the tube. As daybreak came on the West Coast, the true nature of the disaster began to unfold. The first levee breach came at 8:15am, central daylight time (CDT), which was 6:15am in California, resulting in issuance of the first flash flood warnings. By 9:00am CDT, the Ninth Ward lay beneath six to eight feet of water. We stared at the alarming and increasingly horrifying images of people making their way to the Superdome for shelter, being rescued by boat, stranded on the freeway overpass, and wandering the streets—all the time scanning faces for someone we knew. Belinda began to work the Internet, posting countless messages and photos of Russell Sr. in the hopes that some news of his whereabouts would emerge. The messages were simple and plaintive, and because she started early, hers were often among the very first postings looking for missing persons, family, and friends. She returned a day later to find thousands more. She posted one of the birthday photos, with the caption, "80, but looks 60." He would later say that Belinda had made him an "Internet star," clearly enjoying the description and the attention it had garnered. His daughter Janice was also searching, posting this message on September 5,

> I have not heard from my father in four days. His name is Russell Stockard, and he is 80 years-old. He lives alone on Chantilly Drive—New Orleans East near St. Mary's Academy. He could possibly be in the attic. Any information that someone has about him or the condition of the neighborhood would be greatly appreciated.

Rationale for Not Evacuating

When Russell Jr. asked Russell Sr. if he was going to flee the city, we were surprised by his response. Not only did he plan to remain in his New Orleans home in the face of Katrina, but also he fully expected only a temporary disruption of university life and planned to take his place in front of his classroom on Wednesday.

Russell Sr.'s assurances that he had been asked numerous times by friends to join them in evacuation served to remind us that he was well loved by his many friends and had a strong social support network in the city. Among the potential destinations was Jackson, Mississippi, sufficiently inland to be spared the fiercest winds and the threat of storm surge. After the storm, Russell Sr. would say that over forty years of experience with hurricanes and tropical storms had left him with an extensive experiential database. Having lived in the same house since the devastating passage of Hurricane Betsy in 1965, he noted that the little flooding that did occur was concentrated at the other end of the housing development, about a half-mile from his home. He didn't consider himself complacent, but rather a student of the natural events that made living in New Orleans and along the Gulf Coast just a bit edgier than in places where weather was extreme but not likely to trigger the apocalypse. We believed that our father's assessment of the risk he faced grew out of the two professions he had practiced for a half century—geography and journalism. In a way, this professional observer's role was an expression of empiricism and rationality borne of knowledge and experience. Of course, his formula did not factor in what was arguably the most critical piece of data—the risk of levee failure. Notably, the Hurricane Warning issued by the National Weather Service for New Orleans and Baton Rouge on the morning before landfall (10:11am CDT, 8/28/05) focused on the expected catastrophic wind damage but made no mention of the potential for levee breach (National Weather Service 2006, 18)

Geographer Susan Cutter (2005) locates the grossly inadequate emergency response to Katrina's devastation within our society's failure to support its impoverished citizens more generally. Katrina revealed the unique positioning of the economically marginalized Gulf Coast residents who were marked by both geographic and social vulnerabilities. Yet, this storm also demonstrated the precarious nature of class-based protections—particularly given the overlay of racial risk. Firmly a member of the Black middle-class, Russell Sr.'s exposure to the post-hurricane flooding did not stem from a lack of education, grinding poverty, or bodily infirmities. Despite his age, dominant aspects of his identity were his comparatively youthful appearance, and superb physical conditioning. Therefore, unlike many of his compatriots marooned by the Katrina flooding, he was fortified by his vibrant good health, multiple, if modest, income streams, and stimulating involvement in voluntary organizations and community service, which enhanced his support structure. Ironically, however, like so many African American middle-class victims resembling him in the well-off Gentilly and East New Orleans neighborhoods, the treasured fruits of his accomplishments were also a powerful lure to remain in place. In Russell Sr.'s case, his writings and memorabilia from his prolific sports writing career could easily have filled a small museum. What would become of these irreplaceable artifacts should he not be there to protect them?

The preponderance of attention garnered by the Katrina disaster and its dire aftermath was focused on those New Orleans residents who had long endured the constant assaults of concentrated poverty and racial bias. Commentators such as Michael Eric Dyson (2006) have noted, however, that a substantial Black middle-class also suffered horribly from the effects of the storm. Spike Lee included their voices among the poignant observations featured in his acclaimed film *When the Levees Broke* (Lee 2006). Clearly, the vulnerabilities exposed by the disaster, particularly the slow pace of the recovery, reached up the ladder of class.

In their prize-winning book, *Black Wealth, White Wealth*, Melvin L. Oliver and Thomas M. Shapiro (1997) exposed the enormous divide between the resources held by the Black middle-class and the holdings of their White counterparts. The authors assert that when one considers total wealth, rather than simply earnings, including assets (i.e., real estate, stocks and bonds, etc.) as well as liabilities, gross racial inequities across social class are evident. It is not hard to see how access to wealth (translating into capital and credit) would enable one to begin to move beyond the paralyzing immediate consequences of Katrina, including loss of job, residence, transportation, materials possessions, and on and on. Oliver and Shapiro further noted that the wealth that is held by African Americans is limited in large part to the equity in their homes. This suggests that Black middle-class Katrina survivors who lost their homes very likely also lost the only source of wealth they had. They were hardly better positioned than that those who had no home to begin with.

A survey jointly sponsored by the Washington Post, Kaiser Family Foundation, and Harvard University (September 2005), reported that a majority of New Orleans evacuees who were sheltered in Houston answered affirmatively to the question: "Looking back do you think that you could have found a way to leave before [Hurricane Katrina made landfall]?" Russell Sr. would have answered "yes," having turned down multiple offers to leave with friends. After surfacing following the storm, Russell Sr. revealed to daughter-in-law Belinda, a social psychologist, another perceived vulnerability that may have been a crucial factor in his decision to remain. He admitted that he had some reservations about getting mired in the heavy pre-storm evacuation traffic. That is, he believed that it was asking for trouble to be a solitary older person laden with valuable possessions in a vehicle crawling along a crowded highway. Which option posed greater risks? At least one previous storm that had sidewiped New Orleans had triggered a sufficiently large exodus to present a clear picture of the tedium and extensive time involved in evacuation, but also the vulnerability to possible exploitation or attack. Ironically, as it turned out, soon after evacuating post-Katrina to Dallas, Russell Sr. found himself in the position of having to evacuate his temporary residence in Lake Charles in order to flee Hurricane Rita. That trip took many more hours than normal to cover the distance from Lake Charles to Shreveport in the northwest part of the state. Yet, having met up with friends, he was not forced to travel alone.

Facing Down Hurricane Katrina – Missing in Action

Russell Sr. cast his lot with staying in the house that he and his late wife had occupied for nearly forty years. It would be a fateful decision. Having ridden out a number of Gulf Coast hurricanes, he even slept through much of the final phase of the Katrina's passage through New Orleans. He woke up to the sound of rushing water on the morning of August 29. In his own words,

> I talked to my youngest daughter and my sister [on the phone]. I heard what sounded like water running. As I got up from the bed, [I saw that] there was about half an inch of water [on the floor]. So, I walked out of the bedroom into the hall and faced my front door. And as soon as I faced that door, it sounded like a Mack truck had hit the door. I mean, it was the worst sound that I have ever heard.

That this would be "the worst sound" heard by a man who had served during World War II in North Africa and in Italy, and "the worst sound" heard by a man who had gone through a tornado in Nashville, Tennessee as a child is a sobering concept. Peggy J. Miller et al. (1990), who studied narrative practices used by talkers to construct their childhood, believe personal storytelling plays an important role in the social construction of the self throughout the lifespan. Since Russell Sr. is the only one among us who has actually experienced these great storms, we thought that he would have introduced the experience from his childhood into his narrative about his recent experiences. After a probing question, he did refer to the earlier storm but did not make any definitive comparisons. The thoroughly harrowing nature of his Katrina survival may have simply overshadowed any previous experience.

Russell Sr. has collected sports memorabilia since his youth and before 2005 had already donated much of his collection to the Amistad Research Center at Tulane University. Many items remained, however, when

Katrina set her sights on the Gulf Coast. His attempt to save his framed memorabilia probably cost him a final chance to flee the rising floodwaters. He eventually realized the futility of trying to move the valued items away from the inexorably rising floodwaters and thought of escaping in his car. But when he looked outside to the driveway and carport, he saw that the floodwaters had already risen above the door handles. Now there was no time left to do anything except to retreat into the attic. He said,

> And then I of course went to the attic and took a few things with me, like a hammer. And a couple things to take care of bathroom needs. No food now, no food at all. And that water continued to rise, and pretty soon I saw I was going to be in that attic for a couple of nights. And of course, I was there until Tuesday morning.

Staying in the attic until Tuesday morning meant Russell Sr. was alone with the eerie sounds of pieces of furniture as they floated and overturned. Among his thoughts was that this nightmare would have been too much for his late wife to endure. He would later declare that watching their prized home fill with dark, dank water and cover their possessions and memories would certainly have overwhelmed her.

By the end of the second day, remaining in the attic was no longer an option for Russell Sr. He would later confide, "I didn't want to go that way." He made up his mind to descend from the attic and seek out help, regardless of what he would find below. He put the transition this way,

> When I walked out of that attic Tuesday morning, wading through water up to well above my chest, almost to my Adam's apple, it was unbelievable. Everything in the house had turned over: the piano, chest-of-drawers, sofas, everything. Once that water gets in, it turns everything over. So I was able to get out of one of the windows of the house and get to the carport. In that neighborhood, there wasn't a sound. You didn't hear anything. And every once in a while you'd hear something that the water would again claim as a victim; you'd hear something like, "Doop, doop." And I said, "How am I going to get out of here?"

Fortunately, the water would not claim him as a victim since some neighbors remaining in the vicinity heard Russell Sr.'s yells for help from his backyard. After stopping at another neighbor's two-story house for some tennis shoes (Russell Sr. was shoeless and had lost both his glasses and watch in his flooded house) and some food, the small band of neighbors made their way toward the Central Business District, walking through floodwaters and along the freeway for twelve miles.

Russell Sr. would later compare the trek along the freeway to his experience in World War II. While the term "refugees" was rejected in favor of "citizens" for the displaced of New Orleans, what Russell Sr. had seen in North Africa and Italy could be accurately described as endless lines of refugees. Those trudging along the freeway walked mostly in silence. Once at their destination, Russell Sr. and his companions spent two more days camped out on the freeway. He reported no discord, only cooperation among those exiled to the concrete camps. Food in the form of sandwiches miraculously appeared. Russell Sr. was able to persuade an enterprising man, who said he was a taxi driver but who was selling clothing on the street, to give him a light jacket to protect him from the elements. Russell Sr. later said that he didn't have any money and that he had asked the street merchant/taxi driver to "give an old man" one of the garments. Not finding many buyers, the taxi driver tossed the jacket to Russell Sr.

During this time, none of Russell Sr.'s family or friends knew his whereabouts. He did not have a cell phone and, in any event, such service was inoperable by this time. Belinda continued to monitor the burgeoning websites that served as message boards for those looking for kin. Russell Sr.'s youngest sister called phone numbers that promised information on survivors. The common emotions among family members were anguish and heartache, made worse by the constantly rerunning broadcast images of those suffering outside of the Louisiana Superdome and New Orleans Convention Center. Transfixed, we scanned those images continuously though our heads and eyes ached from the effort, ever hopeful that we would catch sight of the family patriarch. The website resource did yield at least one contact from one of Russell Sr.'s friends who had seen the posting from his home in Mississippi. He promised to contact us should he hear any news of Russell Sr.'s whereabouts.

Rescue and Reunion

By the weekend, the agony among family members had reached unbearable levels, but a phone call from Russell Sr.'s sister in Washington, DC finally brought relief. Russell Sr. was safe in Dallas, Texas. He was staying with a friend whom he knew from his Sugar Bowl committee work and who was housing at least three other displaced households. During the initial phone call, Russell Sr. emotionally admitted putting his loved ones through an ordeal by not evacuating before the storm. But Daddy was safe.

Russell Sr. told us over the phone that one of his former students, a military officer, had recognized him despite a five-day growth of beard and the absence of his trademark glasses. The officer had expedited Russell Sr. getting on a bus out of New Orleans. When the bus tried to cross the Mississippi River it was turned away by armed sheriffs' deputies denying passage into their parish—one of several such reported incidents. The bus retreated and the passengers boarded a different bus that eventually deposited the passengers in Dallas. Russell Sr. went to the Veteran's Administration Hospital and finally found safe haven in the home of a friend. His long and incredible ordeal had finally ended.

Frames of Denial, Possibilities of Hope

Despite his careful and rational observations of weather and flooding in his neighborhood over the four decades between Hurricanes Betsy and Katrina, and his knowledge base as a professional geographer, Russell Sr. lived to regret his decision to remain in his home to face the storm. As an observer of the local and state governments, he was not surprised that New Orleans had failed to demand that adequate flood protection measures be taken. To paraphrase the words of Alex de Waal (2005), most modern western societies, as well as the New Orleans/Louisiana/federal governments, invest heavily in "denying the inevitability of disaster." Max Weber's (1978) notions of social action and rationality may provide additional insights. Weber defines social action as including both "failure to act and passive acquiescence;" further, it "may be oriented to the past, present, or expected future behavior of others" (23). According to Weber, social action may be oriented in four ways, but two seem particularly relevant to this context: 1) "action that is instrumentally rational (*zweckrational*), that is determined by expectations as to the behavior of objects in the environment and of other human beings;" and 2) "affectual (especially emotional) action, that is determined by the actor's specific affects and feeling states" (24). Russell Sr.'s actions and reports of his thinking appear to be consistent with the use of instrumental rationality, perhaps as a result of his professional training and his military experience. At the same time, affectual considerations were at play given that he valued his independence and did not wish to burden friends and family; he also did not relish a solitary escape that increased his personal vulnerability. No doubt the emotions that stirred as he practically fought with his family's entreaties to flee the imminent storm were more complex than mere fear. After all, he had survived the horrors of war and the dismal spectacle of racial discrimination and conflict for most of his life.

Despite all of this, Russell Sr. continued to believe in the values of hard work, education, collaboration, and family. Alice Fothergill (2004) has observed the reluctance of middle-class women to accept assistance following a disaster. Asserting his independence and expressing his rationality, Russell Sr. may well have felt some stigma attached to reliance on others, especially before the hurricane had even made landfall.

This story illuminates the complex intersections of race, age, gender, and class, further complicated by personal and professional knowledge and experience in one man's survival of Hurricane Katrina. The fundamental underpinning, however, is family—our emotional bonds, our concerns, and our devotion. We have also highlighted the considerable challenge of finding the best way to secure the safety of a loved one in a time of unparalleled crisis. The two-week heat wave that hit Chicago in 1995, resulting in the deaths of over 500 people, was vividly instructive on this point. Eric Klinenberg (1999) showed that social isolation was a critical factor in the extremely disproportionate mortality of impoverished seniors—particularly those in violence prone areas (where one tends to stay inside with locked windows and doors). African Americans were more likely to die than Latinos or whites, a fact that Klinenberg traced to both systemic resource deficiencies as well as disturbing social changes in certain very low-income African American communities. That is, in the context of degrading environments, residents established a "social distance that enable[d] a preservation of dignity and self-respect" but jeopardized collective support (Klinenberg 1999, 269). The similarities between the outcomes in Chicago and New Orleans are obvious: the elderly were once again the most likely to die, and while the racial divide was not so apparent in the Louisiana deaths (Louisiana Family Assistance 2007a), the visibly stranded were more likely to be Black than white. Moreover, the vast majority of those still listed as missing are African American—65 percent (Louisiana Family Assistance 2007b). Against this backdrop, we are forced to consider our actions with respect to Russell Sr.'s welfare during Katrina and how we should respond if and when we next face this dilemma. A number of family members are potentially in the paths of future storms.

Now, relocated in Baton Rouge, Russell Sr. is still a frequent visitor to New Orleans, often to retrieve items from his ruined house and sometimes to attend events connected not so much with his college teaching career but still active professional career in media. Retirement from full-time teaching has given Russell Sr. more time, but that doesn't mean he is slowing down. Recently, he inquired at a community college in Baton

Rouge about the possibility of teaching geography. He was encouraged to consider teaching there. Most noteworthy, he has recently remarried.

In multiple tellings of his experience with Katrina, we hardly ever heard Russell Sr. mention his age. He does not use pre-existing categories of age in discussions about himself—as if he is neither defined nor constrained by his years. Rebecca Jones (2006) describes this phenomenon (exemplified by older persons talking as if they are not old) in terms of "positioning theory." "Positions" are characterized as similar to, but more flexible and dynamic than roles. Greater use of this conceptual framework could be fruitful as we gather more tales of survival and perseverance in Katrina's wake.

Of course, Russell Sr.'s chances of getting his home back to normal also depend on the diligent performance of various government agencies. Despite the poor marks given to the bureaucracy, Russell Sr. refuses to attribute any specific motives of benign neglect or slow response to the middle-class neighborhoods of Gentilly and New Orleans East during the aftermath of the storm. Rather, he says that the city's response is equally slow across virtually all neighborhoods,

> I don't think much has been done in the city of New Orleans for people at any level. I guess the city is sort of treading water in terms of helping people and returning the city to its pre-Katrina level. What you must understand is that New Orleans was in a very poor state administratively before Katrina. Katrina just sort of accentuated that condition, and because of the disagreement [between] or inability of the city, state, and the federal government to seemingly be at odds, very little has been done in New Orleans. I visit there two or three times a month and very little has been done in terms of infrastructure and of course the mayor and city of New Orleans [has not performed adequately]. I've tried to obtain assistance from other levels of state and federal government. From what I read and what I see when I return to New Orleans, I don't think very much has been done. It seems to me that it will be a very slow process. I think New Orleans, in my estimation, will not... will never be a city of 400,000 people [again].

Russell Sr. readily admits that the government is broken at the city and state levels. He looks at the ruined physical infrastructure and distribution of services and benefits as a direct outgrowth of the dysfunctional New Orleans and Louisiana state governments.

Russell Sr. does think one bright spot emerged in the aftermath of Katrina: the catastrophe brought his family closer together. Except for finally entering retirement from full-time college teaching, he doesn't readily admit to any significant changes in his life or outlook. However, one of the first steps Belinda took after we knew his whereabouts was to send him a cell phone.

References

Bateman, Julie M., and Bob Edwards. 2002. Gender and evacuation: A closer look at why women are more likely to evacuate for hurricanes. *Natural Hazards Review* 3: 107-117.

Blaikie, Piers M., Terry Cannon, Ian Davis, and Ben Wisner. 1994. *At risk: Natural hazards, people's vulnerability, and disasters.* New York: Routledge.

Cutter, Susan. 2005. The geography of social vulnerability: Race, class, and catastrophe. *Understanding Katrina: perspectives from the social sciences.* http://understandingkatrina.ssrc.org/Cutter (accessed July 27, 2006).

De Waal, Alex. 2005. An imperfect storm: Narratives of calamity in a liberal-technocratic age. *Understanding Katrina: Perspectives from the social sciences.* http://understandingkatrina.ssrc.org/deWaal (accessed January 30, 2007).

Dyson, Michael Eric. 2006. *Come hell or high water: Hurricane Katrina and the color of disaster.* New York: Basic Civitas.

Fothergill, Alice. 1996. Gender, risk, and disaster. *Journal of Mass Emergency Disasters* 14: 33-56.

—. 2004. *Heads above water: Gender, class, and family in the Grand Fork flood.* Albany: State University of New York Press.

Jones, Rebecca. 2006. "Older people" talking as if they are not older people: Positioning theory as an explanation. *Journal of Aging Studies* 20: 79-91.

Klinenberg, Eric. 1999. Denaturalizing disaster: A social autopsy of the 1995 Chicago heat wave. *Theory and Society* 28: 239-295.

Lee, Spike. 2006. When the levees broke: A requiem in four acts. New York: Spike Lee Film and 40 Acres & A Mule Filmworks.

Louisiana Family Assistance, State of Louisiana. Hurricane Katrina reports on missing.
http://www.dhh.louisiana.gov/offices/page.asp?ID=303&Detail=7046.

—. Hurricane Katrina reports on deceased.
http://www.dhh.louisiana.gov/offices/page.asp?ID=303&Detail=7047.

Miller, Peggy J., Randolph Potts, Heidi Fung, Lisa Hoogstra, and Judy Mintz. 1990. Narrative practices and the social construction of self in childhood. *American Ethnologist* 17.2: 292-311.

National Weather Service. Service assessment: Hurricane Katrina, August 23-31, 2005. http://www.weather.gov/os/assessments/pdfs/Katrina.pdf (accessed May 25, 2007).

Oliver, Melvin. L., and Thomas M. Shapiro. 1997. *Black wealth, white wealth: A new perspective on racial inequality.* New York: Routledge.

Washington Post, Kaiser Family Foundation, and Harvard University. Survey of Hurricane Katrina evacuees.
http://www.kff.org/newsmedia/7401.cfm.

Weber, Max. 1978. *Economy and society.* Berkeley: University of California Press.

Whitehead, John, Bob Edwards, Marieke Van Willigen, John R. Maiolo, Kenneth Wilson, and Kenneth T. Smith. 2000. Heading for higher ground: factors affecting real and hypothetical hurricane evacuation behavior. *Global Environmental Change Part B: Environmental Hazards* 2:133-142.

Part II

The Managed Self: Identities, Emotions, and the Treatment of the Hurricane "Other"

THE EMOTIONAL MANAGEMENT OF A STRANGER: NEGOTIATING CLASS PRIVILEGE AND MASCULINE ACADEMICS AS A HURRICANE KATRINA EVACUEE

KRISTEN BARBER
SOUTHERN ILLINOIS UNIVERSITY, CARBONDALE

It was late August, and on most days New Orleans was a sticky ninety degrees. The musty, sweet smell of old trash and the aroma of magnolia trees filled the hot humid air; a smell I had actually grown fond of because I associated it with the city I had come to love. It was the smell of New Orleans in the summer. The wet heat slowed life in the city down to a crawl, and was something unfamiliar to me as a native Michigander. Despite this, New Orleans continued to bustle with life as people braved the hot streets in order to go about their daily business.

During this time of year I opted to conduct as much of my business in the air-conditioning as possible, including my physical exercise. Pumping and sweating away on the elliptical machine at the school gym, I tried to take my mind off my burning muscles by staring up at the row of televisions that were affixed to the wall ahead of me. This day, the weather channel caught my eye. The meteorologist pointed to the Gulf Coast and warned that a category 4 hurricane was predicted to make landfall within thirty-six hours; worse yet, it was predicted to make a direct hit to New Orleans.

Not Yet Blasé

I was attending Tulane University as a graduate student in the Department of Sociology and had lived in New Orleans only a year when Hurricane Katrina hit. Being in graduate school, I found myself involuntarily isolated from what was going on in the world. This was a function of spending most (really all) of my time indoors with my nose in a book or in front of the computer screen. I had no idea a hurricane had even materialized in the Gulf. Apparently, this had been big news for the past couple of days and was just now becoming *very* big news. "This could be it! This could be the one New Orleans has been waiting for," the newscasters seemed to shout.

In Michigan, the city of New Orleans is known for two things: First, it is known for Mardi Gras—a.k.a. "beads and boobs." Second, it is known for being situated below sea-level and thus for having the potential to one day flood and sink into nonexistence, realizing the destiny of the lost city of Atlantis. I thought of this reputation as I pumped away on the elliptical machine and damned the television for not having sound. My stomach turned and I felt panic settle in.

I had evacuated for Hurricane Ivan the year before and the storm had left the city unscathed. However, having lived on the Gulf Coast for only a year, I was not yet desensitized to hurricanes; that is, I had not yet adopted the blasé attitude Georg Simmel (1997 [1903]) suggests people assume in order to survive the overabundance of stimuli associated with living in the city. In New Orleans, between the months of June and November, these stimuli manifest in the form of hurricane scares. As I watched the white computerized hurricane swirl into the Gulf and slap its tentacles over my new but beloved city, I decided that I needed to get out of New Orleans, and fast.

Everyone who surrounded me had adopted the blasé attitude, no doubt a consequence of having lived on the Gulf Coast for many years and evacuated for a number of uneventful hurricanes. My boyfriend, Damien, had grown up along the coast in Corpus Christi, Texas, so he shrugged his shoulders at the news of Katrina and told me that this was *just another* hurricane. Baristas at the local coffee shops and random people on the street all seemed to suggest the same thing, "You'll regret it if you go." "Do you really want to waste your time, energy, and money?" "You will just be coming back in a couple of days." I was not back in a couple of days, or a couple of months.

Evacuation

Although it took me "freaking out" for an hour in the coffee shop to convince Damien to evacuee, he did eventually cave and said that he supposed it was "better safe than sorry." It was Saturday and the storm was estimated to hit Sunday evening. We decided we would evacuate to his parents' house in Corpus Christi so that if the storm missed New Orleans we could return quickly and by the end of the weekend. We thought it best to leave in the middle of the night to avoid the incomprehensible traffic that was to accrue that next morning. We headed to our separate apartments to pack and, at midnight, would meet up at my apartment to load the car.

I was not worried about potentially losing my furniture, my own artwork (I paint for a hobby), or my car; rather, one of the most difficult decisions I made was choosing which books I wanted to save from the potential flooding. For a half hour, I stood gripped with panic and indecision in front of my six-foot tall, black and white bookshelf. Finally, I apologized to those books I would leave behind and stuffed a select handful into a gray book bag, making sure not to leave out Karl Marx's *Capitalism: Volume 1*. While I had packed my most important documents (passport, social security card, and birth certificate) and cutest shoes, I later found out that Damien had packed for a fun-filled weekend at his parents—no papers, no photos, nothing of real importance to him; he of course later regretted this. I also made sure to grab both my thesis data and materials for a paper on which I was working for publication. While at the time of evacuation I understood the importance of saving these materials if something were to really happen, I had not thought about having to turn to these materials and continue doing sociology as an evacuee or what that experience would be like.

Damien and I packed ourselves into my brand new Honda Civic. As we drove out of town, we passed a house where a "hurricane party" was being hosted. People were laughing and drinking, and the song, "Rock You Like a Hurricane," thumped out from the stereo. About ten minutes outside of the city police directed us onto the contraflow where they had both sides of the expressway going out of town in hopes to more quickly evacuate people. Tired, and driving in the dark, my eyes became weary and relentlessly went in and out of focus. The red lights from the road reflectors and from car taillights blurred past me. Honestly, I don't know how I stayed awake all night.

We made excellent time and the next morning arrived in Corpus Christi. We went to sleep immediately. After resting from the long drive we watched the weather channel incessantly, and that evening we were relieved to find that the storm had passed without devastating the city. However, the next morning we awoke to find that the levees had snapped in the middle of the night and the unbelievable had happened—New Orleans had flooded. I spent all day on the phone with family; my brother sat patiently on the phone with me as I cried. "I'm sorry, Kristen," he said.

The Archetype of the "Masculine" Worker

The magnitude of the devastation following Katrina immediately shot the CNN newscasters to stardom. I watched with disgust as overnight the broadcasters underwent aesthetic makeovers in order to capitalize on their fifteen minutes of fame—fame that came at the cost of so many lives. Through the internet I was able to access photos of what was happening back home: images of nameless bodies floating face down in ten-foot debris-ridden waters; water where streets and homes had been, where people had built their lives, raised their families, and rooted their identities—where I had just begun to build my own life.

After a couple of days, we realized that we were not going home. Damien had packed few clothes and I had packed only my best suits and shoes, so we wore stained and dirty clothes as we shuffled down to the local coffee shop where we spent our days online and on the phone in order to figure out if friends were alive and how to pay bills we knew were due. I was devastated and in shock. Unfortunately, there was no time for me to mourn, to digest what was actually happening to my life, to the city I now called home, and to the friends and colleagues whom I did not know were alive or dead. The horror and helplessness I felt had to be managed because although my world had stopped, everyone else's had not. Arlie Hochschild (1983) explains that the service worker has to suppress her real and true feelings in order to act out and capitalize on "appropriate" feelings that make others comfortable. This is exactly what happened as I found myself unable and uncomfortable expressing the horror and haplessness that I felt. While I did not capitalize financially on suppressing my true feelings, I did trade them for occupational capital. I still had a paper deadline to meet for the anthology chapter I had agreed to complete and the deadline was just 48 hours after the levee break. Therefore, I managed my emotions in order to be a stoic and professional author, and to be productive so I could complete my paper on time. As a result, I experienced a sort of *role conflict* (Goffman 1971): my unemotional academic self came into conflict with my highly emotional hurricane victim self, and it was difficult to simultaneously occupy each role. I was forced to separate myself from my recent identity as a New Orleans evacuee and instead evoke and make salient my role as graduate student, as a productive "masculine" academic.

The academic institution, along with most work organizations, necessitates the performance of an ideal worker that is constructed as inextricable from the performance of "masculinity" (Vandegrift 2005). This is because, as Hochschild (2001) notes, the workforce expects their employees to have no limitations on their time, nothing outside of work to distract them from productivity. The academic is supposed to be unemotional. We are producers for the academy: tunnel-visioned, efficient, and productive. Emotions simply get in the way of and stunt productivity. This "masculine" character of the academy dubs emotions as irrational and unproductive, and, as a result, unacceptable. Instead of attending to my emotional (and psychological) needs, I sat in my hotel room surrounded by turquoise-colored stucco walls, hunched over my laptop, and frantically editing my paper. Luckily, I had a partner who, despite his own burdens, encouraged me to continue my revisions and assured me that I could and would submit my paper on time.

The paper deadline forced me to be productive despite my fear and confusion. Soon after I submitted the paper, the editors responded with suggested revisions that necessitated more research and a rewrite of the paper. I had approximately two to four weeks to turn the paper around to them. However, I had no access to a university library and the databases I had access to through Tulane were inactive, as were all websites associated with the university. In addition to these obstacles, I became keenly aware that, for most universities, the fall semester was starting that week.

Getting into Graduate School—Again

At the time Katrina hit, Damien was a student at Tulane Medical School. Approximately a week after evacuating, he received news that the medical school was getting ready to relocate all displaced students to Houston so that they could continue with classes and rotations and stay on course as much as possible. I stood on the sidelines desperate and frantic and watched him begin the fall semester despite the hurricane. What about me? Although I was relieved for him, I (not so discreetly) complained that *of course* the school was taking care of the *medical students*; I was convinced that the school only cared about those students who were paying big bucks in tuition. Graduate students on stipends and in smaller programs of study were left to fend for themselves. It seemed Tulane had forgotten us. I later found out that it was the Chairs of the medical school that had organized the enrollment of students into a Houston-based medical school, not the Deans of the University.

No sooner had I reserved myself to a destiny of never finishing graduate school and becoming a homeless wanderer did I receive an email from a good friend of mine, Ashley. She emailed to let me know that the University of Michigan was hosting displaced hurricane college students, waiving tuition, and allowing them to register for classes. This became the case at many universities, and a number of colleges and universities immediately responded to the crisis following Hurricane Katrina. However, there was lag time between host schools accepting displaced undergraduate students and displaced graduate students. One college in Texas told me that they could not help me because they were only taking in Gulf Coast undergraduates, and also because I was not a Texas resident. Another school in Boston was more than happy to help me, but could not provide me with the free housing that I would need in order to attend their school.

After numerous frantic phone calls outlining my desperate personal and academic situation, I was allowed to enroll as a graduate student at the University of Michigan. I drove up to Michigan assuming my tuition would be waived; after all, I was a Michigan native and a Katrina evacuee who no longer had access to the funds in my bank account. However, I soon found out that it would cost me almost $2,500 to take a class there, money I did not have. I called the financial aid office and left messages informing them that even Ivy-league schools were waiving tuition for graduate students. Shortly thereafter, I received a call from a man who worked in the university's financial aid office who told me that not only would the school be happy to waive my tuition, but I could take as many classes as I wanted.

"You're Lucky, Others Have it Worse": Negotiating Class Privilege

Once home, my family greeted me with much-needed hugs, kisses, and good food. Those in the community were quick to ask if I was in need of assistance. I did not know if I had lost everything I owned in the flood; all I knew was that the flooding in my area had reached "undetermined" levels. My mother's friends asked if I needed things such as dishes and clothes. Many people reached out to me via my mother, showing both concern for me as well as horror over the situation. Their thoughtfulness and sympathy was much appreciated.

Their understanding of me as privileged, however, complicated many people's sympathy. That is, although I was an evacuee, I was forced by many I came into contact with on a daily basis to recognize the privilege that came with my position as white and middle-class. This was a constant source of conflict for me as I attempted to access aid that was available to me as a Hurricane Katrina victim. There were three instances in particular where this conflict was most salient.

First, I had heard through a friend that all hurricane victims were eligible for a small but helpful sum of money from the American Red Cross. All of my money was currently tied up in a New Orleans bank and my stipend checks had temporarily stopped coming from Tulane. I had packed only suits and summer clothes, and so I needed sweaters and a winter coat to make it through the long and cold winters in Michigan. However, when I came home from the Red Cross with a money card, as well as blankets and a few grooming products, my family reacted as if I had snatched them from a homeless person off the street; after all, they suggested, I could have just purchased a toothbrush and they had plenty of blankets for me to use. However, I did not know if all I owned had been washed away in the flood. So, while my family perhaps took it as an insult to our ability, as a middle-class family, to afford such necessities, they did not understand my dilemma as a renewed dependent.

Second, in addition to the monetary help from the Red Cross, hurricane evacuees were able to receive food stamps. Immediately, I felt the middle-class guilt and the socio-economic stigma of applying for and using food stamps. This stigma serves to define those who need food stamps as lazy drains on the federal economy, further separating the haves and have-nots. I quickly pushed my pride aside and decided that food stamps would allow me to contribute to the household; after all, I was an adult who was now living at home, eating my mother's food, and could not offer money for bills. When I told my mother I could receive food stamps to help with the groceries, she told me, "We don't *need* food stamps, Kristen." I suspect that my mother did not want to feel or appear that she could not provide for her daughter. Food stamps were for the needy and *we* weren't needy; however, I felt that I was in need. My guilt and my mother's reaction demonstrate how stigmatized and *stigmatizing* food stamps are, even in the face of disaster.

The last instance in which my privilege and my need came into conflict was when the local senior center held a soup-bowl function to raise money for hurricane victims. When they heard that my mother, a local shop owner, had a daughter who had evacuated New Orleans, they were happy to have found someone to whom they could donate their money. It was a wonderful gesture and they raised approximately sixty dollars for me and another sixty dollars for Damien. The senior in charge of distributing the funds soon talked me into re-donating the money back to the senior center so they could take computers to the Gulf Coast in order to help hurricane victims apply for FEMA funds online. A man from the senior center "suggested" to me that if I did not feel I *needed* the money, that his organization could put the money to good use. While I agreed that the money would be better spent helping others, my privilege was a constant barrier to resources and empathy. Although people wanted to help me, I was obviously not the most needy Katrina victim. My position as middle-class became salient within my interactions with town folk and helped contribute to my guilt over taking aid.

Some people in the community displayed a version of Simmel's (1997 [1903]) blasé attitude as I saw them become indifferent to my plight and to the continuing struggles of those along the Gulf Coast. Granted they did live in the North, far from New Orleans, and so their lives were not displaced like those in the South. They went on with their daily lives. I was consistently told that I was "lucky" and that "others have it much worse" than I. Though this is inarguably true (everyone I knew was alive, I had the financial capability to evacuate, I had family who was wonderful enough to take me in), the repetitiveness of such statements reflects people's lack of understanding of what had happened, what continues to happen, and how these happenings affected *every* New Orleanian materially, emotionally, and psychologically (albeit differently). In addition to monetary hindrance, the privilege associated with my class discouraged me from mourning because to do so would be to "feel sorry" for myself and I had no right to feel sorry for myself. In order to not be interpreted as "selfish," I had to perform emotional work (Hochschild 1983), ignoring my own feelings and instead portraying a privileged person not in need of financial, emotional, or psychological care.

Simmel: Evacuee as Stranger

I learned that being an evacuee meant becoming Simmel's *stranger* (1999 [1908]). This was in spite of the fact that I had spent the majority of my life in Michigan and had only moved away a year earlier. In conversations with those I both knew and did not know, my position or role within the community and within interactions with others shifted from insider to outsider; I essentially became the "local New Orleans evacuee." Simmel notes that the stranger comes into a community to which s/he has never belonged and affects the relationship between those who were already there, creating solidarity among the group by representing the "other." Simmel states that,

> his [the stranger's] position within it [the group or community] is fundamentally affected by the fact that *he does not belong in it initially* and that he brings qualities into it that are not, and cannot be, indigenous to it (185; emphasis added).

Based on my experiences post-Katrina, I expand on Simmel's concept of the stranger to include someone who once belonged to the group, leaves, and returns again. With this return, the stranger brings new "qualities" to the community or group s/he has accumulated from life experience while absent from the group, qualities that are not "indigenous to it."

I possessed a reservoir of experience and knowledge that those in the community drew from in order to round-out their understanding of what had happened and what was continuing to happen along the Gulf Coast, particularly in New Orleans. People asked me questions about the state of my life: "Did you loose anything?" How did I know, I hadn't even tracked down all the *people* I knew to make sure they had made it out of New Orleans alive. They also asked me political questions: "Do you think it's the local or federal government's responsibility?" Both. Sometimes, it even seemed as if they wanted to start a fight with me: "Everyone should stop pointing fingers and blaming George Bush and FEMA for the poor response after the hurricane." Or "Well, what do people living below sea-level expect, really?" Grrr!

As Simmel explains, my position as stranger had real consequences on the construction of relationships within the community. As an outsider, my position made salient the location of all those who were not hurricane evacuees (which was everyone). My position as outsider illuminated the commonality of those in the community with whom I interacted; they shared the position of non-hurricane evacuee Michigander. For example, the groups I interacted with constructed their choice of place as a good, safe, and rational choice, and justified the characteristics they did not like about the area in which they lived. Michigan has long cold winters and many people I know suffer from Seasonal Affect Depressive Disorder (S.A.D.D.). This disorder arises in colder climates as people live months without warmth or sunshine. In many instances, while discussing the event of Hurricane Katrina with me, people would often exclaim that, "Michigan may be cold, but at least we don't have hurricanes." Others would nod in agreement, making salient their relationship as proud Michiganders and non-evacuees. Consequently, such saliency reinforced my position as different, as an evacuee, as irrational for living below sea-level, and as a stranger within.

Managed Emotions: Making Others Comfortable

Besides attending class at the University of Michigan, I spent four months of displacement working for my mother in her store. Here, I was a constant source of conversation, "Have you met my daughter? She's from

New Orleans." The attention and conversation was diverted away from my mother who unfortunately performed this sort of emotional labor daily with customers, and instead transferred to me. Although my mother had honorable intentions of illuminating her customers with tales of devastation from New Orleans and encouraging them to care about people who were affected by introducing them to one, I was left to maneuver through conversations about a very personal, sensitive, and emotional topic.

Consequently, not only was I expected time and time again to discuss my situation with complete strangers, but I had to perform evacuee in a way that took the feelings of the customers into consideration. I could not tell them how I was really feeling; that I was sad, confused, scared, angry, and unsure. Rather, I had to "do" evacuee in a manner that kept the customer comfortable. I eventually constructed a universal verbal response in order to deal with such situations. I tried to keep conversation light and diverted away from my real thoughts and feelings, evoking what Goffman (1959) refers to as a "front-stage" performance.

SSS Panel

In March of 2006, following Katrina, Danielle Hidalgo, a fellow former Tulane Sociology graduate student and a good friend of mine, organized a Hurricane Katrina panel for the Annual Meeting of the Southern Sociological Society (SSS), which happened to be located in New Orleans. As a member of this panel, I had the opportunity to share my story, which was essentially a much-abbreviated version of this chapter. Each panelist shared his or her personal experience with evacuating from and later returning to New Orleans. Such personal stories were laced with deep, complex, and often conflicting emotions that came through as a few of us began to cry during our presentations; making it obvious that the emotional and psychological pain caused by our experiences continued long after the winds had passed. Many of us were happy to present our stories, as it was an emotional outlet that allowed us to grapple with and work through our experiences with Katrina (Berger and Quinney 2005).

As Ronald J. Berger and Richard Quinney (2005) note in *Storytelling Sociology: Narrative as Social Inquiry*, storytelling is a way for people to cope with pain and hurt in a productive and therapeutic manner. However, as I mentioned earlier, it is difficult to do hurricane victim and academic at the same time. As panelists, we were expected to simultaneously perform victim/evacuee and academic, one role which is rooted in deep emotional and psychological trauma, the other which requires the disassociation from the emotional and the performance of an ideal "masculine" worker, an "objective" observer.

An example of this emerged as I told my story in front of a crowd of approximately sixty other sociology students and scholars. I stopped many times during my presentation because I was so overwhelmed with emotion I knew I could not say one more word without breaking into tears. I gave myself a moment each time this happened to collect myself; I did not want to embarrass myself by crying in front of colleagues, something not recommended in academics as it is not the appropriate conduct of a "masculine" worker. Then, in the middle of my presentation, I let out a sob. I immediately apologized because crying violated the "masculine" code of the workforce; ironically my apology was "feminine" and marginalized the value and appropriateness of deep-seeded emotion. During the question and answer session of the presentation, one sociology professor politely told me that I did not need to apologize because crying is part of the disaster experience and part of the storytelling process. In listening to the panel, she apparently had been able to separate us, the panelists, out as hurricane victims who were sharing an experience of trauma. On the other hand, she, perhaps as a woman academic, had an appreciation for what is considered feminine and was responding to my socialized and marginalizing response to my sob.

Conclusion

My experiences with Hurricane Katrina illuminates the way the blasé attitude (Simmel 1997 [1903]), the ideal "masculine" worker (Hochschild 2001; Vandegrift 2005), role conflict (Goffman 1971), the stranger (Simmel 1908), and *The Managed Heart* (Hochschild 1983) operate in people's lived experiences. It is important to note how larger social structures such as class and gender influence and shape people's experiences of and reactions to disaster. A disaster such as Hurricane Katrina has the ability to illuminate the workings of society that are otherwise often veiled under a thick layer of popular ideology and social misconceptions. While this story is meant to shed light on how social phenomena work in people's lives and how social theory is useful, this story is ultimately a personal one.

While writing this essay I felt three things: Firstly, I felt uncertain about sharing my intimate, emotional, and personal story. This is because I was aware of the role conflict between being a hurricane victim and an academic. Secondly, I felt guilty because by focusing this story on my trials and tribulations, I do not mean to marginalize the invaluable love, support, concern, and aid that I received from my family, my friends, and those in my hometown. I was thankful that I had the resources to evacuate, family and friends in other states who were willing to take me in for four months, and a university that gave me access to libraries, professors, intellectual rigor, and a graduate school community. This essay reeks of frustration simply because my experience with Katrina was (and still is) rightfully a frustrating one—as well as sad, confusing, and often times lonely. Lastly, I felt relieved to be able to share my story with others and to give insight into what life as a hurricane evacuee was like for a middle-class graduate student. Telling this story, I hope that the trials and tribulations of those affected by Hurricane Katrina will not soon be forgotten and that the lessons that emerged from this story inspire others to search out the social patterns in everyday, and not-so-everyday, life.

References

Berger, J. Ronald and Richard Quinney. 2005. *Storytelling sociology: Narrative as social inquiry.* Boulder: Lynne Rienner Publishers, Inc.

Goffman, Erving. 1959. *The presentation of self in everyday life.* Doubleday: New York.

—. 1997. The self and social roles: Role distance. In *The Goffman reader*, ed. Charles Lemert and Ann Branaman, 35-42. Oxford: Blackwell Publishing:

Hochschild, Arlie. 1983. *The managed heart: Commercialization of human feelings.* Berkeley: University of California Press.

—. 2001. *The time bind: When work becomes home and home becomes work.* New York: Henri Holt and Company, LLC.

Simmel, Georg. 1997 [1903]. The metropolis and mental life. In *Simmel on culture*, ed. David Frisby and Mike Featherstone, 174-185. London: Sage Publications.

—. 1999 [1908]. The Stranger. In *Social theory: The multicultural and classic readings*, ed. Charles Lemert, 184-188. Boulder: Westview Press.

Vandegrift, Darcie. 2005. Mama's always on stage: The absurdity of the pregnant academic. In *Storytelling sociology: Narrative as social inquiry*, ed. Ronald J. Berger and Richard Quinney, 119-127. Boulder: Lynne Rienner Publishers, Inc.

ON MANAGING SPOILED IDENTITY: THE ESCAPE FROM HURRICANES KATRINA AND RITA

STAN C. WEEBER
MCNEESE STATE UNIVERSITY

As a native Iowan, I knew hardly anything about hurricanes except that they were a "coastal thing." When they roared ashore, people evacuated or hunkered down and then rebuilt after the storm passed. Life went on—end of story! I didn't care much about the subject because hurricanes happened to other people, not to me. Inland people generally didn't care very much about hurricanes, and didn't think much about them either. I had never lived on the coast, so they were largely "out of sight, out of mind."

As I interviewed for a new job in Lake Charles, Louisiana in 2000, I thought it wise to ask some questions about this domain that I knew so little about. I needed answers because Lake Charles is about 35 miles north of the Gulf of Mexico in far southwest Louisiana, and two hours west of New Orleans. "A hurricane? It's a drink served at Pat O'Brien's (a well-known bar in the French Quarter). You have to travel two hours to get one but let me tell you, it's worth it." That was the beginning and end of my discussion with a campus tour guide about whether or not people in Lake Charles had anything to fear from hurricanes. I couldn't get anything out of my potential new boss either, "Gawd, it's awfully hot and dry here," he drawled, making it sound like southwest Louisiana's three-year drought would mercifully end if any tropical moisture washed ashore. A new friend, Gwen, dared to mention the "A-word": Hurricane Audrey. Over four hundred people died near Cameron, Louisiana as the storm pounded ashore. A few of the dead floated with the storm surge 35 miles north up into Lake Charles. But that was long ago, in 1957, and few in Lake Charles have taken hurricanes seriously since then.

At interview's end, I was ready to sign a tenure-track contract with McNeese State University to teach sociology, beginning in August, 2001. I had finally finished my dissertation and was ready for my first real job after years of procrastination teaching sociology on the Texas adjunct circuit. I was confident that my family would have nothing to fear from hurricanes.

Hurricane Katrina: The "Town" Frame and the "Gown" Frame

With so much reassurance that I had no need to worry about hurricanes in Lake Charles, I felt safe and confident when Hurricane Katrina roared ashore on August 29, 2005. I watched the storm develop for days and I was very anxious to see where it would land. The Doppler radar was maximized on the computer monitor in my office and I could see the horrible pounding that New Orleans was taking. But I was preoccupied by the selfish question of whether Katrina's westernmost rain bands would reach out to Lake Charles. How would the hurricane affect *us*? Would we have to shut down the school as we had in 2002, when Hurricane Lily approached?

Lake Charles experienced only a brief afternoon shower from the outer bands of Katrina as the storm blew by on August 29th. By the next day, however, we found that the effects of Katrina were more social than weather related. New Orleans evacuees began to arrive here and as a result the third floor of the Teacher Education building at McNeese State was converted into a special needs shelter for these evacuees. As even more arrived, the shelter was moved to the more spacious Campus Recreation Building. In addition, Burton Coliseum, a winter sports venue, was opened to house the busloads of evacuees. Then, we began to see the first of more than 200 college students trickle in from New Orleans who had enrolled at McNeese on an emergency basis in order to continue their educations. We welcomed the new students by extending our late registration for the fall semester, raising the enrollment limits in some classes and keeping a close eye on the students to monitor for signs of anxiety, depression, post-traumatic stress, and any other mental health issues that they may have been facing.

Confronted with newcomers to town, how would the people of Lake Charles evaluate them? I identified two different ways that locals "framed" or organized the experience of the influx of evacuees. Erving Goffman (1974) defined a frame as a schema of meaning that helps us understand and interpret people and situations around us. As the frame takes hold and we rely upon it for a guide to our experiences, it becomes an important part of our decision-making process and how we evaluate certain social situations. The most important of these frames Goffman called "primary frames." More than one primary framework could operate on our experience at once and there could be considerable tension between two frames that appear to contradict one another. In Goffman's classic example, the woman about to give birth faces two contradictory primary frames with respect to a male OB-GYN doctor that is handling the delivery. In a "cultural" frame, it is inappropriate for a male that is mostly unknown to the woman to see her naked body. In a "professional" frame, it is entirely appropriate and in fact necessary for the man to view the woman's naked body if the birthing process is to proceed. In Lake Charles, there were two different primary and competing frameworks that were being utilized to make sense of the social experience of the incoming evacuees from New Orleans; I call them the "Town" Frame and the "Gown" Frame.

The Town Framework appeared to be the frame of choice for most of the people living in Lake Charles who had few ties to the McNeese State community. In this working class town of 71,000, families are generally closely knit, their outlook on the world is shaped by a collectively shared historical experience of having been barred from Acadia, the difficult frontier life in south central and southwest Louisiana, and the unique cultural traditions that their families have established. Suspicion of outsiders runs deep and there is a preference for dealing first with family members that can be trusted. Though superficially kind to strangers, the social currents running underneath the façade of social interactions are strong, with a preference for not getting involved with strangers. Strangers represent danger, and thus the norm prescribed was avoiding meaningful long-term associations with them.

The evacuee strangers headed toward Lake Charles in buses were not just any kind of strangers, they were New Orleanians. The cultural differences between New Orleans and the rest of Louisiana accelerated the fear of these outsiders. Curt Iles (2005), a writer from the small town of Dry Creek, Louisiana, discusses how many Louisianians outside of the Big Easy view New Orleans,

> I love New Orleans but I'm scared of New Orleans. Especially after dark ... I've read too many stories of visitors and tourists being mugged, beaten, robbed, raped, and killed (5).

> New Orleans is part of the rest of Louisiana on the maps only—not in the minds of its residents ... New Orleans is its own world, a city and a state of mind separate and apart from the rest of the country, the South, and the state—especially the state ... (35).

> The average Orleanian will acknowledge there is a state of Louisiana, a vague, distant, desolate hinterland, somewhere "across the lake."

Thousands of adult Orleanians walking the streets have never set foot outside the City... The rest of Louisiana has this love-hate relationship with New Orleans. The farther north you go, the more likely you are to run into people who revile New Orleans as a stinking sinkhole (35).

Unfair as these stereotypical views of New Orleanians may be, they nonetheless became a part of the Town Frame in post-Katrina Lake Charles. Dangerous characteristics were clearly being projected upon the incoming evacuees, based upon something that Lake Charles people had seen, heard, or read about. Behind closed doors, within the confidential talk of family circles, evacuees were being constructed as criminals, vagrants, deviants, outsiders, looters, drunkards, junkies, escaped convicts, child rapists; collectively and as individuals, they were a "spoiled identity" (Goffman 1963). And evacuees were easy to spot on the streets of Lake Charles because they were often on foot, worn and haggard looking, with ill-fitting clothes and wandering aimlessly as to kill time before returning to their shelter.

How could people be so callous as to adopt the Town Frame? What purpose did it serve? As people here have a deep sense of family and of self-protection that is historically shaped by years of maltreatment, the frame embodies love of family and self-preservation of values. These are values that people hold dear.

The frame was employed as I saw family groups gather together, sometimes joined by neighbors and close friends, to discuss the rumors of the mayhem that was supposedly taking place on the streets of Lake Charles soon after the evacuees had arrived. Unruly evacuees were said to be hijacking cars, setting fires, causing riots, shooting at people who were trying to assist them, robbing businesses, and raping women. In the absence of any formal denials from city officials, this rumor-making process substituted for "news" about the evacuees (Shibutani 1966).

Business owners whom I knew operated within the Town Frame as they made immediate changes in security at their businesses. Businesses carrying large amounts of cash hired extra security guards or, as one owner told me, she installed a special permanent lock on the door to her business immediately after Hurricane Katrina. She could press a button to open the door from her desk. She opened the door only for people she knew or suspected to be legitimate customers, and she screened out the "riff-raff" or potential troublemakers or robbers (i.e. the New Orleans people). Further, she whispered to me of the extreme angst of Lake Charles law enforcement as the evacuees settled in, "They respond to calls with more than one squad car—sometimes two or more cars and with eight to ten officers." The lock on her door was evidence that she was gripped with fear, as were many others, over the incoming refugees from New Orleans. The politically incorrect term "refugee" seemed to fit in a sociological sense because locals viewed the people as immigrant aliens who had landed in Lake Charles. A lady on Burton Street, counseling her son not to associate with children evacuated from New Orleans, bellowed, "The fact is, son, you don't know who these people are." The heart of the Town Frame is not the superficial, false veneer of friendliness that may be initially displayed, but the "backstage" fear and anxiety motivated by family and cultural values that drives the frame and shapes individuals' sense of what is real as they encounter the evacuees.

The "Gown" Frame was the second way of organizing the evacuee experience after Katrina. This was a more humanitarian frame. Substantive assistance to evacuees was the norm prescribed and the behavior that was expected and made the most sense within this frame. Evidence of this frame at work was clear as volunteers prepared and/or distributed meals to the thousands of evacuees staying at the Lake Charles Civic Center and the Burton Coliseum. At McNeese State, registration was extended and every possible effort was made to accommodate the 224 new students from New Orleans, including registration in newly constructed independent study sections for certain disciplines. Students, faculty, and staff volunteered their time at the special needs shelter on the campus. Faculty opened their homes to incoming evacuees who preferred a residence setting over the hard concrete of the Civic Center or Burton Coliseum. The McNeese Foundation established the Katrina Hurricane Student Relief Fund to provide financial assistance to displaced students. The McNeese library ensured that computers were available for use by evacuees.

To clarify, the names "Town" and "Gown" are not used to suggest that all "Lake Charles people" with no ties to McNeese represented the Town Frame, or that all the "McNeese people" represented the Gown frame. For example, I knew of some residents of Lake Charles with no ties to McNeese that operated within the Gown Frame, contributing thousands of hours volunteering at the shelters on or off campus. Similarly, I encountered faculty at McNeese whose attitudes toward the evacuees were more in line with the Town Frame than with the Gown Frame.

Settling In: Managing Impressions and Managing Spoiled Identity

Goffman (1963) wrote that some settings are "civil places" where the spoiled identity of the stigmatized or disvalued person is minimized.

McNeese State—where the Gown Frame was the predominant frame—appeared to be such a place, especially for the first wave of evacuees that arrived here; the ones who seemed to have ready access to the economic and social capital necessary to take leave of New Orleans quickly and safely. The setting was not perfect however, as the derogatory term "refugee" was primarily and unwisely applied to the newcomers during the first week. This was clearly an accident, because the McNeese community could not have anticipated that the students would view the term as pejorative. Although the students largely avoided being typecast as troublemakers, as New Orleans evacuees they had been privately typecast under the Town Frame.

A typical line of behavior as the New Orleanians enrolled at their new school was to approach the instructor as an evacuee and to humbly ask how they could "catch up" to the material that the other students had already studied. By deploying their evacuee self, the students were hoping to save "face;" that is, they aimed to achieve a positive presentation of self (Goffman 1967). They hoped that freely admitting their unique status as an evacuee would portend some generosity or leniency on the part of the instructor, and that any shortfalls in student performance might be tactfully ignored or "disattended" (Goffman 1959, 1974). Alex, a 32 year-old senior, stood out as an exemplar of this approach. After his first appearance at my Sociological Theory class, he warmly greeted me and identified himself as a new student from New Orleans. I greeted him back, welcoming him to class and letting him know that I was here to help him during the semester. This approach worked well for both of us. His easy-going, humble, and willing attitude in self-presentation reflected an effort to gain as much "face" as possible and to "establish himself"—or to establish "footing"—on the professor's good side. I reciprocated by letting Alex know how to access the class notes on Blackboard and how to catch up on the assigned readings.

Another student used the introductory encounter as a way to reveal details of her personal biography and evacuation story. This line of behavior carried the advantages of Alex's approach and, by personalizing the account, paved the way for possibly drawing out an extra measure of leniency and generosity from the instructor. Chandra, a 20-year-old freshman, was just settling into a new life in Lake Charles. She was making good progress, judging from her conversation with me on September 14th. Though still in shock, she was slowly beginning to acclimate to her new "home" and accept the irreversibility of her situation. She told me that she had expected to be gone for just a few days when she evacuated from New Orleans. During Hurricane Ivan in 2004, there had been an evacuation of the city, but when the hurricane steered wide, people were able to return after a short time away from home. Chandra hoped that would be the case with Katrina. Now she was trying to accentuate the positives of her situation by discussing some laudatory aspects of Lake Charles such as the low price of housing. She was also looking forward to settling into school and studying collective behavior and other subjects. Because the study of collective behavior involves the study of disasters, I wove in as many references to Katrina as I could into the lecture of September 14th, and Chandra appeared to enjoy that. She seemed to be connecting the subject matter to her own diaspora. Chandra's approach to the instructor successfully initiated her interaction with the instructor on the right foot, and set the stage for her to gain the highest possible grade when grades were finalized.

Several other students approached the situation of their entry to the school by deciding to try to "pass" as regular McNeese students (Goffman 1963). They accomplished this by not making any notation or any other signification at all to the instructor about being students from New Orleans. The evacuated students—224 altogether—were indicated by a special code in the McNeese record-keeping system that designated them as undecided majors. If I was not aware of their status (and I was often too busy to pay attention to the special code), the students could just quietly blend in with the already registered McNeese students, hoping to slip in as late entrants. These students were taking advantage of a long history of socially embedded conversation (Goffman 1981) that goes on between faculty and students during late registration that goes something like this: "Hi, I'm Joe Smith and I'm enrolling late in your class ... what do I have to do to catch up?" With growing pressure for higher enrollments, these late entrants appear more often than ever, even after the late registration period has expired. So, having late, LATE enrollees is not all that rare anymore. Several of the New Orleans students I came to know—Michelle, Lindsay, Renee, Melinda, and Robin—used this figurative conversation as cover to slip into classes unnoticed as Katrina evacuees. Perhaps painfully aware of how Orleanians were being typecast outside the university, these students did not want to suffer guilt by association if they were to reveal their evacuee status. For these quiet and unobtrusive entrants (at least in their approach to me) I discovered their evacuee status well after the fact. By not highlighting it and by not even raising their status during my discussion with them, they chose to forego all the advantages that could have been reaped from making their status known. I believe that they feared a backlash along the lines of the "Town" Frame if they made their status known, although some other factors could have come into play to explain their behavior.

Tension Between Frames: The Case of Cheryse

As the evacuees settled in, McNeese State's faculty, staff, and students often found themselves operating in both the Town and Gown Frames at different places and times, and in differing circumstances. As residents of the town, they went home at night to hear of the anxiety that was spreading through the town. As "McNeese people," they knew what was expected of them. They were to show tolerance, a humanitarian spirit, and generosity befitting an enlightened, educated people.

Goffman (1974) suggested that, with primary frameworks, a choice must always be made. One cannot simply dwell on the tension and fail to take a stand within one frame or another. At some point, action is unavoidable, for better or for worse. The case of Cheryse brought out human imperfections in me of which I was completely unaware. Unexpectedly, I evaluated her under the Town Frame.

Cheryse was a 22-year-old single parent and freshman, who arrived on campus at an inopportune time. First, she appeared well after the first wave of evacuated students had settled in, and second, the mounting responsibilities of taking care of her own needs and that of her two children appeared to be almost overwhelming to her. The shock of her diaspora wore on her distraught face as she wandered from building to unknown building, hoping to find where she could restart her education. Almost by chance, she wandered upon the Registrar's Office where she was able to fill out her student paperwork and enroll in classes.

Her angst intensified as she tried to locate her first class, which happened to be my Introductory Sociology class. She found the building and the classroom, but at the appointed hour, 8:00am, there were no students and no professor in the class. She then went to wherever she could get help: to the Dean's Office of the College of Business, to the Registrar's Office, to the Department Head of Social Science, and, finally, to me, the instructor. The class had been cancelled for the week; I had asked my students to help out in Katrina relief efforts. Meanwhile, I was attending to some committee work that had been improperly and mistakenly assigned to me during the eight o'clock hour. Cheryse felt somewhat better as she was able to find my office and to meet with me for the first time. When I told her the circumstances, she realized that there was a reason that class was not being held. Further, I told her, as I did Alex, how to access the Blackboard, where summaries of the class notes were provided for all of the students. She would be able to access the assignments, the syllabus, and other information that she needed to get caught up. Then, at the end of her conference with me, she inexplicably turned and left suddenly without saying a word or thanking me, still feeling a deep sense of betrayal by the McNeese system. She was clearly angry. Not being used to such behavior, I unleashed the Town Frame in my evaluation of her behavior. At the time, I was disgusted by this rude "flooding out" in which she essentially broke the very civil frame that I was trying to construct for her (Goffman 1961; 1974). I was trying to civilly "remediate" her so that she could catch up with school, and she showed no appreciation for my efforts. I was furious at the commotion she had made over the cancelled class; the class met in the administration building and it is likely that both the Provost and the President heard of her problem. I considered her a troublemaker. I have to admit I was surprised and embarrassed by my own behavior, that I was making such a "big deal" out of the incident. A social science department head that I encountered was equally suspicious of the student, saying, "She's on drugs. Watch her!!" As much as I wanted to treat her like the other evacuated students, I ended up using the Town Frame to interpret and interact with her, at least initially.

Hurricane Rita and Double Diaspora for New Orleanians

The New Orleans students could not have imagined their situations becoming any worse than they already were, but there was trouble as the week of September 18th began. A new storm would become an event that rearranged New Orleanians' lives a second time, and put Lake Charles people through a life-changing experience of their own.

As Tropical Storm Rita became the 17th named storm of the season on September 18th, the news produced no particular angst among the locals in Lake Charles. It was just another storm to watch in a record year for hurricane production. However, the displaced students from New Orleans with whom I spoke were restless and frightened by Rita as it grew into a hurricane. They were not using this new storm as a form of dramaturgy to leverage more sympathy from me as an instructor; their feelings were genuine. A portion of their city was still under water and the broken levees were patched up but not yet repaired. Floodwater was being pumped out, but the process was very slow. Being hit by Rita would mean more water cascading over the broken levees and a double-dose of misery for the Crescent City.

On the evening of September 21st, I held the last class before our evacuation for Hurricane Rita. It was a test review for my class on Collective Behavior and Social Movements. My mind was racing not only to remember the facts of my review but also to ponder who was not there for the class. Chandra and Michelle (a "quiet" entrant) had just started the class a week ago. They were displaced by Katrina and now would end up having to evacuate a second time. Taking no chances, they were already on their way out of town. I also thought about McNeese State baseball player Tommy Stone, another student in the class. His parents lived in St. Bernard Parish and had lost everything during Katrina; he was still tending to their needs. His dad, the fire chief for the Parish, was interviewed by the media frequently and became a local celebrity for his outspoken criticism of the slowness of the federal response to Katrina.

The next morning, I was enjoying the day off from the usual working grind because school had been cancelled. Then, a weather bulletin caught my attention: the storm had turned in a more northerly direction than anticipated. Folks in Houston and Galveston were sighing with relief, but there was more concern by the minute for people in Port Arthur, Orange, Lake Charles, and New Orleans. By 8:00am I learned just how quickly things can change with a hurricane approaching. The mandatory evacuation order was issued for everyone in the parish south of Interstate 10, and we lived about two miles south of the Interstate. My initial reaction was to stay put. However, we got a full dose of peer pressure to pack up and go as all of our neighbors were packing up. Then, our landlord came to announce that we must leave as he and his entire family were leaving. He did not want to be responsible for anyone left behind.

For the New Orleans students, this was a horror more vivid than anything that they could make up or experience in their worst nightmare. The more frightened ones left before the evacuation order, others left only when the bad news was relayed to them. No one that I knew of defied the evacuation order and stayed behind. Everyone was able to escape with someone, some with new friends made in Lake Charles. Indeed, there was much to fear. As students were packing their belongings, Rita turned into a category 5 monster worse even than Katrina. A direct hit from a category 5 hurricane would essentially destroy Lake Charles and McNeese State. As it turned out, even the reduced category 3 fury of Rita completely destroyed some nearby coastal towns in Cameron Parish. After the evacuation, I made phone calls and learned that some of the students had fled to Arkansas. I prayed for Godspeed as they sought a safe place. Since there was some risk that Rita might lead to renewed flooding in New Orleans, they could not go home. The students also wondered what would be the result of this evacuation. Are they leaving for a few days, as they had thought before (as Katrina approached), or was this the beginning of another long period of readjustment and agonizing pain? Unless being delivered to a university town, they were now subject to being treated under something similar to the Town Frame that existed in Lake Charles. I could only hope that it was indeed a "small world" (Pool et al. 1989) and that during their re-evacuation they would link up with at least one other person they knew from back home.

I evacuated with my family to the town of Farmerville, near Monroe in far northeastern Louisiana. In a set of circumstances dripping with irony, the Town Framework predominated here without any Gown countervailing frame. Sure, there was a campus of Louisiana Technical College there, but there was essentially no Gown Frame that accompanied the school. This was a small town of 4,000 people in the heart of farming country. Consequently, I was constantly being evaluated under the Town Frame. There were no four-year colleges or universities there to provide a safe haven for me. The Red Cross shelter serving Katrina and Rita evacuees was on the outskirts of the town, which meant that the poorest of the evacuees would be on foot and townspeople could be forewarned of their approach. I felt secure and loved within the circle of friends who hosted me, but outside, especially when alone and on foot, I could feel the gaze of the townspeople as they tried to assess who I might be and what level of danger I might carry. I imagined them looking at me and thinking, "Is he a child rapist or escaped convict?" The gazes penetrated my soul. The privileged, white male status I carried on the McNeese campus meant nothing here. They did not know me. I was nobody to them, so I could be anybody that they wanted me to be in their own construction of things, or their own framing of the situation. From the small-town perspective of Farmerville, I was from the "big city" of Lake Charles and probably up to no good. When on foot, no one offered me a ride. In a small town where everyone knows everyone else, I was the ultimate stranger: the "other." I tried to blend in with the natives because, fearing backlash, I did not want to make my status known. As several of my students from New Orleans had done at McNeese, I tried to blend in with the crowd. In Farmerville, it was impossible to do this.

After the Evacuation: (Re)establishing Footing

I returned to Lake Charles on October 7th and it would be three more long weeks of waiting before classes resumed. On Monday, October 31st, all of my classrooms passed the vital air quality test and we were finally back in business at McNeese State. When I reconnected with the now "doubly-displaced" New Orleans students, they seemed very willing to talk to me in order to reestablish their relationship. Even though they barely knew me, I was a connection to Lake Charles and to college. They very much wanted to reestablish a connection here in the name of getting something of the "new normal" back into their routine (Brayfield 2006). I was an important piece of the puzzle as they contemplated getting through this nightmare semester with a set of grades that allowed them to feel as if some progress was being made on their degrees. For a few of the students, this was their final undergraduate semester—one they would never forget—and they were very concerned, as most graduating seniors are, with making sure that they had completed all of their course requirements. My heart ached as I discovered that some of the New Orleans students did not return. I felt a compelling need to follow-up with them and to encourage them to complete their educations.

Alex was one of the returnees and was especially grateful to be graduating, but also mourned an experience that had died with the two hurricanes. That semester (fall, 2005) he was scheduled to take a Political Philosophy class that he had looked forward to taking under one of his favorite professors at Tulane. It was this class, above all others, which he was eagerly looking forward to before the storm. He relished the idea of going to class, taking notes, taking the tests, and working on the term paper. I wondered if the Sociological Theory class Alex was taking at McNeese had been equally satisfying; I suspect not, as Enlightenment thinkers important to Political Philosophy were barely discussed. That was one of the aspects of Tulane that he missed—a Tier 1 school with an excellent faculty and the ability of that faculty to teach some specialty classes in which he was significantly interested. Thus, his graduation was bittersweet. He was glad to have survived two hurricanes, but also disappointed in what that meant for him academically.

Importantly, with this conversation, Alex successfully reestablished his relationship with me within the Gown Framework. Though admitting some painful disappointments, he did take pride in his education and his graduation. Once again, he used a line of behavior that emphasized his evacuee status (now double-evacuee) and how he needed to continue to catch up with the material. He asked, for example, if the classroom procedures would be the same as before Rita struck (lecture/discussion format, use of Blackboard). The Gown Frame was the only one left on campus, the McNeese people having been worn down and readjusted in their thinking following their own diaspora.

Cheryse also reconnected with me and was glad to be back in school. She was friendlier now and more willing to talk about the mental anguish of double-diaspora. Due to my own evacuation experience, I softened my view of her and felt that I understood her much better now, especially the emotional strain that she was under. As a single parent, she bore the pressure of providing for her family under these most difficult circumstances. The eight o'clock class that she was taking with me (originally a class from 8:00am to 8:50am) had been changed to a 65-minute course from 7:30am-8:35am. This was so that the class would have enough contact hours in order to finish the semester. I was teaching another section of the course at 4:30 in the afternoon and she asked if she could attend the afternoon class as she was having trouble arranging for child care in order to show up at class on time at 7:30am. I consented to this request, considering the pain that she had been through. Eventually she completed the class and was elated to have finished the fall semester.

Lessons Learned from This Experience

The most bizarre semester in McNeese history ended on December 23rd when 616 students, including several from New Orleans, graduated from the school following an accelerated eight weeks of intensive study. In my diaspora, I can now say that I have something in common, in a minimal sort of way, with diverse peoples much unlike me: sixth century B.C. Jews, famine and flood victims, refugees, Palestinians, people displaced by war and by hunger, and the Acadians driven out of Nova Scotia. I can say that I have experienced such diaspora not only from the standpoint of a native being besieged by newcomers, but also as the homeless wanderer who is exposed to the negative frames of others. I learned much about myself as well as the rural working-class place in which I live. My awareness of human diversity and human nature has never been more heightened. I know that I am capable of a great deal of imperfection. If another hurricane strikes and evacuees come to Lake Charles, I will not use the Town Frame at all when evaluating these people.

The displaced students also underwent a series of changes. They learned more about themselves, especially how tough and adaptable they are. They coped successfully with the crisis of "spoiled identity" that they faced upon their first arrival in Lake Charles. They felt that if they could withstand two hurricanes and two evacuations, they could survive most anything. They vowed never to take their educations for granted. For those returning home, there was a vow to appreciate all the advantages, cultural and otherwise, of going to school and living in the great city of New Orleans. Cheryse told me at our last meeting, "Good old New Orleans! My people are there, my school's there, and my heart is there. Time to go. That's where I belong."

References

Brayfield, April. 2006. Ongoing stories, ongoing struggles. Paper presented at the annual meeting for the Southern Sociological Society, March 23, in New Orleans, Louisiana.
Goffman, Erving. 1981. *Forms of talk*. Philadelphia: University of Pennsylvania Press.
—. 1974. *Frame analysis*. New York: Harper and Row.
—. 1971. *Relations in public*. New York: Basic Books.
—. 1967. *Interaction ritual*. Garden City: Anchor Books.
—. 1963. *Stigma*. Englewood Cliffs: Prentice-Hall.
—. 1961. *Encounters*. Indianapolis: The Bobbs-Merrill Co.
—. 1959. *The presentation of self in everyday life*. Garden City: Doubleday.
Iles, Curt. 2005. *Hearts across the water*. Sulphur: Wise Publications. Kelly. Online image contribution, hurricane digital memory bank. Object #173. http://www.hurricanearchive.org/object/1731.
Pool, Ithiel de Sola, Stanley Milgram, Theodore Newcomb, and Manfred Kochen. 1989. *The small world*. Norwood: Ablex Publishing.
Shibutani, Tamotsu. 2006. *Improvised news: A sociological study of rumor*. Indianapolis: Bobbs-Merrill.

Volunteer Voices: Making Sense of Our Trip to the Mississippi Gulf Coast After Katrina

Jeffrey T. Jackson and Kirsten A. Dellinger
University of Mississippi

It was mid-morning on Saturday, September 3rd, 2005, not quite a week after Katrina had hit the Gulf Coast when five of us—friends and colleagues—sat crammed in the back office of our house discussing an urgent need to "do something." Jeff was put in charge of gasoline, something that made him feel more than just a little bit nervous. In order to get our small, impromptu caravan from the Northern Mississippi town of Oxford to the hurricane-ravaged Gulf Coast some 400 miles away, and to accomplish our newly formed goals—delivering relief supplies and providing rides north to those who might need transportation—we needed to bring our own fuel. We had already heard reports that gas stations as far North as Jackson, Mississippi were completely out of gas and that many people who had gone down in the earliest days after Katrina had become stranded on the coast, their tanks on "empty." Our ad hoc group's emerging motto of "self sufficiency" was to bring everything we needed to get to the disaster zone and back so we were not a burden on the coastal infrastructure or to the people already suffering there. The last thing we wanted to do was become part of the problem.

But this turned out to be no small task. The five of us decided to bring three vans (to carry supplies to the coast and up to fifteen evacuees back from the coast) and a pickup truck (to carry the gasoline). Jeff calculated conservatively that this would require approximately 100 gallons of gasoline, most of which would need to be transported in separate five to ten gallon plastic containers. As Oxford's own supply of gasoline and gas containers was running low, we spent the afternoon contacting friends, asking them to bring us their own gas containers, filled to the top, if possible. Jeff went online to find information on "transporting gasoline" and learned quickly that this was not something that we should take lightly. We were all alarmed to learn, for instance, that it was unsafe to transport gas containers in pick-up trucks with plastic bed liners due to the potential build up of static electricity. We were pretty certain that the last thing the Gulf Coast needed was to have one of its relief convoys burst into flames in the midst of everything else; so Jeff removed the plastic bed liner from the pickup truck and took every possible precaution to make sure we transported our gas safely.

By early evening, we were surprised to find dozens of red plastic containers containing gasoline on the side lawn. While we were touched and inspired by the cooperative effort of our friends in the gathering of gas and supplies, we were all nervous about the quantity of gasoline we would have to take with us. This nervousness left lingering questions in our minds: "Is this really a good idea?" "Should we be doing this?"

We tell our story of "spontaneous volunteerism" during Katrina to shed some light on our motivations for volunteering and, more importantly, to discuss the challenges and anxieties we faced during the experience. Although Katrina affected a very specific geographical region of the country, its impact was national in scope. A focus on volunteerism provides a window into the experiences of people not directly affected by the storm, but touched by the disaster nevertheless. We find John Wilson's (2000) definition of volunteerism useful: "Volunteering means any activity in which time is given freely to benefit another person, group, or organization. This definition does not preclude volunteers from benefiting from their work" (215). We use the term "spontaneous volunteers" to refer to volunteers who, like us, become involved in a volunteer experience very quickly in response to a perceived immediate crisis (St. John and Fuchs 2002, 401). The volunteer experience is an understudied area of sociological inquiry (Lowe 2002; Wilson 2000). We hope that this first-hand account of our volunteer experience not only adds to the overall story of Katrina, but also illuminates the dynamics of relief assistance and volunteerism in general.

The Decision to Get Involved

Six days after the hurricane, it was increasingly apparent that the affected area was not receiving the rescue and recovery assistance it required. By that Saturday morning, September 3rd, after watching endless coverage of mostly black, stranded New Orleanians, one of our friends had had enough. He called us to see if we wanted to take action. His proposed plan was simple: Drive down to the I-10 overpass in New

Orleans and offer rides to anyone wanting to go to the largely empty shelters in Oxford. When we asked for more details, he replied frankly, "To be honest, I haven't thought about it much more than that." In retrospect, what motivated us to dive into a largely spontaneous volunteer relief effort involved a number of factors.

Sociologists have found that people are more likely to volunteer with others than they are on their own (Wilson 2000). Craig St. John and Jesse Fuchs (2002) argue that, "Being connected to a large circle of friends increases the chance that people will learn of volunteer opportunities and be asked to volunteer." Ours is an example of "collectivistic-based volunteerism" which, according to Susan Eckstein (2001), "involves acts of generosity that *groups* (rather than individuals) initiate, inspire, and oversee; individuals participate because of their group ties" (829, italics in original). Our friend's initial plan to drive down to I-10 would not have transformed into the relief effort that resulted without a collective effort. The more people we contacted to donate gas and supplies or for information about the coast, the more real the trip became and the harder it was to imagine backing out. Our group of five began to feel a sense of responsibility to each other and to the people we convinced to join our effort.

We used our house as a home base. After our initial meeting in the small back office, we moved into the living room and spread out around the dining room table. Kirsten grabbed a newsprint flipchart to keep track of the people we needed to call for gas and the number of gallons and containers they were able to donate. The rest of the team pulled out their cell phones to make calls and jumped in their cars to run errands. Throughout the day, we had a continuous stream of friends stopping by to drop off gas, supplies, and money, and just to offer their support. When we realized that this planning session was going to take all day, Kirsten whipped up some bacon, lettuce, and tomato sandwiches. It seemed like eating together further solidified the fact that this was no longer a normal Saturday afternoon and that we were now a team. Emile Durkheim might have explained it as a feeling of "collective effervescence." We were excited to be part of something larger than ourselves.

The social position of members of our group in regard to demographic characteristics and more practical matters such as access to resources also impacted our ability to help. These demographic factors are well-documented in sociological research (Wilson 2000; Wilson and Musick 1999). Susan Eckstein (2001) writes,

> studies concur that the archetypal American volunteer is middle aged, educated, employed, living in a small town, is involved in the community,

is a woman, and in addition is middle- or upper-class and religiously involved (831).

Furthermore, volunteering costs money and time and individuals who have privileged access to resources are more likely to be in a position to contribute necessary resources than those who do not (Wilson 2000). Our main source of financial support and what sociologists call "social capital" came through university and community connections. According to John Wilson and Marc A. Musick (1999), "Social capital... describes resources, such as information, trust, and cooperative labor, acquired and mobilized through social connections" (247). We were able to borrow the Sociology and Anthropology University van, rely on flexible work schedules to recover from and continue our relief efforts, and mobilize friends and colleagues to donate gas, money, and supplies for our trip.

But when volunteers agree to help, the question of boundaries arises. How much should I give? How much *can* I give? Early on it became apparent that we would not be able to bank roll this operation all by ourselves. At 11:00pm on Saturday night, Kirsten and another team member stood at the check out counter in the grocery store with two carts filled to the brim with supplies. We split the cost, each paying about $110 for the diapers, tampons, toothpaste, granola bars, canned goods, juice, and water we bought for people on the coast. While this first outlay of expenses was made without much thought, the question of how much we could afford to donate in terms of both money and time was a recurring issue for the group as our involvement moved beyond the one day trip to include follow-up assistance to the people we brought back from Bay St. Louis. Perhaps the stereotype of the "completely selfless and altruistic volunteer" made it difficult to say "no" to requests for assistance. In addition, it could lead to feelings of guilt if one of us was to decide they couldn't give any more, either in terms of money, time, or emotional labor. While there was little time in the moment to discuss these complicated emotions and feelings, there is no doubt that we were negotiating them, constantly.

In the case of Katrina, it seems clear in hindsight that there were additional macro structural reasons behind our motivation to volunteer. The media images of suffering people in New Orleans infuriated us (as it did many throughout the country and the world). We interpreted this as a story of both racial injustice and governmental ineptitude at national and state levels. The failure of government and non-governmental relief organizations in the aftermath of Katrina was widely understood at the time and is currently the subject of much research (see Shughart 2006; Sobel and Leeson 2006). And part of our motivation for helping was to set out to try to make things right, and to mark our disapproval and disgust with the way things were being handled.

Research on other disasters such as the 9/11 attacks, has found that spontaneous volunteerism often arises out of similar emotions. For example, Seana Lowe (2002) reports that,

> Upon learning of [the disaster,] [volunteers] described feelings of victimization, shock, powerlessness, hopelessness, helplessness, fear, and confusion....the primary motivations for volunteering were a need to better the situation of others, a need to reclaim power, and a need to redefine the circumstances as meaningful (2).

We believe a similar motivation was operating in our situation. Certainly powerlessness and hopelessness were present. Our emotions, however, were less about victimization and fear (of terrorists, for example) and more about frustration at authorities and feeling protective of our region.

It is important to recognize that those of us near the hurricane affected region were particularly sensitive to these issues as local and national news provided constant updates on the status of the relief process. This is consistent with research on volunteerism that finds, "Proximity to [the disaster region]... increase[s] the likelihood of volunteering" (Beyerlein and Sikkink 2005, 2). As citizens of the state of Mississippi, our group felt a particular sense of responsibility to help. In a logistical sense, we were close enough to drive in and out of the disaster area in a day's time. In addition, while the crisis in New Orleans was horrifying, we were increasingly frustrated by the initial (and overall) lack of media coverage of the devastation in Mississippi itself. On the drive down to the coast, as we passed a military convoy, our friend driving the van made vigorous "thumbs up" signs and asked Kirsten to write "Thanks" on a piece of paper and hold it up for them to see. We were intensely grateful for anyone coming to the aid of Louisiana or Mississippi and wanted to feel a connection with them, even if it was behind the glass of our van window at sixty miles per hour on the highway.

Perhaps Randall Collins' notion of "symbolic solidarity" helps explain these motivations. While Collins (2004) does not focus on volunteerism per se, his theoretical discussion of "rituals of solidarity" and the display of "solidarity symbols" in the 9/11 context seems to have much in common with the displays of "voluntary helping" on a symbolic level. Collins writes,

> The key to such a pattern [of solidarity symbols] is the dramatic incident, the attention-focusing event....Solidarity is produced by social interaction

within the group, not by the conflict itself as an external event. What creates the solidarity is the sharp rise in ritual intensity of social interaction, as very large numbers of persons focus their attention on the same event, are reminded constantly that other people are focusing their attention by the symbolic signals they give out, and hence are swept up into a collective mood (55).

We were clearly "swept up into a collective mood" of intense solidarity around a dramatic incident, and it is important to recognize that many individuals and groups throughout the country were spontaneously leaping into action.

But were there other reasons for participating as spontaneous volunteers? Looking back it is important to consider how self-interested motives affected our growing confidence that we should make the trip happen. In addition to the "curiosity" and the "need to participate in the disaster" referred to by St. John and Fuchs (2002, 401), the self-interested motives for volunteering are well-documented within the research on volunteerism (Wilson 2000). For instance, we certainly felt a personal need to feel involved and important (We're better than the government!). And while it is hard to admit, we were driven partially by a deep curiosity and desire to see the devastation first-hand and to experience the positive reinforcement of being recognized as someone making a special effort for others. Soon after, word spread that we were taking a Sunday trip to the coast, we received notes of concern about our safety, offers of money to help fund the trip, and people thanking us for what we were doing. And we hadn't even done anything yet. But it felt good! Not only did we start to become excited about our idea, but we felt that perhaps our trip was becoming an outlet for others who felt the way we did and wanted "to do something" too. After we returned from the trip, we found ourselves telling the stories of survival that the evacuees had told us. In some way, the telling of these stories was certainly about sharing their experiences, but it was also a way to present ourselves as "people who cared enough to listen to those stories," "people who were close to the action," and as "good volunteers." Needless to say, motivations for "helping" are never purely altruistic and involve all of these complicated factors.

The Plan and Preparation

Saturday was filled with two main activities: gathering supplies and gathering information. But the gathering of these things was not as straightforward as checking off items on a "to do" list. This was a day filled with excitement, doubts, and fear. In addition to the phone calls for gas and supplies, we called the local grocery stores and a sandwich shop to ask if they were giving discounts for purchases related to Katrina relief. The sandwich shop donated a dozen turkey sandwich meals intended to feed the Katrina evacuees on our way home in case there were no restaurants serving food. The grocery store gave a 10% discount. Most of the phone calls to friends and local businesses were characterized by a sense of camaraderie. Every time someone agreed to help, whether it was bringing gas or money, or agreeing to donate food or supplies, or giving us another phone number to call to find out the information we sought, we hung up the phone, sometimes with a high five, energized and with more confidence that our trip was the right thing to do. But in the few instances when someone seemed to hesitate before agreeing to help ("I wasn't planning to drive to town today, so I'm not sure we can deliver the gas container") or explained that our plan did not seem to be a good idea, we got off the phone, relayed the tale to whoever was in the room with a sense of anger, agreeing that they were naysayers or that they just weren't as committed as we were. Rallying support for an idea often involves the building of an "in group" and an "out group." Both groups bolstered our goal, though in different ways.

While we needed supplies, we also needed information about where these supplies would be most useful on the coast and where we could find shelters where people were looking for rides out of the area. We made countless phone calls to the official organizations expecting that we would find concrete answers to our questions much more quickly than we did. We consulted the Mississippi Department of Transportation, FEMA, and MEMA, for information about maps, road conditions, roadblocks on the perimeter of the disaster area, and curfews. As we investigated the feasibility of the original plan to drive to I-10 in New Orleans, we learned that the National Guard had closed the roads into New Orleans and they were not letting anyone other than "official aid workers" through. This piece of information forced us to rethink our strategy and shifted our focus to helping people in Mississippi.

We called the Red Cross and the United Way. The national phone lines were often busy or would simply ring and ring. So we tried the local agencies. While they were willing to give information about the location of local shelters, they had little to no information about the location and contact information for shelters on the coast. Many of the people we spoke with were volunteers who, like everyone else, seemed to be overwhelmed by this disaster. When we asked for specific recommendations about where supplies might be most needed, people on the other end of the phone seemed hesitant to encourage volunteers to enter a disaster area;

perhaps they feared litigation or perhaps they simply lacked information due to the lack of telephone service on the coast. No matter what the situation, we were frustrated by our inability to obtain accurate and reliable information quickly. Lack of information, coordination, and communication were widespread problems in the management of the Katrina relief effort (Fischer et al. 2000). These difficulties are often worse for the spontaneous volunteer (Lowe 2002).

Many people we talked to instilled a sense of fear. One volunteer at a non-governmental organization told us we had no business going down there because it was too dangerous and people were getting stranded. Even after we explained that we would be entirely "self sufficient" she told us not to go. Others said the situation could lead us to harm, "With that supply of food and gas, you're going to get mugged." One person even offered us his gun in case we needed to protect our supplies! The misguided assumption, largely fueled by the media coverage, was that most people were taking desperate measures to survive. The assumption that disasters are followed by chaos and a total breakdown of the social order is a common disaster myth (Fischer et al. 2006). While we held tight to the belief that fears of violence were unfounded, we all entertained the thought that perhaps it would turn out to be true. Finally, after a lengthy conversation, one employee at a non-governmental organization gave us an "unofficial" tip, "You didn't hear it from me... but they really need help in Bay St. Louis, Mississippi. They really got hit hard."

We had our destination. But it was not without some misgivings. Some in our group wished we could have gone to New Orleans. In the end, we decided to stay in Mississippi. But the misgivings were about more than the destination itself. The large void in the presence of official assistance agencies (both governmental and non-governmental) led to a lack of guidance and rules for the spontaneous volunteer to follow. We were making it up as we went along. As spontaneous volunteers, we were largely left to ourselves to figure out how to administer relief and this, we believe, led to many of the challenges and anxieties we faced. We debated a number of issues such as whether the volunteer effort was going to be "effective," whether it was going to be autonomous or coordinated with other organizations and authorities, whether it was going to be "one time only" or an "ongoing or long term effort," and, finally, whether such volunteerism was truly helpful and/or altruistic or whether it was self-serving. Similar to Durkheim's notion of anomie (a sense of lack of moral guidance), our group often experienced the feeling that we did not know what our purpose should be and we often found ourselves looking for an overarching authority to guide our actions.

In the end, we decided on a plan of action that we called "micro relief." The idea was that, as a small group, we could do things that the "big relief agencies" couldn't and that, overall, we should be self-sufficient. These guidelines emerged out of conversations with Jeff who was concerned about the possible negative impact of relief assistance in a disaster situation. This concern was largely based on his experience as a researcher studying development assistance in Honduras after the 1998 Hurricane Mitch disaster where he learned about some of the harmful consequences of charity and relief aid in that situation (See Jackson 2005). Jeff felt strongly, and everyone agreed, that we should try to avoid such harmful effects as much as possible in our efforts.

While we did not formulate this philosophy as a written set of guidelines until after the first trip, nevertheless, these were the principles that guided our actions: *(1) Quick in, quick out*: Travel in small self-sufficient groups, have maps and a preplanned route. Be mindful of the curfew and leave well in advance of it. The main goal was not to be a burden on the local scene, even including things as seemingly minor as use of bathrooms or consumption of food. *(2) Provide "Micro-relief:"* Make contact with relief agencies or personal contacts to determine where help is needed. Drop off supplies quickly. Ask whether people need information or if they need to get information out to others. Ask whether people want rides northward. Pitch in whenever possible. *(3) Overall, "Do no harm:"* Relief assistance should not itself become part of the problem. Try to avoid being a burden to the social systems (police, communications, fuel, distribution of food/water, etc.) that are already under extreme strain. Take precautions so that you avoid getting stuck. This includes having the materials/equipment needed to deal with flat tires, fuel, communication, and have at least two cars in case one breaks down. Bring everything you need or will consume with you (gas, food, etc.). Do not compel anyone to take a ride with you. Be aware of your own motivations and keep them in perspective. And finally, follow the instructions of authorities managing the crisis.

The Trip

Our trip to Bay St. Louis is something that is difficult to discuss even today, almost two years later. It is difficult to put into words the scope of what we experienced there. And the feelings and emotions flood back with the recollections. We were only there for four or five hours, but the glimpse into the human disaster that was the Katrina aftermath on the Gulf Coast was vivid.

Our caravan was made up of four vehicles. A University of Mississippi van provided to us by the archeologists in our department led the way. Although well-used, it was the most "official looking" vehicle we had, which we figured would help if we encountered any checkpoints. In addition, this lead vehicle carried a letter on University of Mississippi letterhead from various administrators at the University stating that they approved and supported our trip. Kirsten and another member of our group drove this vehicle and were responsible for navigating our way down. Jeff followed in the pickup truck carrying the gas supply. The remaining two men in our team each drove their own van and brought up the rear. We communicated with each other via cellphone (when service was available) and by walkie-talkie. Before we began the trip, we gathered around the pick up truck and spread maps out across the top of the orange tarp covering the gas containers to double-check our route. We reiterated the need to stay together in the caravan. Despite all of our preparations, we felt like we were venturing into the unknown. We were excited and scared, but we felt confident that we were with a group of people we could trust in any situation.

Ours was not unlike many of the impromptu volunteer groups that made their way to the Gulf Coast in the days and weeks immediately following Hurricane Katrina. As we drove down Interstate 55, we passed numerous caravans and convoys of relief workers, police officers, firefighters, military, religious groups, and medical teams. The license plates were from all over: Illinois, Ohio, Michigan. There were other smaller caravans like us with homemade "Red Cross volunteer" signs taped to the side of the car or "Katrina Aid Relief Supplies" handwritten across the back of small trailers. It seems clear that many people throughout the region had "had enough" and felt compelled to get involved. Research suggests that these groups were spurred by a broad perception that traditional governmental and private assistance organizations had failed (Beyerlein and Sikkink 2005; Collins 2001; Shughart 2006; St. John and Fuchs 2002).

As we traveled south, the lines of cars at gas stations grew longer. Many gas stations were closed or vacant. Our first group disagreement had to do with whether we were going to "top off" our tanks in Canton. We pulled off the highway and found that the shortest line was a two hour wait. Jeff grew nervous because his calculations included topping off our tanks here. Another member of the group disagreed, stating that we were slipping into a needless "gas panic" when in reality we had plenty of fuel for the trip. Could it be that the hoards of people lining up for gas around us made us feel an urgent need to get some too? We grew increasingly aware of the great value of the liquid sloshing around in containers in the back of the pick-up truck, which heightened our anxiety about how desperate people might be for this commodity on the coast.

While we witnessed significant damage from the storm throughout the journey, the destruction from Hattiesburg southward was unbelievable. Trees by the thousands were splintered, broken and fallen; leaning on crushed houses, littering roadways, downing power lines. We drove over the thick steel power cables that criss-crossed the rural highways throughout southern Mississippi with an unnerving "thump, thump." We used the walkie-talkies to say things like, "I hope those lines aren't live!" or "How on earth are they going to put all of this back together?" We saw spray-painted signs with messages like, "Stop—Farm Bureau Help Us Please, FEMA, MEMA welcome!" and "Thank you for your help." Several people stood on an overpass holding an American flag and waving to the oncoming traffic. The scale of the devastation was mind-numbing and we were still two hours from the coast.

In response to these signs of physical and emotional tragedy, the level of tension in the cars ratcheted up a few notches. Driving had now become an exercise of paying careful attention to debris, hazards, and twisted signs, while, at the same time, negotiating the emotional "catch in the throat" that we would feel upon each new encounter with devastation and human suffering.

Using our Yahoo! maps and newly acquired directions provided to us by some Mississippi Department of Transportation workers we happened to encounter during our first refueling stop on the side of the road, we finally arrived in Bay St. Louis around mid-day, Sunday, September 4th, 2005, almost one week after the Hurricane had struck. We couldn't believe our eyes as we entered the city along Nicholson Avenue. Mud covered the roadway and we kicked up a fetid cloud of dust as we passed through. The massive storm surge that had entered St. Louis Bay and its tributaries had spilled over into neighborhoods and businesses and communities, leaving destruction in its wake. There was a pool table in the drainage ditch. There was a tin shed plastered fifteen feet high around the upper branches of a tree. Lining the roadway in both directions, empty, muddy, drowned cars greeted our arrival.

We became part of a growing line of vehicles entering the devastation. At the I-10 overpass, the police momentarily halted our caravan to allow a large convoy of shiny, new "high tech mobile hospital" vehicles from North Carolina to pass in front of us. We followed their flashing lights into the heart of the city.

There were no functioning traffic lights anywhere. A National guardsman policed the busy crossroads at Nicholson Ave. and Highway 90. To the left of us was an encampment of people in the K-Mart parking lot. Someone had rigged up a large sign on a ragged sheet that read "Camp Katrina." Other signs said: "Help Us" "Where's FEMA?" "Need Gas." Straight ahead was another sign advertising "Fresh Water Distribution." We weren't sure where to go so we continued through the intersection and pulled over near some National Guard vehicles on the right side of the road. We observed a number of tents set up in what was previously the Rite-Aid parking lot. Thinking this was a shelter of some kind, we sent two members of our group over to the Guardsmen to ask if anyone in the shelter needed a ride north. "No. No one needs a ride here," one of the Guardsmen replied, "This is the morgue." He directed us across the street saying that the people camped there had been without supplies for days.

As the group confronted our unexpected and sudden run in with the reality of death in the disaster zone, we fell silent and tried not to stare too much at the devastation around us. We had heard about the "Katrina voyeurs" and had even decided not to take photos to avoid being perceived as such. But in the end, it was impossible not to feel like an outsider looking in.

We got back into our cars and made our way to the "evacuee encampment" that we had seen across the street in the K-Mart parking lot. There, we found four members of the National Guard patrolling the entrance. They told us that a religious organization was coordinating the collection of supplies that, finally, were pouring into the area: bottled water, canned food, shoes, clothing, diapers, baby formula, toiletries, flashlights, and just about anything else you could imagine. In the distance, in the middle of the parking lot, we could see pallets of supplies piled up high, making our meager load look almost comical. Nevertheless, we were not allowed to drop our things there. The guardsman informed us that, "They have too much to handle right now." We asked if they knew anything about a shelter, but they said that while they patrolled the area, they had no maps and did not know where it was. Once again, the group was stunned by the fact that those who were supposed to be "in charge" didn't have the kind of basic information one might expect them to have. As we left, we drove close by individual family encampments set up along the edge of the parking lot to see if they needed our supplies. One man asked for gas, which we declined to give him. Others said they were fine.

For some reason, the cell phone reception was working for a moment and Kirsten completed a quick call to one of the members of our support team back in Oxford to let him know we had arrived safely. Although we had been in Bay St. Louis for less than thirty minutes, it was surprisingly comforting to hear a familiar voice on the other end of the line express concern about how we were doing.

Asking around, we learned from some local residents how to get to the shelter. As we made our way East along highway 90, we continued to observe the hurricane's destruction: automobiles at a used car lot tumbled upon one another like a messy kid's matchbox cars, a boat dealership with some of its inventory resting neatly on its roof, someone driving down the road in a car whose doors had been permanently bent open by on-rushing water. Everything was closed. All businesses appeared dark and vacant with few signs of life. We drove past an open field that was being used by the military to land helicopters and witnessed the unsettling "chop, chop, chop" of a Huey helicopter as it took off over us. The sights and sounds, it would be no exaggeration to say, made us feel like we entered a war zone or had just stepped onto the set of a scene from the apocalyptic movie *Mad Max*.

We successfully found the shelter at Bay St. Louis High School, drove around to the back, and began to drop off all of our supplies there. We unloaded the vans along with others who were delivering water, ice, and supplies. Donated clothes were piled high in an outside courtyard area. Mammoth stacks of bottled water sat outside the building, while other supplies were handed through a window in a central cafeteria area to volunteers (or other shelter residents, it was often unclear who was who). When Kirsten brought out the two gallons of cold, donated McCallister's iced tea, Mary, a woman who later decided to take a ride with us, ran up and asked if she could have both of them. Kirsten handed off the containers, with a fleeting concern that others might want a glass, but with a better understanding of how disasters turn everyday items into prized possessions.

Having found a home for our supplies, and uncertain of what to do next, the five of us split up to find people who might need a ride. After one of us worried aloud about the possibility of someone accidentally throwing a lit cigarette into the back of the truck, we experienced a momentary panic and decided it would be best if Jeff stayed outside to keep an eye on the gas containers as well as the other vans.

We should emphasize that this "shelter" had no resemblance to the "neat cots in a row" kind of place that often comes to mind. This was an "unofficial" shelter that was created at the last moments before the storm by hundreds of people fleeing the hurricane who had nowhere left to go. It was a reminder of both the lack of planning by official organizations and the extent to which citizens all along the coast were not sufficiently prepared for the magnitude of the disaster that awaited them.

We learned the story of this impromptu shelter from some of the residents we met there. In the period leading up to the hurricane, the Red Cross had designated several schools further inland as storm shelters. But as Katrina grew closer, those shelters became full. In addition, many people in the immediate vicinity of the school, who had tried to ride the storm out in their own homes and had to flee when the floodwaters overtook them, went to the school in an effort to find a safe haven. Hundreds of people broke into the locked school where they weathered out the storm and waited for relief.

However, because the High School was not a "designated shelter," no one knew about the hundreds of families staying there without any fresh water or food until, we were told, Thursday afternoon—four days later—when National Guard troops discovered it and began to administer relief supplies. According to a Salvation Army volunteer we met at the shelter, no outside help (neither National Guard nor Salvation Army nor Red Cross) had any major presence in the Bay St. Louis/Waveland area until Friday or Saturday (September 2nd or 3rd). He explained that the Salvation Army was told it was too dangerous to go into the area. He doubted this claim and finally insisted that they go serve meals there. On the day we were there, they handed out a meal of chicken breast, wheat bread, carrot coins, and syrupy-sweet canned peaches. Before we left later that afternoon, the Salvation Army volunteers invited us to eat a meal saying that volunteers needed to keep their strength up, too. We protested saying that we didn't want to take food from the evacuees, asserting our role as "volunteers," not "victims." Just before we left the shelter, however, we succumbed and accepted our Styrofoam plates of food, in part because we didn't want to make the volunteer feel badly and also because we didn't know whether there would be another opportunity to eat for the rest of the day.

After four days of being used as the living quarters for so many people, the flood-ravaged inside of the school was a mess. By the time we arrived on that Sunday, just about everyone was now living outside. Most people had staked out areas on the sidewalks under the covered walkways between buildings. They had thin pieces of blue plastic to sleep on, and each family or small group of individuals cobbled together chairs or other bedding to make a living space for themselves on the ground. Inside the school, the hallways were dark and filled with streaks of mud. The odor was horrendous: raw sewage. We learned that in the days following the hurricane, due to lack of running water, the shelter residents had to designate certain areas around the school as "bathroom areas" as the bathrooms themselves had become unusable. Walking through the hallways, we were confronted by eerie reminders of routine high school life at the beginning of the fall semester. A bright red "Freshman Frenzy" spirit sign painted on glass windows and colorful plastic notebooks stacked in hallway lockers were interspersed with twisted metal and downed wires.

As recently as Saturday morning (the day prior to our arrival), there were still 600 people staying there. On that morning, several church buses arrived and transported most of the evacuees to Anniston, Alabama and West Point, Mississippi. So, by the time we had arrived there were not many people left who would need rides. Many of those who remained told us they refused to board the buses, some because they weren't sure where the buses were going, some because they wanted to stay in Bay St. Louis, some because they were told they couldn't take their pets, and still others because they were waiting to hear from family members.

After hearing this news, the team was glad to know that help had arrived, but a little disappointed as we had expected people to be lining up to get a ride out of the shelter. This new reality threw the purpose of our relief mission into question. We didn't expect that we would have to convince people that coming to an Oxford shelter would be worthwhile. We thought they would have jumped at the chance. In retrospect, we should not have been surprised by people's hesitancy to go with us. Who were we? What would people do miles and miles from their friends, family, and neighbors? And on and on. In this situation, sociologists might help us to see that our disappointment was linked to the fact that we had assumed people wanted our "gift." When they asserted needs of their own and rejected our offer for a ride, they were asserting their own agency and power and disrupting the common roles taken on in a gift-giving situation.

As we wandered around the school asking people if they were interested in rides, we tried to make ourselves useful. We began to listen to what people said they needed. People still in the shelter wanted to give us information regarding who was safe and who was missing, and we gathered a list of names for people looking for loved ones (Kirsten later posted these names on a Katrina website and received several responses from family members who were able to find their loved ones as a result). Another member of the team copied down a list of the dead and missing, which had been compiled by a woman in the area. Along the way Kirsten helped an unsteady older woman back to her wheel chair in her sleeping area so that she could eat her meal. Another team member found an oxygen tank at an EMT station to aid a man with cancer whose tank was low and offered the use of a cellphone to make contact with family members (no luck). Along the way, we all listened to people's unbelievable stories of tragedy and strength.

In the end, three people wanted to head north: a single woman, Mary (who had lived her whole life in Bay St. Louis and wanted to get to family in Grenada, Mississippi); and Rose and Mike (a 53 year-old mother and her 25 year-old son) originally from Chalmette, Louisiana. They were all sunburned and tired. Rose and Mike shared with us their incredible story of survival which included being separated during the storm, finding each other again, beating floodwaters and all odds, being transported by barge to the New Orleans causeway on I-10, waiting twenty hours for a bus to the Astrodome, deciding to leave the Astrodome to make their way back to Picayune, Mississippi with a new-found friend, and then being dropped off at the Bay St. Louis shelter the day before we had arrived. They told us the tale with a sense of humor and a spirit of contagious optimism.

We left the shelter at dusk and went to a flooded apartment complex where we had been told there was an older man with a serious infection (some said he had been bitten by a spider) who might want a ride with us. Nerves were on edge as we negotiated downed power lines and trees driving into the parking lot. We found the man with the aid of a few men still living in their devastated apartments, but he decided to stay. Although none of the men in the apartment were interested in a ride, they did ask if we had any supplies. We gave them our remaining water and food. Jeff had asked a police officer about giving out some of our gasoline to the people in the K-Mart lot with signs stating, "need gas" and he was told unequivocally that for us to do that would be a bad idea—we might, "have a riot on our hands." Despite this warning, we decided to leave a five-gallon tank with one of the young men for a generator he was trying to start.

The apartment stop had taken longer than we had expected and we were already well past our pre-arranged departure time of 5:00pm. We had wanted to get out of the worst hit area before dark and our delay made the team tense. In addition, we had three exhausted evacuees in the back of our cars. In the end, we left Bay St. Louis at 6:30pm making only one more stop at a small shelter in an elementary school in Hancock County where a nurse named Maria seemed to have single-handedly maintained a shelter for older patients with medical needs. She walked down the generator-lighted, semi-dark hall and announced to individuals, some laying on cots connected to oxygen tanks or sitting in wheel chairs, that we were driving to Oxford. We didn't have any takers. She asked if we would stop by again if we returned to the coast for another trip.

We stopped at a Wendy's somewhere between Hattiesburg and Jackson, just outside the area where a 7:00pm curfew was in effect. It was the only restaurant open for miles and this fast food joint had transformed into a stopping place for all kinds of individuals coming and going to the coast. As we stood in the long line to order, we talked to other volunteers and to coastal families who had just seen the remains of their homes for the first time. We pushed tables together and sat down with Mary, Rose, and Mike; they hadn't had fast food in days and thought it was a treat, something normal. Out in the parking lot, we funneled more of our gas supply into the 4 vehicles before making our way home.

After a long, bleary-eyed journey on dark roads, we arrived at the Red Cross shelter in Oxford at 2:00am to be greeted by four volunteers ready to receive the people we had brought from the coast. After driving home and crawling into our own beds, most of us thought that our helping efforts were over. But we still had work to do. We cared about the people we had brought from the coast and we were their only connections here in Oxford. The question of the boundaries of giving and the dynamics of human relationships in a volunteer situation started to creep in.

We were unbelievably relieved to find out the next morning that Mary was staying with a local family who volunteered to take evacuees in and that she planned to settle in Oxford or nearby to be close to her children in Grenada. At lunchtime, three of the team members joined up with two of the support members of the volunteer group to debrief about the trip. Telling the story was exhausting and brought some of us to tears. Kirsten, Jeff, and another member of the team went back to the shelter that Monday afternoon to visit with Rose and Mike. We sat in the makeshift TV room eating the donated cupcakes and treats sitting out on the counter. They told us that a young woman volunteer at the shelter did amazing work to find what they called their "adopted" family in a small town outside of Pittsburgh, Pennsylvania. The family had purchased tickets for Rose and Mike and they were scheduled to fly out of Memphis in the next several days to meet them. They had been interviewed by the local newspaper and were proud that they had their Katrina story printed. In the article, Rose told us that she referred to our team as her "angels on wheels." What a compliment. This kind of loving sentiment certainly affirmed our decision to volunteer. But, at the same time, it made us feel self-conscious to accept praise when she was the one who had been through so much. We left Rose and Mike with some "travel money" (and were sure to get some to Mary as well, to be fair). We felt some guilt that we were not taking them to our homes for a Labor Day picnic, but we were exhausted.

On Tuesday morning, Kirsten got an unexpected call from the shelter. Rose called to find out if she could take them to the local Red Cross center so they could get some supplies. Although Kirsten had not realized this was the plan, she picked them up, took them to the Red Cross center and waited in line to find out how they were to get their vouchers. As we sat in the crowded waiting area of the empty WalMart building and they received their numbers, it became obvious that we were going to have to wait hours to be served. Kirsten made a quick decision to forego the vouchers and fund the WalMart trip herself. The group shopped for bras, underwear, sneakers, and a few other supplies and then stopped for lunch at Chili's. We spent the afternoon picking out clothes at the Salvation Army. Rose and Mike left for Pennsylvania the next day. Mary later found a job and an apartment in Oxford. Since then, Rose, Mary, and members of the group have exchanged a few letters and phone calls but, otherwise, have not been in touch.

Epilogue and Lessons Learned

After our trip to the coast we were drained and exhausted. We wanted to get together to talk about all the things we had experienced and seen—to "debrief" about the trip—but in the midst of everything else, we found it difficult to find the time to do so. Perhaps it would have been useful to schedule such a dialogue. To get at our feelings and frustrations right then and there. But, looking back on it now, it is likely that our feelings were too raw and our emotions too close to the surface for such a conversation to have been useful. Instead, we placed our energies on the tasks ahead.

Some members of the group wanted to return to the coast the next weekend. Colleagues and friends who hadn't gone down to the coast with us the first time were keenly interested in planning another trip and had already begun fundraising and organizing the logistics for a return visit. The first person to say he wouldn't go again was our friend whose original idea it was to go to New Orleans. He said it was largely due to family obligations and that he couldn't spend another weekend doing this. But it is also possible that he felt a bit upset that his idea of creating a "Mississippi-Louisiana" connection by going to New Orleans had now become fully side-swiped by the group's growing emphasis on the Mississippi Gulf Coast. Kirsten and another member of the group decided not to return as well. Feeling a bit burned out, both of them stated that it would be better to "give someone else the opportunity."

Jeff and another member of the group did accompany a second caravan down to Bay St. Louis the next weekend. With better logistical planning and a more-carefully assembled load of supplies, the participants in this trip experienced similar difficulties and emotional highs and lows. But by the time we returned from the second trip (this time with a family of nine and their two dogs), it was clear that our period of "spontaneous volunteering" was coming to an end. While most of us continued to volunteer on Katrina-related relief in the weeks and months to come—finding resources and support for the individuals we had helped, working in the local Katrina relief shelter, and, later, becoming involved in Katrina related research projects on the coast—we never did another caravan.

In addition, while all of us have told various versions of our story to interested family and friends, we have never, as a group, tried to arrive at a common account of our experience. As a matter of fact, we must admit that it is still something that we find difficult to discuss. All of us remain close friends but the subject of our spontaneous volunteer experience during the Katrina aftermath rarely, if ever, comes up.

During the process of writing this paper, the two of us telling this tale have realized that there are numerous instances in which we have different emotions and recollections regarding the meaning of what our group experienced on those trips almost two years ago. In an earlier draft, for example, Jeff had written, in reference to the "gasoline lines" in Canton, that our caravan "was unconcerned about the gas lines due to the fact that we had our own supply." Kirsten laughed at reading this and insisted on correcting him, "Don't you remember the conflict we had there? You were so worried that we needed to top off our tanks and we had to make the decision that it was OK to move on." "Oh, yeah," he said, "I guess I glossed over that difficulty, didn't I?" As a result, we changed the section to explore, albeit in an abbreviated and incomplete fashion, the emotions and tensions that we all experienced in that small episode.

There is no doubt in our minds that the difficulty of retrieving such emotional memory is indicative of the need to return to these stories and to explore them at a deeper level. Likewise, it should be obvious to the reader that had others in our group been involved in the writing of this tale, we might find additional omissions or errors and we would most likely discover other vignettes and stories that have different meanings and would lead to different interpretations of our experience as a group.

Nonetheless, we would like to conclude this narrative with just a few brief observations regarding what we think it all means. First, we want to highlight the fact that our group was a part of a broader pattern of "spontaneous volunteerism" that occurred after Hurricane Katrina (and occurs after most disasters). As sociologists St. John and Fuchs (2002) assert,

It is well established in the disaster literature that following most disasters there is a "mass assault" of volunteers on the disaster location. These individuals appear to "converge" on the disaster scene for a variety of reasons, not all of which are purely altruistic, for example, curiosity or a desire to "participate" in the disaster (401).

St. John and Fuchs go on to state that "Although these volunteers can be instrumental in initial search and rescue efforts," the convergence of spontaneous volunteers can also "hinder the performance of trained relief organizations." In relation to this concern, we believe a second lesson from our experience is that by utilizing guidelines of "self-sufficiency" the spontaneous volunteer can avoid this pitfall. By remaining cognizant of the need to be as unobtrusive as possible, we feel proud of what we were able to achieve and feel mostly confident that we did not make matters worse for the people on the Gulf Coast. We say "mostly" because such an evaluation would need to be made by the people whose lives intersected with ours during those trips. And we remain largely unaware of how those people truly viewed our actions.

Third, it is interesting to consider the complex array of forces that motivated us into action. While sociological research has studied the numerous "variables" and "characteristics" that can lead individuals to volunteer, we feel that it was the broader social context that played the most significant role in our group's experience. For us, our decision to act emerged out of the broader political and social concerns that "there was a problem" with the official relief response and that we had to "do something about it." This decision had both practical and symbolic dimensions. We helped where we could by contributing supplies and providing transportation. But we also felt compelled to express our solidarity with one another based upon the common frustration we felt at our government's inaction. In this fashion, our action was also a symbolic gesture and was recognized as such by those around us. This fact might also explain why once we accomplished the trip—once the gesture was done—the spontaneous volunteerism ended.

Fourth, like other spontaneous volunteers, we experienced obstacles, difficulties and challenges related both to the logistics of disaster management (especially poor information) and to the emotional tensions and anxieties that entering a disaster zone entails. Research elsewhere has found that spontaneous volunteers are more likely to encounter such difficulties as they lack the experience of professional relief workers who are trained to deal with such difficulties and because they are often treated as "less important" by the official volunteer workers with whom they are trying to coordinate. We agree with Lowe (2002) and others who argue that official relief agencies need to better anticipate the likelihood of spontaneous volunteers following a disaster and better plan for their involvement. She states, "There could be more rapid centralization and dissemination of authoritative information to community members about where to go and what to do to respond to disaster needs... [as] active community service can be an effective strategy for both individual and community recovery" (4). Better dissemination of information would definitely have helped us and, we are certain, would ultimately be even more useful to disaster victims themselves.

Finally, and most importantly, we have learned through this reflection that spontaneous volunteerism has just as much to do with the helpers as it does the helped. As volunteers, we experienced empowerment and camaraderie with others as a result of our decision to "do something." According to Lowe, the healing and empowerment that spontaneous volunteerism can bring are not only helpful to the volunteer as he or she faces the reality of making sense of a disaster, but, furthermore, acts of volunteerism can help the disaster-effected community at large. She writes,

> The potential healing role of volunteerism is important to recognize... The positive experiences of agency through volunteerism can help transform feelings of helplessness to feelings of efficacy. The new or renewed belief that one has the ability to influence one's environment thereby positively affects the social-psychological state of participants in an affected area (5).

In other words, we may have needed to do this more than we thought. As residents in a state devastated by the Hurricane, we may have been attempting to overcome our own feelings of frustration and hopelessness through our volunteer efforts. This was not something we had fully considered prior to writing this account. But looking at it now, it is easy to see that we were attempting to come to terms with our immediate social context and our need to feel a sense of agency by volunteering on the Mississippi Gulf Coast. In the end, while we may have helped a few others who were dealing with their immediate survival needs after the hurricane, we also ended up helping ourselves.

Notes

1. The "convergence of volunteers who are not self-sufficient" was cited in a 2006 report as one of the "major problems" associated with Hurricane Katrina relief

(Fischer et al. 2006, 8). Therefore, this guideline was probably one of the most important our group had defined. According to the Fischer et al. report (2006), in which first responders to the Katrina crisis were interviewed, "One responder expressed appreciation for those who arrived self-sufficiently: 'I could have kissed them. In they came one day and told me what they came prepared to do; I was expecting another housing and feeding burden, but they told me not to worry about that. They came prepared to take care of themselves, as well as care for those who were in need of medical treatment. I thought, 'finally, something that works, God bless them!'"(9)

2. We use pseudonyms to refer to the people we met on the coast.

References

Beyerlein, Kraig, and David Sikkink. 2005. Sorrow and solidarity: Why Americans volunteered for 9/11 relief efforts. Paper presented at the annual meeting for the American Sociological Association, August 12, in Philadelphia, Pennsylvania.

Collins, Randall. 2004. Rituals of solidarity and security in the wake of terrorist attack. *Sociological Theory* 22:53-87.

Eckstein, Susan. 2001. Community as gift-giving: Collectivistic roots of volunteerism. *American Sociological Review* 66:829-51.

Ethridge, Robbie. 2006. Bearing witness: Assumptions, realities, and the otherizing of Katrina. *American Anthropologist* 108:799-813.

Fisher, Henry W., Kathryn Gregorie, John Scala, Lynn Letukas, Joseph Mellon, Scott Romine, and Danielle Turner. 2006. The emergency management response to Hurricane Katrina: As told by the first responders–A case study of what went wrong and recommendations for the future. National Hazards Center Quick Response Report, No. 189, National Hazards Center, Boulder, CO.

Jackson, Jeffrey T. 2005. *The globalizers: Development workers in action.* Baltimore: The Johns Hopkins University Press.

Lowe, Seana. 2002. Community response in a terrorist disaster. National Hazards Center Quick Response report, No. 144, National Hazards Center, Boulder, CO.

Shughart, William F. II. 2006. Katrinanomics: The politics and economics of disaster relief. *Public Choice* 127: 31-53.

Sobel, Russell S., and Leeson, Peter T. 2006. Government's response to Hurricane Katrina: A public choice analysis. *Public Choice* 127: 55-73.

St. John, Craig, and Fuchs, Jesse. 2002. The heartland responds to terror: Volunteering after the bombing of the Murrah Federal Building. *Social Science Quarterly* 83:397-415.

Wilson, John. 2000. Volunteering. *Annual Review of Sociology* 26: 215-40.

Wilson, John, and Marc A. Musick. 1999. Attachment to Volunteering. *Sociological Forum* 14:243-72

Part III

(Ir)rationality as a Tool for Making Disaster-Related Decisions

DISASTER AND THE IRRATIONALITY OF "RATIONAL" BUREAUCRACY: DAILY LIFE AND THE CONTINUING STRUGGLES IN THE AFTERMATH OF HURRICANE KATRINA

TIMOTHY J. HANEY
MOUNT ROYAL UNIVERSITY

My story begins in the small bayou town of Boutte, Louisiana on September 14th, 2005—nearly two weeks after Hurricane Katrina made landfall. The heavy winds and pounding rains of Katrina had passed and the late-summer heat was stifling. After spending two weeks with the family of one of my colleagues in New Iberia, Louisiana, my spouse and I made it back within fifteen miles of New Orleans. The parishes of Jefferson and Orleans were still closed to residents, so we were unable to return home for any length of time. Even if we had been allowed to return at that time, the lack of electricity, clean water, air conditioning, the debris-lined streets, and absence of open gas stations and supermarkets made permanent return undesirable, if not impossible. Since my spouse was employed in Boutte and her employer was in the process of reopening, we were living temporarily with the grandmother of one of her coworkers (whom we had just met) in the nearby town of Des Allemands.

Strained Bureaucratic Structures

On Wednesday, September 14th, my spouse returned to her job as a high school teacher, and conversations with her coworkers soon revealed that most of them had received disaster assistance in the form of food stamps. We had heard that evacuees from the New Orleans area were receiving such assistance, but previously scoffed at the idea, believing it was reserved only for the destitute and truly needy. Given that we were not in dire need, we initially opted not to apply. However, upon learning that several of her coworkers had received such assistance, many of whom had considerable financial resources, we decided to give it a try. After all, if people with considerable financial resources qualified and received such assistance without fear of social ostracism (it was an extraordinary circumstance, after all), it seemed foolish to turn down free assistance; especially given that we did not know how soon we would be able to return home and what additional costs we would incur.

I walked several blocks to the St. Charles Parish Department of Family Services (DFS) where I encountered a crowd of between 1,000 and 3,000 people waiting under the blazing sun and in 100 degree heat to receive assistance. Tension filled the air. A group of people—appearing to be mostly middle-class by their dress (khaki pants, buttoned dress-shirts which showed the dirt and perspiration of several days' use), demeanor, and the proliferation of class signifiers such as cellular phones, PDA's, and SUV's—waited to collect the free government assistance, something that is often stigmatized within middle-class social circles, even after major natural disasters (Fothergill 2003).

Upon arriving, I was told by a member of the Tennessee Highway Patrol (presumably performing volunteer work) that I needed to fill out the application, but that it was too late in the day to guarantee that I would be seen. I gladly took the application and returned the following day at 6:00a.m., hoping to beat the rush. When I arrived, I was pleasantly surprised to learn that I was about the 40th or 50th person in line. I hurriedly turned in my application and expected to be seen shortly after the Department of Family Services opened at 8:00am. However, the outside staff, which largely consisted of volunteer law enforcement officers from outside of the state, failed to inform me that the disaster assistance was not being disbursed on a first-come-first-serve basis, but rather according to the number printed on the application we had received. This meant that it did not matter when I had arrived; it mattered when I had picked up my application. Since it was now Thursday, I would be called only after everyone who received their applications the preceding week, as well as Monday, Tuesday and Wednesday of the current week, were serviced. Many people who arrived were called within a half hour, while others waited the duration of the day. Rumors circulated that Friday the 16th would be the final day of food assistance for disaster victims, forcing many to wait who otherwise would have presumably taken an application and returned in a few days. It was already Thursday, which meant leaving might jeopardize receiving my slice of the pie.

While waiting, I occasionally saw DFS caseworkers peeking out of the windows at the crowd forming and waiting restlessly. Less frequently, the caseworkers ventured outside to observe the crowd, first-hand. Although the DFS workers were able to observe the size and impatient temperament of the crowd, the processes taking place inside the building were a mystery to those waiting outside. Few applicants had a clear idea what number application had reached the front of the queue (many did not even know to make note of their own number before turning in their application), and no one knew what, if any, criteria were being used to screen applicants. Situations exhibiting this degree of control through visibility are perhaps best described in Michel Foucault's (1977) "Panopticon." In a Panopticonal prison, for example, discipline and cooperation are ensured due, in large part, to issues of visibility; guards can observe prisoners, but prisoners are never aware of who is observing them or when they are being watched. This arrangement is meant to induce a state of "conscious and permanent visibility that assures the automatic functioning of power" (Foucault 1977, 201). Like prisoners in a panopticonal prison, I found myself constrained by my lack of visibility and knowledge about who was watching me, whether my application was being discussed inside, and if I would soon move to the front of the queue. I was under constant surveillance by DFS employees within the building (who I could not see) and by law enforcement officers from around the nation who ensured order outside. Meanwhile the processes at work inside the building remained entirely mysterious. I realized that I could not question or object to processes that I did not understand, and I could not complain about the uncomfortable physical conditions to people I could not see or converse with. Though not expressly tied to bureaucracy in the work of Foucault, Max Weber (1946) acknowledges this maintenance of power, maintained through secrecy and visibility, as a fixture of modern bureaucracy. According to Weber, the "power position of a fully developed bureaucracy is always overtowering," and "every bureaucracy seeks to increase the superiority of the professionally informed by keeping their knowledge and intentions secret" (Weber 1946, 232-233). Foucault and Weber both demonstrate that knowledge, whether gained and maintained through bureaucracy or through physical structures that place individuals under the gaze of the powerful, is utilized as a powerful tool for pacifying and subordinating people. Without direct contact with the decision-makers and without knowledge of the processes operating inside, I was powerless.

By 8:00a.m., the crowd had thickened and the wait was on. The mercury quickly rose to above 100 degrees and shade became a scarce commodity. By mid-day, many people showed visible signs of heat exhaustion, with many laying on the pavement, sweating, and exhibiting facial expressions of duress. But, instead of liberally handing out food assistance in order to thin and quell the agitated crowd, the DFS continued to utilize its standard lengthy screening process for each candidate; this confused me because I had heard everyone in affected areas qualified. According to Weber, the inability to jettison standard practices when they fail is typical of bureaucratic structures; in fact, it is the goal of such structures. To the extent that bureaucracies ensure predictability and calculability—in this instance, clear records of who receives support and how much—bureaucracies usurp emotion and feeling. Bureaucracy dehumanizes business dealings and seeks to eliminate love, hatred "and all purely personal, irrational, and emotional elements which escape calculation" (Weber 1946, 216). Included in this is the emotion of compassion. In the name of calculability and a defined set of bureaucratic rules, DFS employees refused to bend prescribed protocol in order to distribute assistance in a more humane and expedient fashion, even as a group of hungry, emotionally-drained and, in some cases, homeless disaster victims roasted in the blistering sun. George Ritzer (2004) notes that this is one of the irrational consequences of bureaucracy; humans become numbers. Service providers who operate within such bureaucracies never come to know patients or clients as individuals and are, thus, unable to utilize the compassion necessary in such a traumatic situation.

After spending nearly ten hours waiting outside in stifling, humid temperatures with no water readily available, I was called inside via police megaphone where I encountered a *second* waiting area. After another wait, this time exceeding one hour in duration, I met with a caseworker who hurriedly reviewed my application, making sure to note that my spouse and I had assets in our bank account (although we were unable to access them at the time) and that my spouse was still gainfully employed. I did not initially consider that these conditions might be an impediment to receiving assistance, as many of her coworkers had also received such assistance, some who had considerable financial resources. Had our friends, coworkers, and acquaintances intentionally misrepresented their financial situations? Were different parishes throughout the state using different screening criteria to dole out aid? Unfortunately, I was never able to answer these questions. The caseworker performed a number of whirlwind calculations and told us that we did not qualify for the disaster food stamp program: "NEXT!"

After more than 12 hours of waiting, I left the DFS feeling jaded and cynical. Weeks later, when internet service resumed, I researched this series of events and discovered that *all* residents of affected areas qualified for this disaster assistance. As residents of Jefferson Parish (a hard-hit parish that, much like Orleans Parish, experienced widespread flooding), we should have received assistance. According to the United States Department of Agriculture's (USDA) "Expanded Disaster Evacuee Policy," residents of areas affected by Katrina were temporarily granted exemption from both the work requirements and the "Able Bodied Adults without Dependents" limitations (USDA, 2005a). This meant that regardless of one's financial situation or physical ability, *everyone* in the area qualified for disaster assistance during disaster situations. The policy states that, "There are no income or resource eligibility tests. There are no other non-financial tests" (USDA, 2005b). Rather, the only requirements for the food stamp program involved residency in a declared area and date of application.

It is not difficult to understand how such a mistake can be made. The Department of Family Services operates according to a set of institutionalized prescriptions. Faced with scarce resources and overburdened with requests, bureaucratic pressures require rapid calculations and steadfast rules. According to Weber (1946),

> The extraordinary increase in the speed by which public announcements, as well as economic and political facts, are transmitted exerts a steady and sharp pressure in the direction of speeding up the tempo of administrative reaction towards various situations (215).

Thus, when burdened by atypical situations, bureaucracies must choose between circumventing the rules and speeding up the tempo of work; unequivocally they choose the latter. Furthermore, the hierarchical structure of a bureaucracy does not permit those entrenched within the structure to improvise. Instead, the bureaucracy "cannot be put into motion or arrested by him [employee or other non-powerful bureaucratic steward], but only from the very top" and "the ruled, for their part, cannot dispense with or replace the bureaucratic apparatus of authority once it exists" (Weber 1946, 229). But, if those at the top of the hierarchy were likewise exposed to the suffering of persons affected by Hurricane Katrina (some lower-level bureaucrats experienced Katrina at the local level, but certainly all experienced the suffering as filtered through media outlets), why were they unable to alter the bureaucratic structure? Harvey Molotch (2005) suggests that during the days immediately after Katrina, those with the power to disburse aid often retreated into bureaucracy out of fear of reprisal from higher authorities within their given bureaucracy, or, as is most likely the case, out of a lack of compassion for affected groups. Bureaucratic structures provided excuses for those who controlled the resources to remain inactive. In other words, fear of overstepping the limitations imposed by one's job description, coupled with a lack of compassion and understanding, often resulted in steadfast adherence to rules and policies (in this case, income requirements and asset checks associated with receipt of food assistance). Molotch suggests that in large bureaucracies, responsibility for action can always be handed to someone else in hot-potato fashion, often with the net result of inaction. Because of such bureaucratic inflexibility, scores of qualified individuals, many of whom were still uncertain of the condition of their homes, were denied such assistance.

Continued Struggles

During late November, just three months after the storm, I began experiencing car trouble. On chilly mornings (well, chilly by Louisiana standards), I often had trouble starting my car. Concerned that the problem may worsen, I contacted a Ford dealership not far from where I lived. It was one of only two Ford dealerships that had re-opened in the entire New Orleans metro area. The employees at the dealership informed me that they would be happy to take a look at my car, right away. Surprised by the expediency of their service, I wasted no time bringing my car to the dealership where I was then informed that diagnosis and repairs would take anywhere from *four to six weeks*! Additionally, all vehicles were to be left at the dealership until they reach the front of the work queue. If I were to pick up the car to use any time during that period, my vehicle would be dropped back to the bottom of the queue.

Dealerships all over southern Louisiana were backlogged with work and I knew that the storm and construction debris had spiked the demand for automotive services. After calling other dealerships in hopes one would be able to fix my car sooner, I realized that the services would not be performed expediently elsewhere. The service manager at the Ford dealership informed me that three-quarters of their service personnel had not returned after Katrina. Knowing that I would be out of town for two weeks during the next month and would not need my vehicle, I opted to leave my car. As promised, the (extremely minor) repairs were complete in about four weeks. I wondered, however, what effects such processes had on those with limited financial resources, one vehicle, childcare needs, and employment burdens. Could a low-income earner afford the forty dollars per day for a rental car? Were there even any rental cars available in the New Orleans metro area? I escaped with minimal frustration, but for many people these questions were not easily answered.

Throughout the winter of 2005-2006, whatever my goal or destination, I found myself waiting in exceedingly long lines. Lines at the supermarket stretched back fifteen to twenty persons, standstill traffic clogged the area's major arteries, local government offices were overrun by citizens seeking services and stores sold out of product necessary for everyday survival. I found myself dreading my daily drive from Tulane University to my home in the western suburbs of New Orleans: If key stoplights were not functioning, or if I left at the wrong time, I knew it could result in traffic gridlock. New Orleans Mayor C. Ray Nagin echoed these sentiments, proclaiming in December 2005 that, "the 'Big Easy' is not very easy right now" (Haines, 2005).

Shortly before the storm, I had relocated to the westerly suburbs of New Orleans, a smart move given that my former apartment complex was flooded, broken into, and subsequently closed. After moving in, I noticed some water damage on our bedroom ceiling, which I reported to management immediately. The ceiling was also bowing noticeably, which concerned me. Management assured me they would fix the ceiling, but only two days later, Katrina entered the gulf and evacuation plans began. After returning from Katrina, we noticed that the water damage had engulfed our ceiling and sections of moldy, black plaster dangled over our bed. Yet, at that time, the apartment management informed us that, given the more serious damage in other apartments, we were not a priority.

I sent the apartment managers frequent reminders about the rotting ceiling, but the complex management ignored my requests for nearly six months, citing a lack of available workers and materials. Water damage encompassed nearly the entire ceiling, water dripped incessantly, and the mold spots made us doubt our respiratory safety. Sans any scientific tests or hard evidence, the apartment complex staff informed us that the mold did not present a health hazard—yet, research on the topic confirms the danger of household mold spores. With an overburdened legal system, high demand for housing and an extensive waiting list of potential renters, the management knew that any legal recourse on our part was simply not possible. Shortly thereafter, we received notice of a forthcoming $165/month rent increase to keep costs consistent with market prices and to offset increased property insurance costs related to Katrina and the risk of a future flood. Despite living in a damaged, unsanitary apartment, I found myself gradually yet steadily shouldering the burden of skyrocketing housing costs and strained bureaucracies in the months following Katrina.

Habitus, Bureaucracy, and (Extra) Local Struggles

As a resident of the New Orleans area, I frequently encountered a chasm between the rules operating in post-Katrina New Orleans and the bureaucratic rules by which other regions of the United States operated. Some rules in the New Orleans area had been relaxed; for example, due to slow (or non-existent) mail service, the energy company was routinely accepting late payments and waiving penalties. National corporations, on the other hand, were not as forgiving. Tasks as simple as paying my cell phone bill became exceedingly difficult. With no internet service and with delayed mail service, I rarely received bills. Instead, it was my responsibility to find the company's phone number, place a phone call, and attempt to find out my balance and pay the bill via telephone. I learned this lesson the hard way; during late-October of 2005, I received a cell phone bill in the mail that was already five days overdue. Assuming that the company would understand my tardiness (after all, I *did* live in the Katrina-zone!), I dropped the check in the mail. The next month, I found myself paying late fees. Repeated phone calls proved fruitless as the customer service representatives denied my request to both waive the late fees and speak with a higher authority within the phone company bureaucracy. When asked how I should have handled the situation differently (given that I had no mail service, internet, and, ironically, no reliable cellular phone service), I was met with a simple, "I'm sorry. There's nothing I can do."

Not only did I learn that national corporations were often inflexible, even during extraordinary times, but I also saw many of these features exhibited by smaller bureaucratic structures outside of the New Orleans area. Following the spring 2006 Katrina-related suspension of my graduate program, soaring housing costs, and frustrations associated with living in a flood-ravaged city, I ultimately decided to leave Louisiana. Consequently, I transferred to the Sociology Graduate Department at the University of Oregon in Eugene. My spouse and I traveled to Eugene and searched for apartments in the area; and soon received a phone call informing us that an apartment had become available in our desired apartment community. We eagerly seized the opportunity. Having already returned to New Orleans to finish out the spring term, I informed the apartment complex staff member that I would mail out the deposit check immediately in order to reserve the apartment. She cheerfully informed me that the apartment would be held for four business days while my check was in the mail. My jubilation quickly morphed into restrained fury. I politely informed her that although our mail situation in the New Orleans area had improved markedly since the fall, I could not guarantee that my check would arrive in four days. Naturally, I assumed that she would waive that rule for us; after all, Katrina is an exceptional situation that requires exceptional patience and compassion. I was coldly informed that the waiting list was a mile long; either I find a way to get the check to Oregon in four days or the apartment goes to the next person on the list. Sending it overnight delivery was not only expensive, but the United States Postal Service had been affected so profoundly by Katrina that I still had some doubt as to whether the check would even arrive in time, or at all. Simply put, the services I was accustomed to as a United States citizen could not be counted on any longer. I immediately became furious and lashed out at her for her inflexibility, not yet grasping the two very different paradigms from which we were operating.

At the time, the lack of compassion exhibited by the apartment complex employee was shocking. How could anyone who saw the events of Hurricane Katrina unfold on television not be sympathetic? How could she not have bent the rules for us? Then, I was reminded that Hurricane Katrina was already nine months in the past. Since that time we, as Americans, have experienced skyrocketing gas prices, mountains of celebrity gossip, a tense middle-east situation, nuclear threats from North Korea, blizzards, tornados, deaths, births, sports championships, floods in the northeastern U.S., stories of genocide and a myriad of media mini-sensations that have shifted America's focus away from the horrific images of New Orleans' devastation. The brief nation-wide shock of Hurricane Katrina had ended, the life of the woman at the apartment complex had returned to normal, and naturally she must have assumed that mine had as well. Thus, compassion was no longer necessary. Unfortunately, for residents of New Orleans everyday presents new challenges. The local newspaper and television stations continued to prominently run stories on Hurricane Katrina tragedies, levee improvements, FEMA trailers, family separation, federal assistance, and flood insurance. Residents were, and continue to be, bombarded with reminders of Katrina, and for us the images of August 29th, 2005 were not yet usurped by more recent events.

Social theorist Pierre Bourdieu (1977) would suggest that the roots of the misunderstanding I encountered with the apartment community managers can be traced to the concept of *habitus*, which includes the material conditions of a person's environment that all or most people within that environment share. According to his theoretical schema, our perceptions and actions are shaped by these shared material conditions and past experiences. Since not all people share exactly the same past experiences, everyone's habitus is somewhat different, but people who live in similar environments would logically act in similar ways. We apply our habitus (i.e., the combination of our past experiences) to different situations or problems, and use it to make decisions regarding similarly shaped problems. It is a way of turning past experiences into future-shaping frames. Past experience with disaster recovery might therefore help me interpret and react to future disasters I encounter. Someone lacking that experience would therefore logically react much differently to news of a disaster.

Having long forgotten Hurricane Katrina, the woman with whom I spoke about the apartment possesses a habitus shaped by her readily available images and experiences, which did not include the everyday struggles of living in post-Katrina New Orleans. My habitus, on the other hand, includes rich, vivid images of flooded buildings, traffic jams, long lines, FEMA trailers, boarded windows, deserted streets, and rampant inefficiency. I understood that some courses of action to which we were accustomed prior to Katrina were simply no longer feasible options. For her, images of Katrina are restricted to a few passing days of media coverage and photographs from helicopters. Absent from her habitus are the detailed experiences of everyday life in the post-Katrina New Orleans.

Although part of our misunderstanding was embedded in our very different social milieus, like the DFS employees, the apartment employee filled a role in a bureaucratic hierarchy. As an official embedded in bureaucracy, she could not dispense with or replace aspects of the bureaucracy (Weber, 1946). Even if she had understood my predicament, she was bound by a bureaucratic structure that did not allow for improvisation and in which the rules were determined by the highest-ranking officials, some of whom she may not have even known personally.

Conclusion

The check to secure our apartment in Eugene did arrive in time, and like many of my colleagues, I have since left New Orleans to continue my academic work in another region of the country. Nevertheless, for many New Orleanians who lived through Hurricane Katrina, the images and experiences garnered during that time will remain vivid, permanent fixtures of our habitus and will continue to inform and shape our decisions for the rest of our lives. Disaster scholarship generally assumes that disasters do not produce new "social facts" or patterns, but merely magnify and give clarity to the processes already at work in society

(Mauss, 1916 [1979]). If this is true, Hurricane Katrina exposed deep and profound irrationalities in what were supposedly rational, efficient, and calculable bureaucracies. These irrationalities, far from providing annoyances for Gulf Coast residents such as myself, served as a *social* disaster, further complicating the lives of people who already had to deal with flooded homes, lost jobs, and displaced neighbors. A "natural" disaster such as Hurricane Katrina can therefore spawn a series of social disasters that complicate daily life long after the storm.

References

Bourdieu, Pierre. 1977. *Outline of a theory of practice*. Cambridge: Cambridge University Press.

Fothergill, Alice. 2003. The stigma of charity: Gender, class, and disaster assistance. *Sociological Quarterly*. 44: 659-680.

Foucault, Michel. 1977. *Discipline and punish: The birth of the prison*. New York: Random House.

Haines, Erin. 2005. New Orleans mayor asks frustrated residents to return. Associated press state and local ire, December 3.

Mauss, Marcel. 1916 [1979]. *Sociology and psychology: Essays*, trans. Ben Brewster. Boston: Routeledge.

Molotch, Harvey. 2005. Death on the roof: Race and bureaucratic failure. Social Science Research Council. http://understandingkatrina.ssrc.org/Molotch/.

Ritzer, George. 2004. *The McDonaldization of society*. Thousand Oaks: Pine Forge Press.

United States Department of Agriculture. 2005a. Expanded disaster evacuee policy. http://www.fns.usda.gov/fsp/rules/Memo/05/ee-policy.pdf.

—. 2005b. The national enhanced policy for evacuees. http://www.fns.usda.gov/fsp/rules/Memo/05/nationalenhancedpolicy.pdf.

Weber, Max. 1946. *From Max Weber: Essays in sociology*, ed. Hans H. Gerth and C. Wright Mills. New York: Oxford University Press.

MY AUNT PO:
COLLECTIVE MEMORIES SHAPING COLLECTIVE RESPONSES

SARAH STOHLMAN
NEW ORLEANS, LOUISIANA

My Aunt Po, also known as Pauline Munch, was your quintessential New Orleanian. She spent her childhood and most of her adult life living on St. Maurice Street in the Ninth Ward, but like many others, moved to St. Bernard Parish after she lost everything in Hurricane Betsy in 1965. She and her firefighter husband, my Uncle Phil, bought a tiny little house on Pakenham Drive in Chalmette just a few miles away. They figured that they'd be a lot safer from hurricanes in "The Parish," and since many other Ninth Ward expatriates were moving to the then newly-developing area, they decided to follow. To be quite honest, I'm not sure she ever got over leaving the Ninth Ward. I think she missed being able to take the RTA bus from St. Claude down to Canal Street to shop at D.H. Holmes and Krauss department store. She always talked about how she, my grandmother, my dad, my Aunt Sue, and my Aunt Joann would get on the bus and spend their days away shopping and sometimes seeing movies at the Joy Theatre. I'm not sure if she ever knew that the old Holmes store was now the Ritz Carlton, and that the Joy was in a sad state of disrepair. I assumed she did because she knew a lot about the city, but I never wanted to be the one to upset her memories of the way things were. Plus, I always liked the fact that she was a bit of a living time capsule and an oral historian, to boot.

My Aunt Po, like many New Orleanians, had the great New Orleans gift for storytelling, for turning mundane recollections of everyday events into unbelievable tales even the most skeptical of skeptics would repeat to anyone and everyone who would listen. She was, and I'm sure she wouldn't mind me saying so, a bit of an Ignatius Reilly—the ironically heroic melodramatist from the book, *A Confederacy of Dunces*. She could make a daily trip out to "make groceries" seem like a three-ring circus. I can say this, I suppose, because I've got some Ignatius in me, too. It must be in the water…or in the blood.

To this day, I revel in recounting her story of the time she saw a bright white light hovering in front of her car late one night on the Old River Road in St. Charles Parish. She was certain it was a UFO and, based on the conviction of her testimony, so was I. I can remember her words almost exactly,

> Oh *Lawd*, Sarah, ya'll never believe it. Never. But it happened, I tell ya'. Your Uncle Phil and I were drivin' down the Old River Road out in St. Charles, and this bright white light just appeared in front of the car. It was so dark; and I had no idea where it came from. I was so scared, and it would not move from the front of the car. I can remember tellin' ya' Uncle Phil that if any little green men came out of that thing that I didn't know what I was gonna do…It was right around the time when ya' mama and ya' daddy were gettin' married…

As she told the story, her pale blue eyes were as big as the saucers she spoke of and she waved her hands in front of her as though the words and intonations coming out of her mouth weren't nearly expressive enough on their own to convey the significance of the situation.

She was such a good storyteller, and I suppose that's the reason she was chosen on a pretty regular basis to serve as one of the call-in supporters for items being sold on the QVC home shopping network—you know, the ones who call in and say that they just *couldn't live* without their microwavable neck pillows or their body-shaping slacks or their Diamonique brooches. Most recently, my Aunt Po was invited to lend her support for Suzanne Somers' ageless beauty cream. She spoke with such an earnest sincerity as she told a smiling Suzanne, and the QVC host and audience, that she had been using this cream for years and that her skin is absolutely and indefatigably gorgeous. To be quite honest, I'm not sure that Suzanne Somers' beauty cream has been around for years, and I'm even less certain that my Aunt Po had been using it for all those years, but I do know that she sold her fair share of units that day and I'm pretty positive that her storytelling skills landed her a prime position on QVC's product-supporting speed-dial.

The Big One

In August of 2005, my Aunt Po got the fodder she needed for the most outrageous and unbelievable story she would ever tell. And unlike her many QVC confessions, every word of this story was true. I'll do my best to tell her story here, because it's an important one and because she would be telling it now if she could. I'll try to tell it the way she would want it told because that's only fair, and because I believe there are a host of sociological implications that emerge from her experience and from those of the many other elderly people in New Orleans who are just like her. I think her story reveals something significant about the culture—or, more precisely, the *spirit*—of New Orleans, and why some of the city's most treasured residents were unduly subjected to Katrina's most deadly wrath. I also believe the story speaks to the ways in which *collective memories* can leave certain groups of people, particularly the elderly, vulnerable to the devastation of such things as hurricanes and other disasters, shedding light on the ways in which urgent warnings should be communicated to people who have grown accustomed to thinking of things in terms of socially constructed narratives of the past (Halbwachs 1992; Zerubavel, 2003).

Katrina's in the Gulf—Should we be Concerned?

A few days before Katrina hit, my Aunt Po began feeling some mild pains in her chest. While this wasn't altogether surprising—she was in the earliest stages of congestive heart failure—the pains were strong enough to warrant her going to the emergency room at Chalmette Medical. She figured she'd be in and out, but her doctor seemed worried about the chest pains, so he encouraged her to stay for a few days for observations. As she lay in her hospital bed, she watched news story after news story about a big storm brewing in the Gulf. She became a little uneasy about what could potentially happen over the next few days, not because she feared the storm, but because she feared what would happen if there were a mandatory evacuation and she were still in the hospital. For the ninety or so years she had lived in New Orleans, she had never been in the hospital while a hurricane was on the horizon. But, as she told me, she figured this was just another "false alarm" and that the storm would skirt the city, just like it always did, and would go to either the Florida panhandle or to Texas. She, like many other New Orleanians, operated under the impression that New Orleans was somehow magically shielded from hurricanes. Betsy, in all of her devastation, was nothing more than a fluke; a fluke that had occurred over forty years ago. Since then, New Orleans had not sustained a direct hit by a powerful hurricane. All this lead to a collective understanding that the city was somehow immune to hurricanes. News broadcasts urging "Everyone leave the city immediately!" were understood as nothing more than a reflection of what Barry Glassner

(1999) deemed a "culture of fear." These fears are often unjustified because they are culturally constructed and perpetuated by the media and, to a lesser extent, groups of influential people.

This "collective memory" that made people believe New Orleans was somehow magically shielded from hurricanes reflects Maurice Halbwachs' (1992 [1925]) view that certain memories are constructed and shared by social groups, and that these memories can have a powerful impact on how people act. These memories do not necessarily reflect the way things actually are (or have been), but are instead the product of social processes and interactions between and among distinct groups of people (Halbwachs 1992 [1925]; Zerubavel, 2003). The fact that many residents believed New Orleans was magically shielded from hurricanes reflects a collective memory that grew out of both a long period when no "disastrous" hurricanes had hit the city and an alarmist media that had repeatedly encouraged people to evacuate when even mild thunderstorms were approaching the city. In addition, for many New Orleanians, particularly elderly people like my Aunt Po, frequent evacuations are not a realistic option because evacuation often means driving long distances, staying in a hotel for a number of days, abandoning pets and leaving your home vulnerable to invasion. This collective memory that New Orleans is safe from hurricanes provided many New Orleanians with a solid justification for not evacuating for Katrina—something many of them couldn't do for logistical and practical reasons, anyway. Logistical constraints, for many, helped to construct a collective memory that justified not evacuating. In this sense, the collective memory that encouraged people to believe New Orleans was safe and that the media were, once again, spewing "false alarms," can be viewed as a primary reason why so many people did not evacuate—particularly the poor and elderly.

Since my Aunt Po had lived in New Orleans her entire life, she didn't fear hurricanes, per se. In fact, she and her husband didn't even evacuate during Betsy. They weathered the storm in their tiny house in the Ninth Ward, but evacuated quickly after the storm when people started running down the streets shouting that the storm surge was coming. I remember her telling me how it happened: she and her husband were sitting in their home, relieved that they had "survived" the fierce winds of Betsy. They figured that they had beaten yet another storm. Then, all of a sudden, a group of neighbors began running down the street shouting that people needed to pack up their important belongings and get out because the surge was coming. Upon hearing this, she, my Uncle Phil, my grandparents, and my Aunt Sue (my Dad and his cousins were in college by this point) jumped in their cars and quickly headed out to the nearby middle school where my grandfather was then serving as principal. The ground was slightly higher at the middle school, but the surge still came, forcing them up to the second floor. They remained up there until the surge subsided and then returned to their flooded homes, only to realize that they had lost everything. Over the next few months, they lived at the middle school while they sold their flooded-out homes and purchased new ones in St. Bernard Parish.

But, what my Aunt Po was hearing on the news stations as she laid in her hospital bed late in August of 2005 made her uneasy. The meteorologists were predicting that this storm could be "the big one." While this wasn't the first time that weather people had claimed that the "big one" was coming, this one seemed a little more likely. With her mind wandering about what was going to happen, my Aunt Joann and Uncle Bobby came for a visit. My Aunt Po asked them what they were planning to do about the hurricane, and they told her that, of course, they weren't going to evacuate. They, like many other long-time New Orleanians, figured that the storm would probably just hit Florida and that they would never even consider leaving with her in the hospital. They told her that they were planning to stay home in Meraux and that they'd be fine. They reminded her of all of the times that newscasters and government officials have called for mandatory evacuations, and they assured her that she had absolutely nothing to worry about. Nothing was going to happen, but if by some slim chance it did, she'd be in the best place: the hospital.

After they left, my Aunt Po felt slightly relieved. She figured that if the storm were really going to hit, then my Aunt Joann and Uncle Bobby would be evacuating; they were rational, so they wouldn't risk their lives by sticking around for a huge category 5 storm that was definitely coming. But, as she told me, she continued to watch the news coverage and the situation seemed to be getting increasingly dire by the hour. The newscasters were saying that the storm was definitely coming. Mayor Morial was telling people that they needed to take up emergency shelter in the Superdome or, at the very least, make sure that they had a hatchet on hand so that they could hack a hole in their ceilings and roofs to escape the massive flooding that would likely accompany the storm. All of these images and sound bytes unnerved her. Though she retained a collective memory that the media tended to sensationalize hurricane situations and that hurricanes never *really* hit New Orleans, she started to think that Katrina was going to be a lot different (Halbwachs 1925 [1992]).

Later in the evening, the hospital staff began rushing around urgently. My Aunt Po asked one of the nurses what was going on; the nurse told her that the storm was coming and that they were going to have to evacuate everyone from Chalmette Medical to Memorial Baptist Hospital, a few miles away in the city. Since St. Bernard was so vulnerable to flooding as a result of coastal erosion and its location right on the Gulf, the hospital staff agreed that it was best to evacuate all of the patients before the flooding came. It was already raining heavily, but they nevertheless loaded all of the patients into ambulances and hurried them along to Memorial Baptist. By this time, my Aunt Po was in a state of panic. How would she be able to let my Aunt Joann and Uncle Bobby know that she was being relocated? The phones weren't working now and everything was moving so quickly. The nurses and doctors were preoccupied with arranging the transport of all of the patients, many of whom were on life support or attached to other sorts of cumbersome medical machinery, so they weren't available to answer questions or to help patients contact loved ones. According to my Aunt Po, it turned into pandemonium right there in the hospital.

It was my Aunt Po's turn to be evacuated. She was quickly placed in an ambulance with another woman and driven a few miles away to Memorial Baptist. While she was in the ambulance, she realized how bad the weather had become. The wind was blowing fiercely and the rain was coming down in sheets. While the hurricane had not yet made landfall, they were experiencing the early wind gusts associated with the outer hurricane bands. As they drove in the ambulance, she saw that the streets were beginning to flood. She worried about my Aunt Joann and Uncle Bobby; they hadn't evacuated because they thought the storm wasn't coming. She wondered what they were going to do now. Would they go to one of the schools for shelter? Would they go to the Superdome?

After a frightening drive through abandoned and flooded streets, my Aunt Po's ambulance arrived at Memorial Baptist. She was hurried inside on a gurney and placed in a hallway. The nurses and other medical staff tried to find ways to accommodate all of the incoming patients. At this point, the hospital's generators were still working so they had light and air conditioning—a near-necessity for those muggy summer nights in New Orleans. But the frantic pace of the hospital made it difficult for her to relax. She watched as hordes of people were herded into the various wings of the hospital, left alone in hallways, or crammed into hospital rooms. She couldn't believe what was going on. She never really thought that the hurricane would hit New Orleans, but now it seemed like it was really going to happen and she was worried. What was going to happen to her home? Her possessions? Since she hadn't thought she would be in the hospital for very long, she had left all of her important papers, like her birth certificate and the deed to her house, at home. She worried that they would all be lost in a big, Betsy-like flood. Most importantly, though, what was going to happen to her and her family? These questions, and the dizzying pace of the hospital, kept her up all night.

Landfall

Sometime in the early hours of the morning, the storm made landfall. The wind picked up speed, the rain shot down in sheets so thick it was like nothing she'd ever seen before. Then, all of a sudden, the windows started breaking. The force of the wind put so much pressure on the windows that they simply exploded, like they were being bombed out. This sent the medical staff into a panic as they scurried to evacuate all of the patients from the rooms. It was too dangerous for the patients to remain next to the windows, so they were all moved into the hall and other protected areas of the hospital. Then, the generators stopped working and the electricity died. I remember my Aunt Po telling me that it became so incredibly hot in that hospital that she didn't think she was going to make it. She said that the hospital was crowded with people and there were no lights. The nurses walked around with flashlights to check on all of the patients. She was amazed by the bravery of the medical professionals that assisted her during the storm. Faced with their own potential losses, they remained in the hospital to help serve their sick, and often elderly, patients.

After a few hours, when it seemed like the situation was starting to wind down, the truly horrendous and unimaginable part of her story began. Early on Monday morning, while the patients and staff of Memorial Baptist were struggling to maintain their composure amidst stifling heat and no electricity, the water started to creep in. At first, it was only the first floor. Since the staff had strategically kept everyone off of the first floor, this didn't particularly alarm them. But then, it started to rise. And rise. And rise. And then, it started to spill over onto the second floor. Panicked, the hospital staff told the patients that they were going to have to get to the top floors of the hospital to wait for medical rescue. Anyone who could walk would have to walk up seven or so flights of stairs and wait for their turn to be evacuated to yet another hospital. My Aunt Po, though she was more frightened and nervous than she had been in a long time, was helped off of her gurney and shuffled up the stairwell where she joined a queue of people waiting for rescue by helicopter. She told me that climbing those stairs was one of the most difficult things she's ever had to do. She was ninety years-old and suffered from chest pains associated with congestive heart failure, making the climb to the top of the hospital difficult, especially given the heat and the commotion of the situation. Nurses and other medical staff carried those who couldn't walk up the seven flights. Individuals on life support were also carried up the stairs. She stood there in worried amazement as she awaited her turn to board the helicopters.

After waiting for a few minutes on the stairwell, it was her turn. Since she'd never been in a helicopter, and since she had only flown a few times in her life, she was apprehensive about the ride. Once she was in the helicopter, she felt relieved. She felt like this ordeal was over. They were probably just going to drop her off at a nearby hospital and there she'd get the care that she needed. She was worried about her home, but right now she just wanted to escape the stifling heat and the putrid odors that permeated Memorial Baptist. Much to her surprise, however, they didn't drop her off at another hospital; they didn't even drop her off at another building. Instead, they dropped her off at a makeshift hospital located under an overpass on the Interstate-10 in Jefferson Parish—right in front of the Galleria building.

Now, I should interject here that I remember watching the news coverage of Katrina. I saw the horrific images of hordes of people gathered on the I-10 in front of the Galleria building in Metairie. I couldn't believe that this stretch of road I'd driven probably ten million times before had become a horrific drop-off point for thousands of evacuees—people abandoned by their government and their fellow citizens. I certainly never imagined, *never in a million years imagined,* that I had a family member among those teeming masses. While I didn't know exactly where my Aunt Po, Aunt Joann, and Uncle Bobby had evacuated to, I was certain that they had evacuated and that they were safe. I couldn't fathom that my Aunt Po, whom I'd known and loved my entire life would be subjected to such a horrifying experience. While I felt connected to the people that I saw on television because we were all New Orleanians, I couldn't connect to their experience. Now, after learning that my Aunt Po was stranded under one of those overpasses, I look at those images differently. It's painful for me to watch that news footage and realize my Aunt Po was there, and that there was nothing I could do for her. As I sat in my tiny apartment in California, glued to the TV and the internet, making frantic phone calls trying to locate missing relatives, I never thought that I should have been closely looking at the abandoned masses right there on the interstate. It is, to this day, an unfathomable reality for me.

My Aunt Po told me that once they dropped her off on the interstate, she was told to lie down on a cot with all of the other people who had been evacuated from the hospital. She told me that the woman in the cot next to her was in a very bad state: her husband was by her side, wiping her sweating face, but her breathing was shallow and it seemed as though she couldn't possibly live much longer. Eventually, this woman did die—right there under the overpass on the I-10. The doctors and nurses moved her away to a makeshift morgue, somewhere out of sight. My Aunt Po told me that the woman's husband was distraught; he had no idea what to do, what was going to happen, or where they were all going to go. It was an incredibly painful experience for my Aunt Po. After seeing this woman succumb to the physical and emotional trauma of Katrina—right in front of her eyes—she realized that it was possible she wouldn't make it either. She was scared.

During this time, people were getting understandably restless. They were dirty, tired, anxious, dehydrated, and hungry. Many of them knew that they had lost everything. Many had been recently stranded in their hot, flooded attics for hours prior to helicopter rescue. Many more were unsure where their friends and families were, and if they'd even survived the storm. My Aunt Po shared these concerns. She didn't know where Joann and Bobby were. As she laid on her cot for nearly eighteen hours under the overpass on the I-10, so many things came to her mind: where would she live if her house had been flooded? At ninety years-old, she was hardly capable of rebuilding another flooded house. She had done it once after Hurricane Betsy and she knew she didn't have the energy to do it again. Would she die right there, under that overpass? She had to tell herself that she *would* live through this. She couldn't die right there. No one would know where she was!

Displacement

Late in the evening, another helicopter arrived to transport her to yet another location. She had no idea where she would be going, but she figured that any place would be better than the scorching interstate. As many who have been through hurricanes can attest, the days following a storm are unbearably hot and humid. Lying on a cot with congestive heart failure in the muggy heat was certainly not a pleasant experience, so she was ready to go wherever they planned to take her. As she boarded a second helicopter, she felt another sense of relief. *Finally*, this ordeal was over, she thought. The medical staff on the helicopter then told her that they were taking her to the airport where she would be more comfortable. When she arrived at the airport, she was taken directly to *another* makeshift hospital that was set up in one of the terminals. The heat inside the terminal was unbearable, but there was nothing that she could do. She told me that she was feeling very sick at this point and that she couldn't think straight. All of the commotion of the past day was too much for her and it was finally taking its toll. She told me that she really thought she was going to die in the airport. A few people in the airport told her that they were flying people out of the city, to hospitals in Baton Rouge and elsewhere. The pains in her chest were returning and she began to hallucinate.

After a short rest, my Aunt Po was informed that she would be taken to another hospital, but no one could tell her where exactly. At this point, she didn't care. She was tired and she needed to get out of that airport immediately. She had been displaced for almost two days now, and she didn't think that she had the physical or emotional wherewithal to last much longer. I think the medical staff sensed this and expedited her final evacuation. Her asthma was acting up and she told me she had never felt so close to death. People were dying, people were crying, and people were running around frantically. It was all too much for her to bear. She had never even considered the possibility that she might die as a result of a hurricane. After all, hurricanes never *really* hit New Orleans.

She finally boarded the helicopter. When she got on board, she asked where they would be taking her and they said they were taking her to Atlanta. Atlanta?! It made no sense to her. She wondered if she was hallucinating this whole experience. Why in the world would they fly her to a city so far away where she knows no one? How would she get home? How would anyone know where she was? She couldn't believe they were flying her so far away, but she had no choice. The helicopter pilot followed the orders of someone unknown, and my aunt's preferences were completely ignored. It was as though she was not a person—a sentiment expressed by many Katrina victims with whom I have spoken.

After the long helicopter ride to Atlanta, she was dropped off at some hospital; she couldn't remember the name or the location. The staff in this hospital, according to my Aunt Po, was mean and inhospitable. They treated her and her fellow evacuees (many of whom were African American, per her description) as though they were criminals and thieves. The perception was that they were the indigent masses who didn't make the "smart choice" to evacuate. This unfair bias was reflected in the type of care that they received. After having experienced such a significant trauma—being airlifted out of the hospital only so she could spend hours on the hot interstate, approaching death in the airport, not knowing where any of her friends or family were, and knowing that she probably had lost every possession she ever owned—there were no mental health professionals made available and the evacuees were treated as burdens. She told me that evacuees were having nervous breakdowns left and right. Some of them cried for days, some of them were violent with nurses and other medical staff and some of them acted as though they had given up on life. My Aunt Po was among the latter of those people.

After spending nearly one full month in an Atlanta convalescent home, she was returned to New Orleans via helicopter. She came home to her worst nightmare: Joann and Bobby had not evacuated. They had been stranded in their home for three days following Katrina, escaping only after Bobby had hijacked a neighbor's abandoned boat and had rowed them all the way to safety. My Aunt Po had lost everything: her home, her community, her material history, and her spunk. Nearly everyone in our family had lost everything. Only one home in our entire family escaped unscathed.

Coming Home

After coming back to New Orleans, my Aunt Po was forced to live in a dingy convalescent home in Lutcher, far away from her life and friends in St. Bernard Parish. I visited her in the home and couldn't believe the conditions. The floors were dirty, the food was inedible, and patients were jam-packed into the rooms. My parents offered to let her stay with them, but she, Joann, and Bobby refused. They knew that she needed medical care consistently. Her mental and physical health had deteriorated from the stresses of Katrina; she didn't seem like the Aunt Po I had known and loved for so long.

I remember riding in the car with her to Thanksgiving dinner at my Aunt Joann and Uncle Bobby's new rental home in Prairieville (far, far away from New Orleans). She spent that whole day telling me her Katrina story. It was as unfathomable as her many QVC and UFO stories, but this one was undeniably true. I could not, for the life of me, comprehend that anyone would ever have to go through what she had gone through, let alone one of my relatives. The whole experience of Katrina was just completely implausible, but my Aunt Po's recollections gave it a tangibility that I could no longer deny, and this was hard for me. It was as though I were there, lying amidst shattering windows and interstate overpasses. I was one of those abandoned individuals, clinging desperately to life wondering who was going to save me from this misery. I guess that's what a good storyteller does: takes you to an unimaginable, faraway land and makes you feel as though you are there. That's what my Aunt Po did for me that day, and that is why I tell her story here.

A few days after I returned to California, my parents called to let me know that my Aunt Po had died. It was a traumatic moment for me; I was completely devastated that she was gone and I couldn't believe she would no longer be around to tell her outlandish stories at family dinners or gatherings. She was an integral part of who I am; and so, in a sense, Katrina took a part of me. For what it's worth, my Aunt Po was a spunky, QVC loving, UFO believing, lifelong New Orleanian, and I loved her. She was one of many unsung casualties of Katrina—those people who didn't necessarily die during the storm, but died after they realized what this heinous monstrosity (both the storm and its response) had done to both the city and the spirit of New Orleans. Katrina robbed my Aunt Po of her *spirit of New Orleans* and that, in a nutshell, was enough to kill her.

Notes

1. In this essay, I've tried to preserve the "voice" that I've come to associate with New Orleans--that particular cadence and sentence structure that is, in my opinion, unique to New Orleans. As such, I've included quite a few tangential appositives and organized my sentences in ways that I wouldn't in other sociological writings. Using this voice, for me, was cathartic, but also allowed me to infuse my "New Orleansianness" into my essay; which, for me, is an important part of the experience of "sociological storytelling." For clarity, an example of this voice can be found in the second paragraph of this essay.

References

Glassner, Barry. 1999. *The culture of fear: Why Americans are afraid of the wrong things.* New York: Basic Books.

Halbwachs, Maurice. 1999. *On collective memory,* ed. and trans. Lewis Coser. Chicago: University of Chicago Press.

Zerubavel, Eviatar. 2003. *Time maps: Collective memory and the social shape of the past.* Chicago University of Chicago Press.

USING SIMMEL TO SURVIVE: THE BLASÉ ATTITUDE AS A DISASTER REACTION AND RESPONSE

JESSICA W. PARDEE
ROCHESTER INSTITUTE OF TECHNOLOGY

Saturday morning, 8:30am, I awoke at my boyfriend's apartment where he called for me to "come and see—the storm's headed right for us." He laughed dismissively and prepared to go to his Saturday morning class. I dressed and went straight home, turning on the television. The entire Gulf of Mexico was covered by an enormous, spinning cloud; then the image flipped—now a storm track path—and New Orleans was still at the center. I realized that this storm was big…bigger than a category three…bigger than what the levees could hold…big enough to be the storm we all joked about but secretly feared. And the storm was headed straight for us.

New Orleans had been my home for the last 11 years. As an undergraduate, I played in three feet of water that accumulated on Willow Street after just a few hours of heavy rain. The next week a faculty member scolded the class for playing in the toxic soup, "Don't you know there's backed-up sewage, rats, snakes, and trash in that water?" he clamored. We didn't. Nor did we understand that the city was a fishbowl, susceptible to flooding from rain or a levee break…at least not until his impromptu lecture on the importance of the levees for New Orleans. That class—that lecture—transformed my understanding of the geography of New Orleans. I'd evacuated for Hurricane George before, but mostly it was the sight of the Mississippi River flowing upstream, *from* the Gulf of Mexico *into* the city, that was the motivating factor. Until that class, with the sewage and floodwater and rats and snakes, I had never really thought about levees, or flooding, or devastation before.

Building the Blasé: Choosing Action over Reaction

With that knowledge in my back pocket, I went home Saturday morning to prepare for Hurricane Katrina. Intimately, I moved between waves of overwhelming, almost paralyzing panic, to technical, pragmatic planning. I knew the danger. Katrina had been a category 5 hurricane for a large part of that day. I imagined flooding. But, even then it was hard, and dangerous, to react, to let myself feel the fear of the situation. I was so deeply afraid it was almost paralyzing to let myself feel anything during that time. I imagined the water rising. I worried for people I loved, people I hated, and everyone in between. In particular, I worried for people without the means to leave. I knew a broken levee would inevitably mean death, as floodwaters were estimated to reach twenty feet in that case. So severe would be the consequences of a storm this size, a category 5, that the fear was paralyzing. So, I did my best to contain those emotions and ignore them. I rationalized the situation. I made lists. I blocked out the overwhelming nature of the constant stimuli on every news channel. I turned off the television, began my preparations to leave, and focused on the unexpected tasks the storm thrust upon me. Emotionally, I chose not to react, instead centering my attention on the technicalities of survival. I used breathing techniques from yoga to "center" myself and attended to the task at hand, preparing my cats, my house, and myself.

This power, this capacity to choose our reactions, was what Georg Simmel (1995 [1903]) called the blasé attitude. His wording so completely describes what I experienced: an "intensification of emotional life due to the swift and continuous shift of external and internal stimuli" (Simmel 1995 [1903], 31). Every news channel had constant streaming loops of information. Friends and family called to see what I knew, if I would leave. My mom wanted assurance that I would go. I promised, and at that point I had decided, to leave. I then called my friends in Texas, who had previously agreed to be an evacuation location. They joked, saying they wondered when I'd finally call. The humor was very much appreciated, since it cut through the reality of the storm's danger. Then my aunt called. She lived an hour south of New Orleans, and had been hesitant to evacuate in the past. I was relieved when she said she had made hotel reservations with another couple from their gardening club; they were headed to Mississippi. She gave me the hotel phone number, and we promised to make contact once we got to our final destinations. Finally, I called my friend who lived around the corner. He was planning to stay in town with his girlfriend. This made me nervous; I urged him to reconsider. I also borrowed a Harry potter book, just to get my mind off things. Later that afternoon, he called me to say that he and his girlfriend were going to Baton Rouge. I was tremendously relieved.

In the midst of all this phone-calling and preparation work, it was difficult to concentrate. Eventually, I chose to shut down my emotional side, forcing myself to breathe, and make lists: rational, bureaucratic style lists—Weber would be proud. The list included things like: move planted pots, wash dishes in sink, pack photos, get cat supplies. Then, I began to pack. I gathered photos. I moved potted plants inside and against the house. Mechanically, I took down yard decorations. I moved my patio table to the back corner of the fence and locked the lawn chairs to it with some twine, hoping the fence would block the wind since the twine clearly would not hold. I followed the list. I checked the television for updates. I moved all the other lawn furniture, plants, and empty pots I could into the little shed on the side of my house to prevent them from becoming projectiles. Of course, this shed, like the twine, was practically useless in its rusted state, but the point of all this work was to diminish the potential for the wind to pick up small objects and toss them like cannonballs into the house. With a category 5 storm, you know that you can't stop the damage, you just do the best you can to reduce it. In many ways, the blasé attitude functioned in the same way; I couldn't stop the feelings of helplessness, I could just minimize them by taking control where I could. So, I kept working on my lists; I listed things to bring like research materials, books, bills, checks, cat food and litter, and photo albums. I sorted through my keepsake trunk selecting the memories I would want, just in case: my grandmother's yearbook, my great grandmother's letters, and my B.A. and M.A. diplomas. I bought food and water for the road. I planned out my evacuation route—I would head south on Interstate 90 to avoid the traffic standstill of Interstate 10. I called my boyfriend to ask him to leave with me. He held out. Working for the power company, he had work responsibilities, even though he was supposed to be the "evacuated guy"—the one who leaves in case the guy who stays is killed by the storm. In the end, he left with me, at 8:00pm that Saturday night. We were to stay with a college friend in Northern Houston. Normally the drive is five hours, but with the I-90 route and evacuation traffic, I didn't know when we'd get there. I just knew we had to leave. By the time we left, I was already exhausted.

The Long Drive West

My evacuation path took me first to my friends' house in Houston, TX. The drive itself lasted ten hours, from 8:00pm to 6:00am, but usually takes six. The last four hours were filled with painfully slow traffic. People were speeding and braking, speeding and braking. The drivers were weaving and changing lanes. Still, in New Orleans evacuation time, this is excellent. The year before, one of my friends drove for eight hours to go thirty miles from her house to the airport as Hurricane Ivan approached. Another friend drove for 24 hours just to get to Baton Rouge, a mere 75 miles away. She could have literally walked there faster! So, like I said, ten hours to Northern Houston was excellent.

The journey was long and stressful. Leaving so late, we were driving when we should have been sleeping. We were also in separate cars because he refused to have *his* flooded out and I refused to have *mine* flooded out. In the worst case, my car would become my only possession, and the only means to get myself and my pets back to Connecticut, where I had grown up. So, my boyfriend and I used our cell phones to talk with one another in order to help us stay awake. Periodically we'd stop off at a gas station to nap. If I got sleepy, I'd play the Pearl Jam song "evacuation" a dozen times to wake myself up; I appreciated the irony and had selected the album purposefully while packing. It was a long, slow journey. The traffic was thick, but flowing. People changed lanes often, but maintained a speed of around sixty. Around 3:00am, as we neared Houston proper, the traffic became atrocious. For several miles, I was stuck behind a car swerving across the lines on both sides of our lane—three feet to the left, two to the right. I couldn't tell if they were drunk or falling asleep. I tried to stay as far back from them as I could, and prepared myself to swerve off the road if necessary. Eventually, I had the chance to gun past the car, and I did. The erratic driver, the time of night, the stress of the unknown; these little things added to the strain. Exhausted, physically and mentally, we arrived in Houston at 6:00am.

Unlike other disasters, such as floods or tornadoes where the warning and evacuation period is brief (Drabek and Boggs 1968; Erikson 1976), hurricane evacuation is longitudinal, spanning several days. Hurricane forecasting has improved so much over the years that we can actually see a storm in its infancy, as a wee little tropical depression, evolving to its teenage years as a tropical storm, and then fully develop into a powerful and influential hurricane. This temporality, the growth and emergence of a storm, extends the stress and anxiety over time. Still, evacuation is important. During Hurricane Andrew in 1992, evacuation saved lives. The severity of the storm ripped houses to pieces (Gladwin and Peacock 1997). So we continue to evacuate, no matter how exhausting the experience. We evacuate to stay physically safe, but we become emotionally vulnerable to the uncertainty. The day after a tornado people can immediately see what damage has been done. Yet, when you evacuate to Texas, you can't get back the next day. You have to wait, to dwell in uncertainty. Life is suspended. Your patience is demanded. Waiting, waiting, waiting...It's like having your own little purgatory of uncertainty here on earth.

The hospitality of my Texas friends was simply beautiful. They cooked delicious dinners for us, let us use the entire upstairs of their home, and were patiently supportive while we waited for Katrina to make landfall. Much of Monday is a blur, spent sleeping and watching stupid newscasters on television get blown down Canal Street as they hid behind postal boxes. There was also reported damage to the Superdome's roof; a few video feeds of water pouring in, but no serious acts of violence. There was the shattering of windows at the Hyatt hotel due to the powerful winds. Eighteen months after the storm, those windows still haven't been replaced. Finally, there was the flooding—localized rain flooding of two to three inches, but nothing newsworthy. After all, New Orleans gets that type of flooding from passing thunderstorms.

By Monday night, the storm had passed and most reports declared New Orleans spared. I felt a great sense of relief... What a great feeling! My friends, boyfriend, and I went out for dinner—fajitas and margaritas. We made plans to go home Tuesday afternoon or Wednesday morning since I still didn't know if I'd have to teach on Wednesday. After all, the semester was about to begin.

Tuesday morning, I turned on the television; I was ready to go home. Instead, I saw water. I saw water streaming, pouring, continuously, like a waterfall...a muddy, brown waterfall of disaster, pouring through a hole in a levee. In this moment, I knew, e*vacuation had become displacement.* New Orleans' survival had become its drowning. In this moment, the blasé washed away.

"The blasé washed away." What does that really mean? Well, since the blasé attitude allows us to choose our emotions and is a form of rationality, then imagine the pain you feel in the moments of your life when you can't hide behind the rationalizations, the unknown facts, or the statistical odds. Imagine or remember the moment you *knew* your lover was unfaithful. Or you *knew* you had to leave a relationship because the fighting would never stop. Or the moment when someone called you to say a family member had passed away, and you *knew* before they said it, but to actually *hear* the words was utterly devastating. In these moments, you can only experience pain. They are so intense, you react emotionally first, and become rational second. This is how I felt when I saw the water flowing through the levees. It was nothing I could control; nothing I could stop; nothing I could change; and nothing I could rationalize. I was completely helpless, possibly homeless, and my emotions were overwhelming and sickening. It was real; it was painful; and it was one of the most horrible moments of my life.

Displaced, Disheartened, and Distressed

Tuesday night, my friend took us to a liquor store. It must have been the biggest liquor store I had ever seen. They had a deli, a cheese selection beyond my wildest dreams, and bottles of tequila so expensive you could rent a car for a week for the same price. With the levees still breached and water still streaming into New Orleans, I just wanted to escape. So, I purchased about fifty dollars of beer, wine, and cheese with the pure intent of getting wasted. The image of the levees, and this catastrophic disaster unfolding on every television set in all of metropolitan Houston, was too intense, I couldn't even keep my focus enough to drink; and I really wanted to be drunk. Mostly though, I wanted to do something that would not just numb the pain, but make me forget it altogether. Yet, all I could manage was to drink a single beer impatiently and watch movies. I couldn't tell you now what they were, and it didn't matter because I wasn't watching. I was doing whatever I could figure to stop my mind from spinning over the reality of what was happening and the reality of what it meant. Again, I was doing my best to be blasé.

As Wednesday to Friday melted together, my boyfriend and I tried to make series upon series of contingency plans. He attempted to get relocated to Houston for work; I scrambled to find out if Tulane would reopen, or if I could enroll in school somewhere else. Without enrollment, student loans come due, and my subsidies would be permanently lost. Neither of us could access the money in our bank accounts because, having used regional banks, the accounts were temporarily frozen and the balances unavailable. Imagine: homeless and no money. You feel utterly helpless. I finally contacted my aunt. She told me that our insurance company was cutting checks to help pay for hotels. I found a local branch and took my rental policy. It wasn't much, just $2000, but it was all I had until, well, whenever. I felt fortunate. I had left New Orleans with just $300 in cash. Of course, later on I would learn that this meant I would be denied any further assistance—despite lost and damaged possessions, a legitimate mileage reimbursement claim, and food and hotel costs. I also never received an "official" copy of my claim either, meaning I could not dispute it. In the end, the insurance run-around was so exhausting that I gave up. Sometimes in life, you have to surrender the battle to save yourself for the war… this was one of those times.

Everyday following Hurricane Katrina, about ten times a day, I tried to register with FEMA. The local news had said some aid was available and that everyone from the hurricane-damaged areas should register. Some reports said FEMA was giving people $10,000, others cited more modest numbers. Either way, any help would be much appreciated. Yet, when I tried to log on, the server was always too busy and the webpage wouldn't load. When I called, the call wait-time was in the hours. Amid all this, I just kept hoping they would reopen the city, and I could just go home. But, each day the violence seemed to increase, the flooding continued, and no one sent any help. I remember the mayor swearing on a news interview because we needed assistance. It was something to the effect that the president and military needed to get their asses into New Orleans to bring food and water, and to get people out of the city "yesterday." I agreed and couldn't understand why, in the face of such an extraordinary disaster, it wasn't obvious to the President that the City couldn't fix its problems alone. Broken levees exceed the type of emergency any city can handle. No one expected New York to go it alone following 9/11, and that was just one city block. This was flooding across miles and miles of dense metropolitan development! Nor was this a state-level problem. Louisiana is one of the poorest states in the Nation. We lack behind the nation in income, educational attainment, and public teachers' salaries—just to name a few. However, we do rank *second highest* in the nation for the numbers of persons in poverty in 2005 (U.S. Census). So, of course, why couldn't Louisiana handle it alone? It's only one of the worst disasters in the entirety of U.S. history. To be serious though, how hard is it to figure out that the city, the state, and the entire Gulf Coast region needed help and needed it yesterday? To this day, I cannot understand the delay. I can only suspect that a conservative administration had little sympathy and motivation to save the lives of democratic African Americans in a crime-ridden city. I agree with Kanye West; the delay occurred because the victims were black—no more, no less.

Defining Displacement and Its Effects

In the coming days, U.S. citizens of New Orleans and the Mississippi Gulf Coast were redefined as "refugees." Refugees are individuals who are forced from their homes due to political unrest, war, and other atrocities; they are forced migrants (Wood 1994). The victims of Katrina were not refugees; they were displaced, and this is significantly different. First, citizens have rights. Second, they have a government that functions and has the power to support and assist them. Displacement means residential relocation occurs due to the physical destruction of a living environment. It does not mean you stop paying taxes or become "un-American." Thus, the use of the term refugee is an infuriating INSULT to every American citizen who lived and died during the Hurricane Katrina disaster. To call evacuees "refugees" denies our right and claim to governmental support. It is also a sophisticated form of blaming the victim, since most nations feel they owe nothing to refugees in terms of assistance, shelter, food, or amnesty rights. By contrast, citizens can demand these assistances from their government under such extreme circumstances. As citizens, we have a legitimate claim for help from our government and elected officials. We gave them their jobs and we should not be forgotten in return.

My lived experience of displacement meant staying with friends and family. For others it can include similar living arrangements, or even living with strangers in shelters for extended and unknown periods of time; limited or no access to your own bank and, therefore, no money; having only the clothing you evacuated with; ruptured daily routines, or no routines at all; not knowing if you have a job, employer, school, or home to return to; spending inordinate amounts of time trying to find information about what remains of your daily existence, if anything at all; waiting endlessly to register with FEMA; and, finally, locating the people you love, like, and even hate, just to know if they are okay—as if somehow they're being okay can make you okay.

This feeling, the need for "okayness," reflects a collective sentiment among Katrina evacuees. It crosscuts gender, race, and class, which I've learned through my dissertation research on the survival strategies of low-income African American women from New Orleans during and following Hurricane Katrina. They, like me, share deep feelings of loss and pain, complicated experiences in their efforts to gain assistance to help recover, and the same uncertainty of what the future will bring. What underlies the entire experience for all of us is a sense of collective trauma. In his meta-analysis of the common effects of disasters, Kai Erikson (1994) deftly observes that there are,

> ...familiar symptoms of trauma–a numbness of spirit, a susceptibility to anxiety and rage and depression, a sense of hopelessness, an inability to concentrate, a loss of various motor skills, a heightened apprehension about the physical and social environment, a preoccupation with death, a retreat into dependency, and a general loss of ego functions. One can find those symptoms wherever people feel left out of things, abandoned, separated from the life around them (21).

I feel a sense of intimacy most anytime I meet someone with connections to Katrina. It's a depth of shared pain that is only truly understood by those who lived, loved, and respected New Orleans and its people. To live in New Orleans was to live in a city with a deep soul, a sense of history, and a complicated past. It was somewhere you could lose and find yourself, transform at will, and rebuild at any time. The destruction of houses that were 100 years-old, the new construction that will inevitably replace them, if they are replaced at all, the population loss, and new groups who have entered in replacement, all of these transform the old city into something that is new and unknown. To Katrina evacuees and citizens, the flooding of New Orleans represents an entire change of everything you once knew to be true in your life. To everyone else, it seems like it was "just a little water," a brief moment from which the city will eventually and inevitably recover.

"How Long Will You Be Staying?"

My boyfriend and I spent two weeks total with my friends in Houston. After ten days, we finally got access to FEMA's online application. Tulane University had cancelled fall classes. Neither of us knew anything about our homes, our lives. What we did know was that we needed to move forward; my boyfriend went back to New Orleans on a work permit, while I went to South Carolina to live with my college-aged siblings.

As an evacuee, a common question from family, friends, and social service providers is "How long will you be staying?" The thing is, you don't know. Evacuation is not a vacation. It is not planned. Furthermore, the question is laced with a duplicitous meaning on any given day. Sometimes it means, "We really don't want you here so take the hint and make it brief." Other times it means, "I'm really happy to see you, your company is a joy." The thing is, as an evacuee, you don't know the meaning, or the answer. You can't. That decision is simply out of your control. The question is more complicated when service providers ask, since many of their services are contingent upon residency requirements. So, you feel like your supposed to say you're staying a long time, despite your intense personal desire to go home, to your home, and not be an alien in someone else's community. One of the biggest challenges the question creates: there is no actual answer.

Katrina created a level of destruction our government and our society were not prepared to handle. More important, the extended mandatory displacement put people at odds with themselves and their place attachments. People bond emotionally to the locations where they live their lives (Pollini 2005). As such, asking people to declare new residency under seemingly temporary circumstances runs directly against this attachment, creating conflict. New Orleans is a place to which people are deeply attached. Louis Armstrong illustrates this place attachment in his song, "Do you know what it means to miss New Orleans?" People love New Orleans so deeply; they are so attached that some have never left the city, ever. And I can understand why. If you can love a city, can meld yourself with it—with its music, its food, its culture, and with everything that keeps humans alive and creative—then I did. I love New Orleans. Which is what makes it so difficult to express the trauma of leaving, or the greater trauma of being asked to declare somewhere else your "home."

The Second Displacement: Surviving in the Southeast

Each week following Katrina it seemed like I'd be able to go home soon. My neighborhood didn't flood, but there were rumors of looting. The next town over, technically a neighboring parish, allowed folks back after just two weeks. It was mid-September then. The town line was only two miles from my house. A friend had "snuck in" to the city to clean his apartment and throw out his damaged things. At the two-week point, I had moved to South Carolina to live with my siblings. There, I was in a world where Katrina already felt forgotten. People were "so sorry," but they really didn't seem to understand. Moreover, they didn't even try. Their utter indifference, their absolute blasé attitude towards me and my plight left me feeling isolated and completely alone. I was afraid, my future unclear, and no one knew or cared about how tremendously ruptured my life, routines, plans, and reality were and would continue to be. Similar to survivors of Hurricane Andrew in Florida, I was "living between two worlds" where I had to balance being in the "normal" world South Carolina offered, while my life was grounded in the disaster world of New Orleans (Smith and Belgrave 1995). It was hard to explain to people that Hurricane Katrina created catastrophic damage, killed over 1,300 people, and devastated survivors, the city, and the region; it was all too much to consider and more than most people truly could, or wanted to, understand.

At this point, I was emotionally and physically worn down, exhausted, listless. I wanted to go home. I went to the local unemployment agency to see if I was eligible for unemployment compensation. I had with me signed letters of offer for two adjunct classes. Instead, I was told I had to apply to the state of South Carolina and be actively looking for work there. "But I'm not staying. My part of the city didn't flood," I said. It didn't matter. My pleas were met with indifference. This typified the blasé attitude of people who saw me as just another charity case. So, I had to apply as if I were a resident. In the end, I never received unemployment. In fact, I never even received an official answer concerning whether or not I was even eligible; I basically wasted another half hour of my life on the phone in an effort to get help that never came. The follow-up number I was given to call actually went to a mortgage company, not the unemployment office. When I called the Louisiana office months later, I could never get a person on the phone, so I could never find out if I was even registered.

My experience with health care was even worse. While at the unemployment office I was funneled through a "one-stop" shop of social services for evacuees. I managed to give my social security number away to everyone, but seemed to be unqualified for many forms of assistance. While talking to a health care worker, I tried to get a prescription filled. She made an appointment for me and called everyone I would encounter to smooth out the way. I thought to myself "finally, some relief." I was told I would have an appointment in a half hour. I drove quickly to get to the clinic on time, yet no one knew anything about who I was. Plus, there was no appointment. I spent over an hour past my estimated waiting time. I was also told the prescription would be free. After waiting two hours for the clinic to fill the prescription, they asked for payment. When I explained I had been told it would be free, and I actually didn't have the money to pay for it, the workers went from being friendly to treating me like any old charity case. Just five minutes earlier, they were asking about Katrina and how the animals had been saved. I was dumbstruck at their emotional transformation and shift in my treatment from friend to foe, equal to subordinate.

This transformation in their affect, this resistance, made me feel like it was somehow my personal fault a levee broke and I needed a refill. But this is how the blasé works. People sense the overwhelming nature of the constant and overwhelming stimulation of life and shut those feelings out, dulling their reactions and redirecting their mental energies on the trivialities of daily life. Meanwhile, for me, I had no energy left to preserve my own blasé, and thus, no protective barrier against their indifference. So great was the stress of the "run around," that I broke down sobbing in the waiting room—and I don't cry in public, at work, or walking down the street. Yet, these women didn't even look up at me. Only patients, South Carolina's poorest, were willing to try to help me. They knew the desperate need you feel when you have to resolve yourself to take a handout, and the way it cuts at your pride. They also knew that the poor and needy are treated in an unconscionable way and that it was normal and to be expected. In this way, they can be understood as blasé in their own waiting for help. Yet, I was not prepared. Worn down and vulnerable, when they asked if I was okay, all I could say was "No."

The city of New Orleans was flooded by a broken levee and neglected by a federal government with alternate spending priorities. 1,300 people died in the city alone (GAO 06-934). Yet, this is how we treat our citizens in the face of a catastrophic disaster. Our service provision model clearly has a problem. At the point of tears, of trauma highlighted in a public space, over a prescription refill, I insisted that the clinic workers give me a phone number to call. Without detailed explanation I simply said to them, "I cannot stay here any longer, will you give me the phone number or not???" They asked me to wait a just few more minutes. Without a pause, I repeated myself, "May I *please* have the number? I *can not stay here any longer.*" I did not yell, I did not cry, but I did not back down either. I would come back tomorrow to pick up the prescription, but I would not wait any longer that day. Hesitantly—almost argumentatively—they obliged. Looking back, this moment in the health clinic, crying before a room of strangers and apathetic "helpers," was my Hurricane Katrina rock-bottom. Nothing before or since made me so angry, so hurt, so exasperated, so exhausted, or so deeply furious. This *almost* broke me. I say almost, because after I walked out of that clinic, I got in the car and I screamed as loudly as I could for a full minute. Then, I took a breath, and I screamed again. Then, I felt like a fool because I thought someone across the parking lot saw me. I didn't care. I was taking care of myself and not hurting anyone else in the process. Collected, I drove with intent to the unemployment office and reported my mistreatment. I waited in no lines, but just walked back to where the "one-stop" Katrina evacuee relief system was set up. In response, the original nurse I spoke with drove to the clinic to get the prescription herself, an act for which I will be eternally grateful.

Despite this incident, not everyone was so blasé and insensitive that day: the food stamp booth at the one-stop center overheard my saga and gave me a purchase card on the spot; Catholic charities provided gas vouchers and a clothing voucher to the Salvation Army store; Red Cross gave a debit card that I could use anywhere, and on anything but alcohol. These small pieces, embarrassing as they were to accept, were a deep relief and a beginning to recovery. Having been financially independent since age eighteen, accepting help—even under the extreme circumstances of Hurricane Katrina—cut my pride and sense of self-sufficiency deep. I had worked so hard to educate myself out of the working-class. Now, I was homeless, financially broke, and unable to support myself. Though I was well-educated, this education was ironically worthless at this time. Sure, I could have found a job, but in those early days having a master's degree provided nothing towards meeting my basic needs. For the first time in ten years, I had to let strangers and my family care for me—and my younger brother and sisters at that. My survival was linked to the same networks the urban poor rely upon to make ends meet, and I knew it (Stack 1974; Edin and Lein 1997).

Despite all the chaos of this day, I met one woman who became a saving grace. She was a career counselor for the county, and made the most meaningful gesture of any during my weeks as an evacuee. Having overheard the ordeal of my afternoon at the clinic, she took me to a steak dinner at a restaurant where she worked part-time. And we just talked as adults, about life, things, what we did, who we were independent of the storm. Humans need interaction; we are social beings. And I needed a space to just be myself, not a charity case, or "poor girl." Her support was perhaps the most restorative in South Carolina. With her, I was an adult, a human, myself. For a few hours, I was able to shed the label of "Katrina victim." I met someone connected to my humanity, a woman who was not hiding behind the blasé attitude engaged by the clinic workers. For a few hours, I was free to just exist as my "normal" self.

While I lived with my siblings, they were busy leading college lives. The next few weeks were uneventful, and passed quickly. I went to a wedding for my boyfriend's sister. I enrolled at the University of Central Florida (UCF) as a visiting student, and I began a new dissertation. The flooding destroyed one of my research sites, a low-income public housing community that had been covered with nine feet of water, and thus invalidated my old project. My days were mostly spent picking up the pieces of my life. I checked on the status of my Tulane student loans, which were my pre-Katrina means of paying my bills. I applied for new loans at UCF, and slowly began to build a new financial network to cover my bills, since returning to live in New Orleans would make me ineligible for FEMA rental assistance. Finally, in the third week of September, the mayor announced that I could go home.

Returning to a "Home" that Wasn't

Returning "home" was not what I had expected. The damage was severe, extensive, and deeply emotional. It far exceeded the video footage. Block upon block of flooded, damaged, and in some cases missing, houses stood vacant among the dusty, mud-caked roads. Everywhere you looked something was amiss: a tree with large branches hanging, grass overgrown or completely dead, cars on their sides, roofs covered in blue tarps, or with gaping holes where no tarp had yet been placed. In Lakeview, there was a mountain of debris over thirty feet tall and extending almost two miles. In my neighborhood, as in others, there were houses that just collapsed on themselves or were missing walls so you could view the contents inside. The streets were littered with dozens of refrigerators, each filled with decomposing food. As a collective, the refrigerators replaced the neighbors who used to talk on the sidewalks and emitted a noxious odor so intense that it made burning hair smell like roses. In my boyfriend's house, the landlord had removed the refrigerator, but had left the stream of liquid from the melted food and meat to fester on the floor. It had sat unattended for three weeks. We returned to a thousand maggots, crunchy under the paper towels, disinfectant spray, and rubber gloves we used to clean them. I took a single picture of myself at this time. I looked like death walking. I wanted to remember how I felt, because it is likely I may never feel that bad again; and I was very lucky. Ironically, amidst all this debris, destruction, and decomposition, my basil plant was now four feet high. Even in death, life emerges.

While the blasé helped keep me calm during evacuation and backlashed against me during my exile in South Carolina, it was nowhere to be found in recovery. With each passing moment, it eroded. I returned to a home that was not home. New Orleans became a new space, neither simulacra nor nostalgia, nor anything I knew. Although the city was more than a shell of its former self because of the collective sense of pain and struggle, New Orleans was altered fundamentally to its core, its soul. For example, once a walking city, it now felt unsafe. From nails in the street under your shoes, to strange men acting openly offensive and sexist, this place was not my home. In an effort at normality, my boyfriend and I dressed up and went to dinner at the newly reopened Red Fish Grill. Downtown, on Bourbon Street, a stranger approached me, telling me, "I'd like to take you home in that dress." My boyfriend and his roommate were standing next to me. While to the outsider this may seem harmless, there was a vulgarity in the comment and accompanying glare that I'd never experienced on a New Orleans public street before. It was as if this man thought appropriate New Orleans behavior was the content of a Girls Gone Wild video. No native of *my* city had ever spoken to me that way, and the offense was intensified because my boyfriend was standing right there. It was barely mid-October and I was already disgusted.

An equally jarring set of experiences occurred at the local neighborhood bars. I had waitressed at one, but no longer knew any of the customers there; they were not locals. They were, however, extremely racist. Because I am white, they would tell me about "what those niggers did" at the mall or at the grocery store—as if the only "looters" in the whole entire city were black, or as if the government hadn't failed to bring food or water to people for five days. The final straw in this new environment was when the police harassed me while I was talking to my neighbor, who was being evicted. She is Black and was getting in her car as I was returning home. We started talking and were there for about fifteen minutes when a police cruiser pulled up next to us and just stopped. The officers asked what we were doing. My neighbor responded that we were going to lunch and asked if they had eaten. Then the car just sat there, blocking my narrow street for almost 45 seconds; it felt like an eternity. The officers said nothing. Finally, I looked at both and said, "Can I help you?" I knew that as a white woman, with no criminal background, attending Tulane University, I was empowered to politely challenge their harassment with minimal consequence. After all, I was repopulating the city. By contrast, my neighbor could only joke with them to ease the tension. They paused for another fifteen seconds and then drove off slowly. My neighbor and I remarked that we didn't really understand what that was about. I suspected openly that perhaps they thought I was buying drugs from her. She agreed and we parted ways. Apparently white people and Black people can't be friends, especially after Katrina. The negative imagery of Blacks looting during the storm created such a deep prejudice that relief workers, visitors, and even local citizens seemed to buy into racial stereotypes. A week later, my neighbor was forced out as a new tenant replaced her, someone who would pay a higher rent.

In all of this, I felt vulnerable and raw. The daily reminders of Katrina, the local news reports of bodies found in attics, and my harassment on the streets just washed the blasé away every time I'd start to reconstruct it. So intense were the racial frustrations, the blatant comments, the glares from national guardsmen toward Blacks in the city after the storm, that all I could emotionally do was retreat. I cleaned up my yard, rented movies, and hid from the city. I was hiding from the strangers, those invasive souls who came to New Orleans to "save us" and to help us "recover," but who seemed to stake claim to a new home without a thought for those who were displaced. Like the survivors of Hurricane Andrew who felt angered at "the appearance in devastated areas of empty-handed voyeurs," I too felt resentment at the profiteers who were making extra money by "serving" in the disaster zone and by renting apartments that residents could no longer afford or access (Smith and Belgrave, 255). In this shifting space, life after the blasé was complicated, difficult, and contradictory. My sense of displacement pervaded and continued, as home just didn't feel like home anymore.

A Survivor's Continuing Sojourn

Writing about my experience with Hurricane Katrina, I realize how I can now, again, engage the blasé attitude. The choppy, quick feeling the writing takes in many places reflects the fact that the overall experience, no matter how much I rationalize it, caused me a deep, ensuing trauma. Yet, I've distanced myself and write in many moments without reaction to the words I commit to the page. It's almost as if I tell you quickly how afraid I was, how difficult the experience, how hurt, how angry I was, that I won't have to feel it. It's been almost two full years, and I still feel anger, sadness, frustration, and fear. There is not a single day I don't think about Hurricane Katrina. I want my city back. I want to be home. Yet, I know that home no longer exists and I am left with an altered life (Smith and Belgrave 1995). Unable to recreate the past, or recapture what once was, I face an uncertain future. Some days, this freedom excites me; other days it terrifies me. For me, since Katrina, only the unpredictable has been predictable. At the time of this writing, I live in Central Florida—attracted here by a one-year visiting professorship. Just yesterday, I learned I will work here for another year. But like New Orleans, I am not completely recovered; my life is not predictable or stable, I no longer plan more than a couple months in advance. I, too, am a work in progress.

People often ask me if I will go back. I say I would, but I am not sure what I would go back to. My life in New Orleans was wonderful and rich. It was filled with culture. It was also filled with pain, love, and growth. When I tell people I lived in New Orleans for eleven years, what I really mean is that I *lived* in New Orleans. I trace both my most fulfilling and painful moments to that city, and everything in-between. While sociology has helped me frame my experience and has connected me with the normality of my reactions when compared to other hurricane survivors, what sociology has not yet resolved for me is this: how do you leave a city you love?

In an evacuation, you are told to leave. You have to leave. And Katrina forced everyone to leave. We were displaced. We were left outside our homes and in many ways outside ourselves. Displacement disarmed the defenses and it displaced the blasé. Now when I hear the song, "Do you know what it means to miss New Orleans?" I understand. I ache for my city, my home, my old life; only to realize that like Louis, I must walk away from the racism, the anger, and the disappointments of the city because, in the end, the damage is so deep, so fundamental that I am left to question if home can ever truly be restored.

Notes

1. Simulacra is a postmodern concept that refers to an entity that simulates some social reality, originated by Baudrillard (1998). It is a copy of something that never existed.

References

Baudrillard, Jean. 1998. Simulacra and simulations. In *Selected Writings*, ed. M. Poster, 166-184. Palo Alto: Stanford.
Drabek, T., and K. Boggs. 1968. Families in disaster: Reactions and relatives. *Journal of Marriage and the Family* 30: 443-451.
Edin, Kathryn, and Laura Lein. 1997. *Making ends meet: How single mothers survive welfare and low-wage work.* New York: Russell Sage Foundation.
Erikson, Kai. 1976. *Everything in its path: Destruction of community in the Buffalo Creek Flood.* Simon and Schuster: New York.
—. 1994. *A new species of trouble: The human experience of modern disasters.* New York: W.W. Norton.
Gladwin, Hugh, and Walter Gillis Peacock. 1997. Warning and evacuation: A night for hard houses. In *Hurricane Andrew: Ethnicity, gender, and the sociology of disasters*, ed. Walter Gillis Peacock, Betty Hearn Morrow and Hugh Gladwin, 52-74. New York: Routledge.
Government Accountability Office. 2006. *Hurricane Katrina: Strategic planning needed to guide future enhancements beyond interim levee repairs.* Report Number: GAO 06-934.
Pollini, Gabriele. 2005. Elements of a theory of place-attachment and socio-territorial belonging. *InternationalReview of Sociology* 15: 497-515.
Simmel, Georg. 1997 [1903]. The metropolis and mental life. In *Simmel on Culture*, ed. David Frisby and Mike Featherstone, 174-185. London: Sage Publications.
Smith, K., and L. Belgrave. 1995. The reconstruction of everyday life: Experiencing Hurricane Andrew. *Journal of Contemporary Ethnography* 24: 244-269.
Stack, Carol. 1974. *All our kin.* New York: Basic Books.

Wood, W. 1994. Forced migration: Local conflicts and international dilemmas. *Annals of the Association of American Geographers* 84: 607-634.

THE FIRST MAJOR U.S. URBAN EVACUATION: HOUSTON AND THE SOCIAL CONSTRUCTION OF RISK

PAMELA BEHAN
OUR LADY OF THE LAKE COLLEGE

The fall of 2005 was a strange season in Houston. The news images of victims and survivors of Hurricane Katrina repeatedly and vividly reminded all Houstonians of the Gulf Coast's vulnerability to disaster; then, thousands of evacuees from New Orleans were brought to Houston and their unmet needs kept the local news focused on disaster stories throughout September.

As a university professor, my main point of contact in all this was with displaced college students who were trying to make the transition to new courses several weeks after the semester had already begun. As a former nurse, I also paid attention to the arrangements being made to meet evacuees' health care needs; I was proud that our mayor had insisted upon taking in whoever needed refuge and that the medical community had responded to the evacuees' extraordinary needs by setting up service arrangements.

Houston is big enough that the evacuees were absorbed fairly invisibly into the city. As a resident of Houston Heights, though, I realized that the boarded-up apartments down the street from my middle-class home were likely to be reopened to help fill the increased need for inexpensive housing, which meant that displaced kids might be walking through our neighborhood on their way to the local high school. Change was afoot in Houston, and I began to hear colleagues, students, and neighbors express anxiety about the effects of so many New Orleanians on the city. A few of my African American students were the most vocal in their condemnation of the areas of New Orleans from which the poorer evacuees had come; their fears appeared to be rooted in social class, and upon a firm conviction that all "those people" were criminals and deadbeats who would cause problems for Houston.

The Threat of Hurricane Rita

Into this already tense racially and class charged atmosphere of Houston came a new concern. Another hurricane had made its way into the Gulf and had begun to grow, heading straight for Houston. For several days, the local weather casters were simply keeping an eye on Hurricane Rita, directing any warnings solely towards the coastal areas. Then the mayor's and county commissioners' offices announced plans for the mandatory evacuation of those areas and our island neighbor, Galveston, in stages and by zones. I found myself thinking about the effects of a direct hit on Houston; the mayor's actions made the risks seem more real. At least the authorities were learning from Katrina, I thought; they were starting early, emptying the low-lying areas first and organizing buses to help carry those without cars out of the city—these people included some of the recently resettled evacuees from New Orleans.

Wondering whether we needed to do anything about the approaching storm, my husband, Ed, and I talked it over with some of our neighbors, who had lived there much longer than we had. They told us that the category 3 hurricane, which had hit Houston years ago, had knocked out the power in the neighborhood for a week—very unpleasant in the heat, but about the worst risk anyone expected fifty miles inland. Since this was consistent with what I had heard from my brother in Florida, who was regularly affected by hurricanes, there was no sense of urgency. It was early in the week and Rita wasn't due until Saturday. There was a sense of anticipation, but, to me, it felt more adventurous than dangerous. We filled up our cars with gas, just in case.

Then the mandatory evacuations began. Tuesday, the evening news showed lines at gas stations and traffic jams on the highways going north. They showed Hurricane Rita building in strength and heading straight for Houston. They warned of danger in a more breathless, almost hysterical tone. By Wednesday morning, I felt enough urgency to run some preparatory errands on my way to school. My first stop was the local drug store, where I planned to pick up batteries and bottled water. Instead of what I wanted and needed, though, I found a lot of empty shelves. It seemed absurd; there was no visible change in activity in the stores or on the streets, and no one I saw was acting particularly anxious, yet clearly the crunch had begun. I settled for the smaller water bottles that the store still had, and tried a few other stores before I found batteries.

Even after that first dose of reality, it still surprised me to arrive at the university and find that classes had been cancelled for the remainder of the week. It was obvious that I wasn't from hurricane country. I had grown up in Kansas with the threat of tornados, which appear fairly quickly out of visible storms and dissipate in just a few hours. I found the three days' wait for the hurricane unsettling; too long to keep treating it as an emergency, but just as disruptive and potentially lethal.

Apparently, I wasn't the only one having trouble taking the situation seriously. The authorities repeatedly expressed their concern for citizens who were not making appropriate preparations and, later, for folks who refused to evacuate their homes. Houston had not been hit by a hurricane for almost two decades, and only about half of its residents had any memory of how frightening and destructive that category 3 storm, Hurricane Alicia, had been. The local TV stations ran interviews with people who planned to weather the storm at home and with authorities who predicted that such residents would end up risking the lives of others sent to rescue them. In retrospect, I am pretty sure that those interviews and concerns were only about folks living near the coast, but the strong impression they left was about the dangers of staying.

Nevertheless, my husband and I began making preparations for riding out the storm at home. We were not in an evacuation zone and knew from our Tropical Storm Alison experience that our house was unlikely to flood; therefore, we concentrated on finding plywood to cover the windows, a few sandbags to keep water on the patio away from the back door, and appropriate foods to get us through a power outage. This took both persistence and luck, and, finally, a willingness to not be too picky about what we would eat. Ed began measuring windows and I began to go through the freezer, pulling out stuff to thaw and cook before the storm arrived. We also filled every water container we could find.

Uncertainty and the Social Construction of Risk

The risks to our area soon began to seem less predictable, making us question our decision to stay. On Thursday morning, Rita was reported to have grown in power to a category 4 storm, and was predicted to progress to a category 5 before it hit Houston's coast. As its power grew, so did our sense of vulnerability. Our house was a solid one, fifty years-old and in good condition; we wanted to trust that it could protect us. However, it had never been through a category 4 or 5 storm. We knew of no way to tell whether it could withstand such winds, and there was no internal room in which we could find safety away from the windows. On the other hand, the storm wasn't due for another day and a half; it could still change course or lose power before reaching land. In the face of such uncertainty, we were unsure if we should stay or evacuate. We felt urgency to decide;

we would have to make different preparations if we were going to leave.

Risk and uncertainty are social variables that have been frequently examined by sociologists and other social scientists. Most agree that both concepts are social constructs; that is, that people decide in interaction with one another how to define, think about, and respond to aspects of life which they cannot control. Agreement upon the meanings of risk and uncertainty are passed on to children, friends, and coworkers as ways of coping with dangers and doubts, and eventually become largely unquestioned parts of societal and organizational culture (Dake 1992; Hunt 1995; Richardson 2001; Wilkinson 2001).

From what I saw in the days before Hurricane Rita's arrival, it seemed that most Houstonians were coping with the uncertainties by gathering information from the media, talking with family and friends, and attaching meanings to the decision to go or stay. Those meanings appeared to revolve around bravery and prudence; those who had decided to stay talked about not being afraid of the hurricane, an admirable trait in south Texas, while those who had decided to evacuate talked about uncertainty and safety, especially if they had small children. Ed and I were no different. We kept checking the latest hurricane news on the local TV stations which were our main source of information on the storm and, therefore, on the relative risks of staying versus evacuating. We consulted with friends and learned many of them were leaving, either because they lived in a mandatory evacuation zone or because they had decided to avoid the risks of staying. In the late afternoon, our son Nathan, who was 24 years-old, showed up with his girlfriend and announced that they would be evacuating to Austin with her family. Nathan urged us to leave too, saying that he would worry about us if we stayed. We certainly didn't want to cause anxiety for him, but we weren't yet convinced that leaving was necessary. Ed and I began to seriously consider evacuating, but remained ambivalent until we received a call about two hours later from some friends near San Antonio; would we like to come to their house until the storm passed? Their concern and the prospect of a friendly refuge ended our ambivalence; we decided to leave. Deciding to evacuate felt like accepting the inevitable; if the media, our son, and our friends thought it was too dangerous, too risky, to stay, then, of course, we needed to leave. It wouldn't be reasonable to worry everyone and cause extra trouble for the authorities by staying. The social constructions of risk all around us had shifted and, as a result, our decision to stay had shifted as well.

That night, the media reported an increase in the storm's measured power. This seemed to support our decision to leave, which we no longer questioned. However, the decision to leave brought new anxieties; if we thought our house could not protect us, then we certainly could not rely on it to protect our possessions. Accepting this new construction of risk meant acknowledging that everything we didn't take with us might be destroyed by the hurricane. In one day, we went from feeling relatively secure at home to wondering if our house would be there when we got back. We didn't sleep well that night.

Evacuation

Early the next morning, we had a new concern. Apparently, a lot of other people had also made the decision to leave voluntarily, a development the authorities had not anticipated. We had not paid much attention to reports of gas shortages and traffic jams the day before, assuming they were caused by the mandatory evacuations and limited to the coastal evacuation routes. However, both problems had escalated; the main roads out of Houston were now backed up for fifty miles, and many people were running out of gas en route, creating further congestion. The local TV channels showed four and six-lane highways full of traffic at a standstill, with people sleeping in their cars and walking dogs on the shoulders of the road. Reporters interviewed families beside their cars, sometimes returning hours later to find the same families in the same places. There were reports of deaths on the roads from dehydration and heat stroke; people weren't using their air conditioners for fear of running out of gas, and few had brought enough water for long exposures to Houston's muggy heat.

Our neighborhood's streets were now unnaturally empty, with few cars or people. Our closest neighbors evacuated only to come back hours later, telling us that they hadn't even gotten to the city limits in all that time and had become afraid of running out of gas before reaching shelter. The question for us now was whether we could get out at all.

We'd heard on TV that the city had begun working on turning the main area highways into one-way roads away from Houston and its coast: "contraflow" lanes. However, this was going to take some time to arrange, as several jurisdictions were involved, and the interstate entrances pointed towards Houston would have to be blocked all the way to San Antonio, Austin, and Dallas. We covered our windows with plywood and made room in the garage for the car we wouldn't take while we waited for the contraflow lanes to begin and the traffic jams to clear.

We were still waiting at noon on Friday. We had decided to take our smaller car, because it used less gas. It was all packed, with photo albums and other irreplaceable items, an ice chest with perishables we could eat on the way, and clothes for a few days. All that was left to do was to put our cats in their carriers and climb in. However, being unable to go yet, we could not relax, so we found things to do around the house; I busied myself with cleaning the refrigerator, figuring that the power would be off when we got back and hoping to avoid a stinky mess.

By early afternoon, we were both too antsy to wait any longer, so we packed up the cats and left. The streets of the city were eerily quiet; there were no people on the sidewalks, businesses and public buildings were closed, and there was almost no traffic. We avoided the highways and took city streets and back roads as far as we could to the west. A few miles from the city, though, we began encountering other traffic heading outward; enough people had also thought to avoid the main highways that our county road was soon bumper-to-bumper, with especially long delays at intersections with stop signs. Both Ed and I are fairly calm people, but the slowness of our progress began to frustrate us, just as it clearly did other drivers. Several times we saw people take crazy chances, usually to pass long lines of cars. Some drove by on the shoulder; others raced around on the left in the face of oncoming traffic. Fortunately, after an hour or so, the radio reported that the contraflow lanes were working on the highway to San Antonio, so we turned south and made our way to the interstate, where traffic was moving at its usual pace.

However, a number of vehicles had already run out of gas, and empty cars and trucks were scattered all over the grassy roadsides and the median strips. Many people were sitting or lying on blankets or lawn chairs beside vehicles, with others stretched out across the seats with both doors open. Some had ice chests and thermoses out, and were eating. No one looked acutely distressed, but everyone looked hot, tired, and worried. It appeared that the normal rules of travel had been suspended, and the scene reminded me of a post-apocalyptic movie—a cross between a highway and a nightmare. We saw no police or highway patrol cars at all, and wondered who would help all these people escape the hurricane. It felt cold to pass by so many stranded travelers, but we did so anyway; it suddenly seemed plausible that we could get stuck there too.

For the first time, we began seeing "out of gas" signs at the gas stations we passed, which were all either totally empty or crowded with vehicles. When we later stopped for a bathroom break, we learned that the crowds meant that those stations still had food, or drinks, or an open bathroom, but not necessarily gas. We were thankful for our little car's fuel efficiency, since the risk of running out of gas had become very real.

After we stopped at a wrong-side rest stop and switched drivers, again, the whole scene began to feel surreal to me: the odd view from the wrong side of the highway, the contrast of glaring traffic lights with the dark of the night, and the frequent glimpses of abandoned cars and stranded people. The feeling ended when we found an open convenience store with a working bathroom, a symbol of normality. A family we met there told us they had left Houston 24 hours earlier; they had weighed the risks and decided to leave Thursday, but had only gotten exactly as far in all that time as we had in six hours. They looked half asleep on their feet and very uncomfortable, scratching irritably at sweat stained clothing and bug bites. Part of our motivation to evacuate had been our son's concern, and he had thought our preparations at home and delay in leaving were foolish and risky. However, in retrospect—and coincidently—our delay had saved us a good deal of stress, and ultimately gotten us further along the road in a much shorter time.

Lessons in the Storm's Aftermath

Ten hours after leaving home, we reached our safe haven, and had our first good sleep in days. The next morning brought a new twist to our story, as we learned that Hurricane Rita had both turned aside and lost strength in the hours before it had made landfall. Houston had been spared altogether, and the evacuation of thousands, including us, had been unnecessary. All our careful weighing of risks and options had been faulty, and our actions to avoid disaster useless. It was oddly depressing to have been so wrong, in spite of the relief that our house was all right. Too tired to do anything else, we spent the day at our friends' house watching the news obsessively, learning about Rita's devastation of the East Texas/Western Louisiana coast and various evacuation crises, including a bus full of elderly folks that had caught fire on the road, killing many. We heard the evacuation critiqued, including all the things that the authorities might have anticipated and set up ahead of time. We also learned that many families had, contrary to expectations, tried to drive all of their vehicles away from the storm instead of only themselves and their most irreplaceable possessions. Apparently, many people felt that a ruined vehicle would be an intolerable financial burden to replace; this had been one of the factors swelling and complicating the interstate evacuation.

As our critical faculties returned with rest, we noticed that there was no critique of the urban development of the Gulf Coast and its residents' reliance on personal vehicles. This seemed to us a glaring omission, considering the role that those factors had played in complicating the evacuation. After all, weren't hurricanes expected in the Gulf Coast, a matter of "when" rather than "if?" And didn't everyone who moved in know that they might have to get out when a hurricane hit? Weren't buildings and roads in coastal zones simply destroyed every so often by such storms? And wasn't the destruction clearly worse when development was allowed to disrupt natural ridges, drainage patterns, and wetlands? This sort of prediction is, after all, a staple in sociology, which tends to advocate using technology in ways that will not create future problems. That is, nature works in certain ways; we can either anticipate its more extreme events and shape our activities in ways compatible with survival, or risk turning natural events into manmade disasters (Hilgartner 2007; Maganda 2003; Murphy 2001). Yet the Gulf Coast had been steadily built up since the last hurricane, with little regard for either the number of people who could realistically evacuate in an emergency or the additional destruction likely to result from new development.

But we heard no such critique. During the days of hurricane coverage after Rita, the notion that people could continue to do things in the same way, except in a crisis, was never called into question. We began to wonder if an equivalent evacuation under more severe time pressure would even be possible, and to suspect an unhealthy level of overconfidence in Houston's apparent belief that it could "rise to the occasion" to handle almost anything. What if a category 3 Rita had been projected to hit further down the coast, and had then both strengthened and swung into the Houston area on the last night? This was at least as likely as what had actually happened. How many unnecessary deaths would have then resulted, with no one able to do anything about it? The social construction of risk began to feel as inappropriately low between hurricane scares as it had been inappropriately high with a hurricane approaching.

The media were preoccupied with the Gulf Coast drama of the preceding few days. Yet even on that topic, we noticed another odd disparity in coverage. Eventually, the total human death toll of the evacuation would pass one hundred, a number that would be regarded as a true disaster if the cause of death had been the hurricane itself; the same number of deaths from heat and dehydration, however, seemed oddly taken for granted. There was no attempt to assign responsibility for them. The implication was that those deaths had been somehow inevitable and could not have been prevented. Perhaps this should not have surprised us, as the media and authorities seemed as implicated as anyone else in those deaths; their overblown public construction of risk had certainly contributed to the evacuation crises, whether they ignored that fact or not. We speculated that the authorities might regard those deaths as acceptable losses, just one of the risks of engineering such a mass exodus, and comparable to the military's dismissal of civilian deaths in wartime as "collateral damage." If they regarded this attitude as reasonable, however, we did not.

When the news coverage finally moved on, it focused on returning to normal life as it had been before the hurricane threat. The mayor's office tried to manage the traffic back to Houston, asking citizens to wait a day or two so that gas, supplies, and essential personnel of various types could be in place first. Ed and I were content to rest and wait at our friends' house, but many would or could not stay where they were—thousands returned immediately, ignoring the authorities and creating a risk of more traffic jams on the way back.

By the time we returned on Monday, most of the cars on the sides of the roads had been moved, traffic was moving normally, and the gas stations were restocked. Both my husband's workplace and mine stayed closed another day, which gave us time to yank the plywood off the windows and unpack. The university reopened on Wednesday at noon, exactly one week after closing, and I began learning through my students about how the hurricane threat and evacuation had affected other Houstonians.

My Students' Experiences

Several of my students had been caught on the highways for 24 hours or more, unable to use their air conditioning because of the gas shortage, and had became uncomfortably hot and sweaty. Some had children with them, and one family had to use containers in the car to relieve themselves, as there were no bathrooms available. Another student's family had made it sixty miles to the north after 24 hours, but were still in the path of the hurricane and with no place to stay, until a stranger led them to a fairground shelter set up for evacuees. They had a good experience there, with many unexpected comforts and much kindness from the locals: including donated soup, military ready-to-eat meals, and even a place to safely house pets.

Other students didn't leave, and had experienced a deserted city for several days, with no businesses open to provide food or other necessities. One student described this scene as belonging in a zombie movie, with its striking emptiness producing an eerie atmosphere. Another student had taken her chances with an elderly relative who refused to leave, saying she was sure her big old house would withstand the storm. One student had procrastinated because of workplace responsibilities, creating tensions with his family and, after all that, found no one else at work when he showed up. Another described a tense few days sheltering with too many family members in too small a house; conflict kept breaking out over relatively small irritants, like their pets' fighting and the work of feeding everyone. Two students had evacuated to family in the border region where the hurricane had actually struck; those students didn't get back for weeks.

Finally, one student, a young woman, vividly described the struggles she had witnessed over gas in one of the evacuation zones. Apparently, many of her neighbors had never experienced long lines and waits for gas, and in the heat became frustrated and irritable. Some disagreements escalated into physical fights in those lines, as people became frantic about obtaining gas. When one station put a limit on the amount of gas people could buy, the customers cursed and shouted; some even discussed beating up the attendant! My student concluded that many of her neighbors had behaved in ways that were quite out of character. Their discomfort and fear of the hurricane had apparently overridden their usual concerns about disapproval and other negative sanctions for "bad" behavior, producing less inhibited behavior.

The only hurricane "theme" my students had in common was their anger at the role the media had played in making everyone so fearful; many felt that the 100+ evacuation deaths were the media's fault, directly attributable to the repeated warnings and images of death and destruction that had taken up so much airspace as Rita approached. Although the city authorities were part of this repetition on the dangers of staying, the students held the media more responsible. In this, research supports them; showing us that media provides us with the raw materials, such as selected images and facts, with which people socially construct the risks associated with different courses of action (Spencer and Triche 1994; Stallings 1990).

However, the meanings attributed to such materials are rarely accepted at face value; they are instead contested and reinterpreted by their recipients in complex ways (Garvin 2001; McLeod et al. 1991). For instance, those who chose to stay in Houston had, in asserting that they weren't afraid, challenged the media's exaggerated construction of hurricane danger and reinterpreted it as a lesser risk. We therefore can't simply attribute the overblown social construction of risk to the media; if some of us accepted that construction uncritically, then we also bore some responsibility. Ed and I, for instance, had decided at the beginning to base our evacuation decision on safety; depending heavily on the mass media for the information to gauge the relative risks of different possible courses of action had made us vulnerable to any exaggerations on their part. Similarly, my students' neighbors in gas lines had apparently accepted the social construction of safety that suggested a full gas tank was the way to escape the storm; this made them feel vulnerable to the point of panic when they then experienced gas shortages. Finally, as a result of the social construction of risk, many of my students experienced the irony that came with their evacuating only to end up at risk of a manmade evacuation crisis or in the actual path of the hurricane.

An Overall Assessment

In retrospect, Houston was very lucky. In this, the largest evacuation of a U.S. city to date, much more could have gone wrong, especially if Hurricane Rita had struck the city as powerfully as feared, with thousands unable to leave or stranded with their vehicles beside the roads. The city authorities could also have been much less proactive; in this event, the mayor's office had been relatively farsighted and efficient about managing preparations, except perhaps for the late opening of the contraflow lanes.

As it happened, the event served as a sort of "dress rehearsal" for planning such evacuations in the future, and taught local authorities much about the many ways citizens can and will upset city evacuation plans, creating new uncertainties and risks. Although human behavior is often fairly predictable, such predictions deal with probabilities, not certainties, and never encompass everyone. We know that people tend not to behave normally in abnormal situations; since modern Americans are rarely threatened by uncontrollable events such as hurricanes, their behavior in such situations is very likely to confound normal expectations and can only be predicted by studying behavior in similar emergencies.

However, we also know that governmental and scientific authorities are unlikely to remember and utilize all of these lessons in the future; organizations tend to develop their own agendas and internal dynamics, which may get in the way of their meeting more basic social goals (Healy 1999; Maganda 2003). The risk here is that the reasons for well-made plans will be forgotten and new plans will be revised in unwise ways. In particular, the more time that elapses from the traumatic event that leads to lessons learned, the less likely it is that the lessons will be remembered. Houston could, if not threatened by a hurricane again for ten or fifteen years, go through all the same mistakes that result in deaths, again.

One main lesson many citizens learned from this experience is how dangerous mass evacuations can be, especially when they involve more people than planned. The thousands of people who were stuck on the road, suffered from the heat, or gave up on leaving in the face of endless traffic jams, learned how helpless they could be in such a situation, and talked endlessly about how to avoid such helplessness in the future. The 100+ deaths became vivid lessons to the rest. As a result, I heard a great deal of skepticism afterwards about the ways the authorities and media had encouraged voluntary evacuations by keeping Houstonians focused on the hurricane danger. It seems likely, in retrospect, that these sources underestimated the effect their repeated warnings would have on citizens conditioned by catastrophic images from New Orleans and Hurricane Katrina to construct hurricane risk in extreme ways. It also seems that if the conditioning had been understood, the media could have stepped in with sources of different types of expert knowledge, balancing the hurricane warnings with some warnings about the possible dangers of too many people joining the evacuation. The authorities could have warned those of us not in mandatory evacuation zones to wait until the mandatory evacuations were complete, or even restricted access to the main routes out until that time. Instead, their decisions contributed to an exaggerated social construction of risk from the hurricane, creating new, potentially avoidable manmade dangers in the evacuation itself. They also created new levels of skepticism towards information sources on which citizens' lives may depend in the future.

Future Evacuations

For better or for worse, Houstonians' experiences during the scare of Hurricane Rita will shape the ways they may respond to future crises. The authorities would be wise to consider experts about citizen responses to perceptions of risk in future evacuations. However, they will also have to consider how long it has been since this formative event, and how much its lessons have already worn off. Finally, they would be wise to take action to shape the media coverage of such a future event in useful ways, a tricky enterprise that could backfire if mishandled, but an apparently necessary one.

We have a great deal more to learn about how individuals, families, employers, authorities, and the media contribute to the social construction of risk in different types of situations, and about how representations of risk should best be handled by those actors under different circumstances to minimize manmade threats to life and property. The social construction of risk shapes people's actions, and so must be handled in a publicly responsible way that does not expose citizens to new, "manmade" dangers that authorities can't anticipate or manage. To put it plainly, the social construction of risk is as real a source of danger to citizens as any hurricane, and we must learn to handle it as carefully as information about the storm itself.

References

Dake, Karl. 1992. Myths of nature: Culture and the social construction of risk. *Journal of Social Issues* 48: 21-37.

Garvin, T. 2001. Analytical paradigms: The epistemological distances between scientists, policy makers, and the public. *Risk Analysis: An International Journal* 21: 443-456.

Healy, Kieran. 1999. The emergence of HIV in the U.S. blood supply: Organizations, obligations and the management of uncertainty. *Theory & Society* 28: 529-558.

Hilgartner, Stephen. 2007. Overflow and containment in the aftermath of disaster. *Social Studies of Science* 37: 153-158.

Hunt, Jennifer C. 1995. Divers' accounts of normal risk. *Symbolic Interaction* 18: 439-462.

Maganda, Carmen. 2003. The politics of regional water management: The case of Guanajuato, Mexico. *Journal of Environment & Development* 12: 389-413.

McLeod, Jack M., Gerald M. Kosicki, and Zhongdang. Pan. 1991. On understanding and misunderstanding media effects. In *Mass Media and Society*, ed. James Curran and Michael Gurevitch, 235-66. London: Edward Arnold.

Murphy, Raymond. 2001. Nature's temporalities and the manufacture of vulnerability. *Time & Society* 10: 329-348.

Richardson, Kay. 2001. Risk news in the world of internet newsgroups. *Journal of Sociolinguistics* 5: 50-72.

Spencer, J. William, and Elizabeth Triche. 1994. Media constructions of risk and safety: Differential framings of hazard events. *Sociological Inquiry* 64: 199-213.

Stallings, Robert A. 1990. Media discourse and the social construction of risk. *Social Problems* 37: 80-95.

Wilkinson, Iain. 2001. Social theories of risk perception: At once indispensable and insufficient." *Current Sociology* 49: 1-22.

Part IV

After the Storm: Navigating New Meanings of Self and City

TRAUMA WRITTEN IN FLESH: TATTOOS AS MEMORIALS AND STORIES

GLENN W. GENTRY
THE STATE UNIVERSITY OF NEW YORK COLLEGE AT CORTLAND
AND DEREK H. ALDERMAN
EAST CAROLINA UNIVERSITY

On October 29th, 2006, I drove east on North Robertson Street and merged onto North Claiborne Avenue through the Ninth Ward towards Chalmette. There is no way to adequately describe New Orleans since Hurricane Katrina devastated the city. I wish I had a camcorder pointed out the passenger window to capture the devastation that whipped past me as I drove around the city. The homes that hug the narrow road through the Ninth Ward gave way to wide medians and gas stations as I approached the Jackson Barracks where the National Guard had been trapped by floodwaters during the storm—deep red bricks and iron gates damaged. Traveling through Arabi and into Chalmette, I recognized a Wal-Mart from the media blitz following the storm; the neighboring Home Depot had just reopened. The St. Bernard Civic Center stood empty and tomb-like above a sea of white FEMA trailers. It reminded me of the post-apocalypse zombie movie, *28 Days Later*. My destination was a neighborhood of long, straight streets with brick homes, solidly middle-class and replicated across the United States—suburbia.

That particular day I helped a family re-grade their lot so that their home would not flood during downpours. Later I cleaned and busted bricks. During this time, and at the end of my trip, I contemplated the New Orleans landscape as it has been transformed both on the ground and in my mind. I thought particularly of the Ninth Ward with its many wooden homes and churches punctured and toppled by wind and water; I wondered how it might look next year or ten years from now. Areas near the canal have been cleared and the vegetation, which grows quickly in the warm and humid climate, has begun to reclaim the empty spaces that once held homes. Kenneth E. Foote (1997 [2003]) suggests four possible outcomes for sites of tragedy: sanctification, designation, rectification and obliteration; all of which either demonstrate or hide the memory of past tragedies. The Ninth Ward is too large to become a memorial (sanctification) and I suppose a sign will be put somewhere to remind others of the tragedy of the floods following Katrina (designation); but what concerned me were rectification and obliteration. In order to be rectified the site has to be returned to its pre-tragedy condition, with the same recognizable look and use. I cannot imagine that will occur as politicians, planners, and others with good (and not so good) intentions struggle over how the Ninth Ward and other sites in New Orleans will be rebuilt, if at all. Many locals, displaced and otherwise, fear Foote's final category, obliteration. Will the Ninth Ward and other spaces be left as green-space or rebuilt with architecture and residents foreign to its soil and history? What concerns us is how memories are retained, repeated, or lost in the city. Or, more directly, how are Hurricane Katrina-related memories made visible in a city where repair and rebuilding erase sites that act as witness and memorial to this historic tragedy?

The city's neighborhoods, structures, and spaces are still in flux. While the French Quarter sustained little structural damage, a weakened economy continues to drive out many businesses. The Garden District, an area wealthier than much of New Orleans, also had little damage and its residents generally have the monetary means with which to properly bandage the cosmetic damage to their homes. But other areas such as Uptown, Midtown, Lakeside, and Gentilly, still have significant damage to the structures and communities that occupy these places. These sites have been "tagged" in spray-paint by both rescue officials marking searched buildings and by residents who scribble messages to Katrina and government officials on plywood, windows, doors, junked refrigerators, and in debris piles along the road side. Slowly, very slowly, these messages and reminders are being leveled and hauled away. They were spontaneous memorials (Azaryahu 1996) that will soon be lost in time. However, a more permanent and mobile form of visible memory work is etched in the skin of many of the survivors, rescuers, and volunteers of Katrina.

The Tattoo Storm

In the wake of Katrina, tattoos have become a popular means for people to express their trauma, honor the deceased, and pay tribute to the city of New Orleans. Tattoo artists interviewed by the *Associated Press* a year after the hurricane indicated that as many as half of their customers wanted storm-related inscriptions (Plaisance 2006). The tattoos include images of crumbling buildings, broken hearts gushing floodwater, explicatives about Katrina or eulogies such as "9th Ward, RIP Lower 9" (See Image 13-1). People with hurricane tattoos include both first-timers and experienced collectors. Family members and friends come in together to be tattooed. For instance, after being rescued from New Orleans by the National Guard, Sean Jeffries and two other friends got matching tattoos. Jeffries was quoted as saying: "I'll probably never get another tattoo, but this one means something to me. I got it because it has meaning behind it" (Plaisance 2006).

Image 13-1: Andrea Garland displays her tattoo that reads "9th Ward RIP Lower 9," a memorial to those lost during Hurricane Katrina near her 9th Ward neighborhood in New Orleans. October 2006. Photographer: Cheryl Gerber. Reprinted with permission from Associated Press/World Wide Photos.

Tattoos provide a means by which those affected by Katrina can express and deal with their memories of trauma and place attachment, a way to make these feelings visible not only to themselves on a daily basis but also to a larger public. Annette LaRue, the owner of Electric Ladyland

Tattoos in New Orleans, captured the mood of much of the surge in Katrina-related tattoos when she suggested that it represented "a way for people to wear their pain." This observation has been further substantiated by the research of Marline Otte of Tulane University, who conducted post hurricane interviews with citizens. She characterizes these tattoos as a "phenomenon of mourning" and suggests that they occur across class, gender, and racial lines. Otte also observed that amid these feelings of sorrow are attempts to reclaim the memory of New Orleans and its distinctiveness. Underlying many of these body inscriptions is fear that the city is becoming a "'forgotten place in America'" as response and recovery efforts continue to be frustrating and disappointing (MacCash 2006, 1). It is little wonder, then, that the fleur-de-lis is a common motif in Katrina tattoos, often represented alongside or inside the standard hurricane symbol or swirl (See Image 13-2).

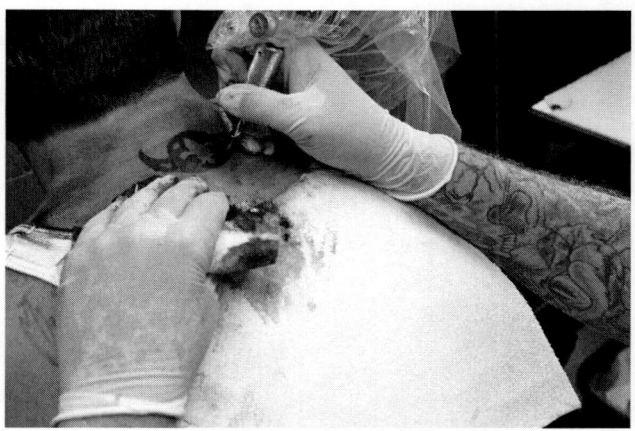

Image 13-2: Steve Soule gets a tattoo shaped like a hurricane graphic with a fleur-de-lis as the eye of the hurricane. October 2006. Photographer: Mel Evans. Reprinted with permission from Associated Press/World Wide Photos.

Derek, after reading an article by Doug MacCash (2006) in the *Times-Picayune*, a local New Orleans' newspaper, began talking with me about how people were using tattoos as a way of uncovering the memories and stories about Katrina and its aftermath that they wished to make visible. As cultural geographers, he and I share an interest in vernacular expression, specifically the ways in which ordinary people inscribe their experiences and perspectives into visual symbolic forms. Being seen and heard is important to people, but it is particularly important when coping with the psychological, social, and physical stress of a disaster (Alderman and Ward, forthcoming). In the case of tattoos, people respond to trauma by writing their story into flesh, thus creating a highly personal memorial to Katrina and its impact.

In order to explore the cultural importance of Katrina-related tattoos and what they mean to the people who get them, Derek and I contacted several tattoo shops in New Orleans. We asked tattoo artists to help us understand this phenomenon, as well as assist us in finding people with storm-inspired tattoos. I visited New Orleans in the Summer and Fall of 2006, and interviewed tattoo artists and customers within the city. From the number of tattoos that artists said they or their shops had done, we estimate that there have been thousands, if not tens of thousands, of Katrina and New Orleans-related tattoos inked into flesh since the hurricane. Some artists told us that these tattoos are generally larger, more detailed, and more visible than ones before Katrina. This suggests that tattoo wearers may be seeking to make public memorial statements, in addition to creating personal reminders of the tragedy.

We initially thought of New Orleans' tattoo artists as gatekeepers who would help connect us with people who had received storm-inspired tattoos. However, it quickly became apparent that the artists were a much richer source of insight than we had originally assumed. Artists gave us a valuable perspective on trends in New Orleans tattooing both before and after Katrina. Perhaps more importantly, artists were often victims of the hurricane and had their own stories of loss and displacement to tell. In some instances, artists—like their customers—were motivated to mark their trauma by getting a tattoo, allowing us a special understanding of the process of designing and wearing the final product. The following narratives are from interviews that I did with three tattoo artists in October 2006. The first two interviews, with Tom and Brock, focus on their experiences during Katrina and how their stories became inscribed into the tattoos they now wear. The third interview, with Jody, demonstrates how the inking of someone else's tattoo can serve as a point of emotional reflection and storytelling for both the artist and the client.

"X" Marks the Spot

We met a bit accidentally on the city street outside of the tattoo shop, Art Accent Tattoo, where I went to do interviews. I approached a man to ask about parking on Rampart Street without paying the parking meter (it only took credit cards—but not mine). He informed me that "they don't come this late on Wednesday. They don't boot yet. Anyway, that's a rental car...why worry, what they goin' do?" When I mentioned why I was there, he introduced himself as Tom, a tattoo artist at the shop, and that he was waiting for me. The interview began right there on the sidewalk with the story of his latest tattoo. After a few minutes we moved into the tattoo shop where I began to ask my questions.

The conversation moved quickly to the "rescue X" tattoo that covers the outside of his right calf and takes up most of his lower leg (See Image 13-3). Tom's tattoo requires an audience for it to achieve its intended purpose. Although clear to those who recognize the symbolism, tattoos do not speak for themselves, but require audience interpretation. Some tattoos are more easily "read" than others. Though Tom's X tattoo is powerful for those who followed the media coverage on television and the Internet, a fuller understanding of the symbolism and meaning behind any tattoo can be learned through the personal stories that accompany it.

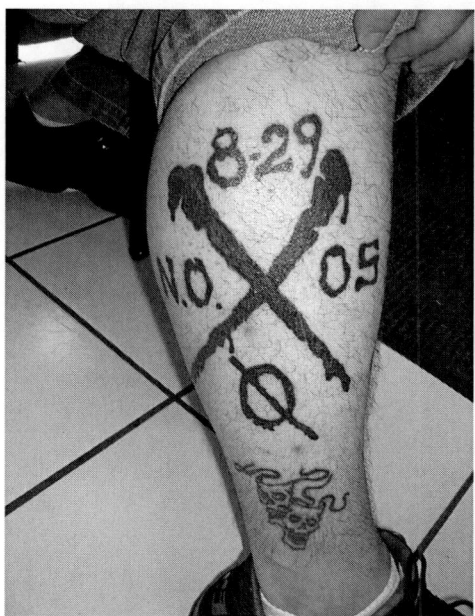

Image 13-3: Tom's memorial "rescue X" tattoo. October 2006. Photographer: Glenn W. Gentry.

Immediately after the storm, rescue responders searched homes for both survivors and the dead, and marked each building they searched with a spray painted "X" (See Image 13-4). Among other things, this X indicated the date of the search and the number of bodies found dead. The markings, while originating from a practical need to facilitate search and rescue, took on deeper psychological meanings to those in New Orleans as a sign of death and the beginning of FEMA's long and often frustrating intervention in the city. For some, including Tom, the X marks the spot of their trauma brought on by both the floods following Hurricane Katrina and the "Federal Flood" of governmental failures that continue to deeply affect the city.

Image 13-4: House in the 9th Ward bearing the ubiquitous "X" mark to indicate that it had been searched by officials. October 2006. Photographer: Glenn W. Gentry.

As a local tattoo artist, Tom was well aware of the surge in Katrina-inspired tattoos, and since he rode out the storm in his 9th Ward home with his pregnant wife, Tom was there when the shop opened shortly after the storm. "A lot of thought was put into this tattoo," he said. "I didn't want something reactionary and just like everyone else. I already had a NOLA on my arm and Mardi Gras masks," he told me as he grabbed his left arm and showed me the tattoo. "This was so people could not forget what happened...what *is* happening. We musn't forget."

Tom used pictures taken of post-Katrina New Orleans homes to design his new tattoo. This is not his first nor will it be his last tattoo memorializing the storm. At the time of the interview, he planed to have another one inscribed as a full back piece. The X tattoo is especially important to him because of its connection to his daughter, who was born a couple of weeks after the storm. Pointing to the tattoo, he told me,

> My daughter walks up and points to my tattoo…and she points at the houses when we are going home [in the 9th ward]. She knows they are related. My daughter was born a couple of weeks after Katrina. This is part of her legacy. She has no idea how hard it was to keep her alive, the struggle it was without electricity, clean water, diapers…nothing man. I mean we were just trying to keep her alive. She was just so little…

As Tom told me his story, he became visibly emotional as tears welled up in his eyes; I struggled with my composure as well. I struggled as a researcher who was supposed to "objectively" listen to this man's story, but found myself wanting to *really* listen and experience the emotion and poignancy of the moment. He continued,

> We didn't even have clean water and you couldn't boil it…That is why this tattoo is so important. She does not know it yet, but the city's struggle is part of her lifetime, it is part of her legacy…She could have died…We just struggled to keep her alive…This is why we cannot forget what happened.

The tattoo bridges generations. For Tom, it represents the experience of Katrina while also representing the birth and life of his daughter. The story of Katrina will be passed on to his daughter; it is part of her legacy, permanently written on her father's leg. Tom told me that his tattoo has meaning to others as well. "I cannot go anywhere without people staring, or pointing, and people always have a story. Man, everybody. I got this because it is too important to forget. I can't," he said slapping his tattoo, "It is right here."

Tom took the design and placement of his tattoo seriously. It stands not only for his own experiences with Hurricane Katrina, but for the experiences of all of the victims and the city that he loves. The tattoos represent badges of pride and survival, as well as markers of the traumas that unfolded on the landscape and in people's lives. The loss of house and home, family and friends, and the struggles to help others are encoded upon their skin. They demonstrate pride in a city, their city, which has been critiqued and criticized in the media and by politicians.

Watching It All Go Down

Tom's tattoo was a product of serious reflection and was inked several months after the storm. Brock, a tattoo artist who had been living in the city for only a few years, was more reserved when talking about his own tattoo. This is not to say he shared with reluctance, but relied more on my own understanding of how someone can become attached to a place, telling me, "You're from Texas, you understand." Brock received his Katrina-inspired tattoo soon after he had evacuated, letting his love for the city of New Orleans guide the design more than making a particular statement.

I met Brock at the tattoo shop he works at on Magazine Street, an area that did not flood during the storm and its aftermath; it was one of the first shops to reopen after Katrina. Brock got his tattoo soon after evacuating to Kentucky the day before the storm made landfall. A friend and fellow tattoo artist, with whom he was staying, completed the tattoo. "I did not know if I would return," he told me, "[but] I needed a tat, something to remember the city and the way it was." This was not his first tattoo, and he noted that he lets his tattoos "tell stories about [a particular] time in [his] life." He collects tattoos as both reminders and as pieces of art. In this case, he felt the need to commemorate his experience of Katrina and his life in New Orleans.

Brock's Katrina-tattoo includes a crawfish and a fleur-de-lis inked on the top of his right thigh (See Image 13-5). He wanted the tattoo to "be more for myself...to commemorate the happy things." He told me that he was "not trying to represent the city to anyone else," but to remember his city—the city he did not know, at the time, whether or not he would see again. The *fleur-de-lis* is a French iris, both a symbol of France and an icon for the city of New Orleans. To speak to the damage inflicted by the storm, Brock's *fleur-de-lis* appears worn and is missing "petals." Curled around the fleur-de-lis is a crawfish, a happy and recognizable symbol of New Orleans for Brock and for others. When I asked about the crawfish, he smiled and told me that, "Every year we [at the tattoo shop] have a crawfish boil. Those are always good times, sitting around eating, drinking, and talking. Those are the best times here and I didn't want to forget them."

What is perhaps the most interesting aspect of Brock's tattoo is its placement. According to Brock, he chose to have the tattoo placed onto his thigh so that he could watch the tattoo being "inked" while simultaneously watching the coverage of the flooding of New Orleans on television. Hours of inward reflection, sharing his stories with others, and viewing the stories of thousands of others being played out in front of him on the television were all part of his Katrina tattoo experience. So while Brock's tattoo is meant for him (where Tom's was also meant for others), the memories involved in the tattoo are both publicly shared (images and messages from the media coverage) and private.

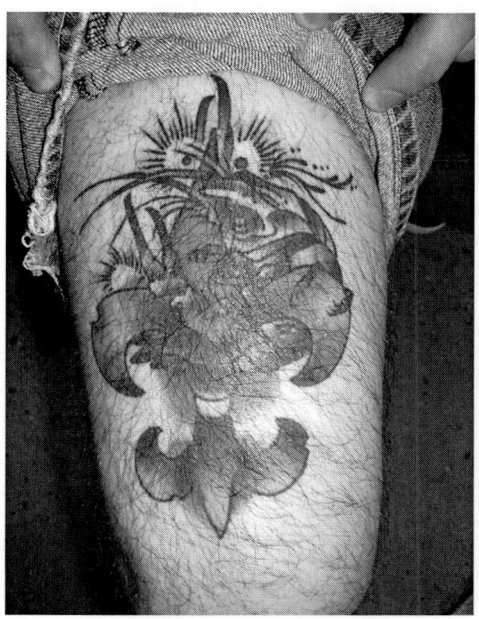

Image 13-5: Brock's crawfish and fleur-de-lis evacuation tattoo. October 2006. Photographer: Glenn W. Gentry.

Brock's tattoo is personal and is commemorative of his love for and feared loss of New Orleans. Whereas Tom's X is intended as more of a public memorial, Brock's is envisioned in more private terms, but readable by others as related to New Orleans. In both cases, the process was important to the final product. In Brock's case, the ability to see the tattoo in concert with the images of his flooded and neglected home is pivotal to understanding its significance. His tattoo marks a particular time and event in history. In contrast to Tom's tattoo, which marks his struggle to save his family from floodwaters, Brock's inscription came from a different point of trauma as he watched it "all go down."

Who Sent You?

This last vignette is as much about the tattoo artist as the tattooed. This story comes from my questions to tattoo artists about memorable tattoos they inked onto others since Hurricane Katrina. Since Jody told me the following story about one of her clients, there is no picture or analysis of the tattoo. At this point in the interview we had been talking for well over an hour in his shop on the Westbank. The interview included another tattoo artist/piercer and was very conversational as they took turns answering questions, often disagreeing with one another. During this particular story, Jody had left to an adjacent room and was speaking through an opening. We could not see each other during the exchange.

"It was the first tattoo I did once I got back," Jody said. He was working as an independent tattoo artist in another shop because his pre-storm shop had burned down. He went on,

> A Red Cross dude came in and wanted a red cross, no outline, with Japanese waves behind it and "Katrina" underneath. The man cried after he saw the tattoo when it was finished. He had me sign the tattoo [which is unusual in tattooing] because he said that being in New Orleans was the most important thing he had ever done and wanted to remember who gave him the tattoo. On his way out I asked him why he had come to me to get the tattoo. He said his [Jody's] friend R****** had suggested him. They had met when the Red Cross dude pulled R****** from the water. He had saved his life. I just tattooed the guy who saved my friend's life. This was after I had only been back two days. Doing this tattoo meant the world to me.

This account illustrates the emotionally charged nature of both getting and giving storm-inspired tattoos. By inking the tattoo described above, Jody not only memorialized the experiences of the Red Cross worker, but also the story of his friend's rescue from the floodwaters. In asking who sent the rescue worker to him, Jody reflects on how the shared trauma of Hurricane Katrina brings people together in unexpected ways. This forced him to reevaluate his personal relationship with the tattoo and its wearer. What started as perhaps just another tattoo for Jody, turned out to be a "tattoo that meant the world" to him, and was now part of his own storm-related recollections. By signing his name on the tattoo, Jody became an indelible part of the Red Cross worker's remembrance of New Orleans, creating a bridge of memories and stories that transcend "just" one person.

Perhaps it was the effect of the disembodied voice, but more likely the brevity in delivery and the unexpected aspect of the answer that gave Jody's story such an emotional impact. Rarely did tattoo artists provide long stories about their most memorable tattoos, yet each story evoked powerful emotions; I began, almost automatically, to brace myself for the telling. Despite this, I was overwhelmed by each story and the depth at which they struck me. As a researcher, I have been told to strive for rich detail and long, involved stories. The power of Jody's story reminds me that stories bare in length and detail are far from sparse in meaning and impact. In much the same way, many of the Katrina-inspired tattoos I saw mean far more than their visual weight suggests. This is not a case where "less is more." Rather, it is a reminder that we must be open to the seemingly little things if we are to understand the full breadth of how individuals reveal their identities and experiences to others. They are not simply little things, but keys that unlock larger landscapes and worlds of meaning.

Tattoos as Memorials and Stories

In understanding the cultural power of tattoos as modes of expression in New Orleans, it is necessary to see them as memorials. The city's landscape presents a special challenge to the project of memorializing the disaster that followed Hurricane Katrina. In contrast to other nationally significant tragedies such as the Oklahoma City Bombing of 1995 and the destruction of the World Trade Center in New York City in 2001, New Orleans has been unable to engage in large-scale monument building or even smaller, more temporary memorial construction. As a result, New Orleans is a site of tragedy not easily memorialized. In such an environment, tattoos have emerged as an alternative site for people to remember and reflect on the disaster, a way of symbolizing and retelling their stories in the absence of a stable social and physical landscape upon which to memorialize. Tattoos may not have the same physical or symbolic gravity as large, planned memorials or even small, spontaneous shrines; yet, it is important not to ignore or underestimate the "microfeatures of everyday life…[because] the small can serve as a marker for the large" broader systems of collective memory and trauma (Fine and Hallet 2003, 12). Moreover, the body—although long treated as a "biological given"—is now understood as an important site for representing and participating in the social world (Reischer and Koo 2004, 298).

There is a strong connection between tattoos and storytelling. Tattoos, as visual narratives, communicate important messages about the cultural experiences and identity of the inscribed persons (Atkinson 2003, 2004; Burton 2001; Demello 2000; Kosult 2000). As Judith Sarnecki (2001) suggests, receiving a tattoo may be an especially appropriate way of marking tragic stories. On this point, she asks: "Does pain, loss, and suffering require more drastic ways of [story] telling, ways that involve our entire being? Does writing in the flesh in some permanent way help us both to let go and to memorialize a particularly painful or traumatic event in our life" (Sarnecki 2001, 39)? New Orleans remains a landscape of trauma. Memorial tattoos are popular ways of dealing with this trauma and marking the loss of people and places both tattoo artists and clients hold dear. The vignettes presented in this chapter demonstrate the potential of tattoos to serve as significant and emotionally charged expressions of memory. The events of Hurricane Katrina are written permanently on the bodies of many whose lives have been affected by the disaster. Many, if not all of the tattoos, represent an effort by individuals to set their trauma in time and place. For some, it was motivated by a defensive pride in their city in light of the social inequalities and political inefficiencies that have been revealed. Regardless of the reason behind the tattoos, they are steeped in stories that are in need of being told—stories communicated through the images themselves as well as the discussions they provoke between the tattooed and other people. Katrina-related inscriptions are not just windows into understanding a single personal traumatic experience. As evident in examining Brock's story, the tattoos also take on a collective or social quality as people reflect on the potential loss of their community of friends or their entire city. Stories surrounding Katrina-related tattoos are often touching, at times lengthy in explanation, and hit you like a swift and painful blow to the gut.

Notes

1. We have permission to use the real names of tattoo artists interviewed for this chapter. In Annette's case, her last name is used because several media outlets quoted her. In all other cases, we provide first name and shop location to give the artists credit for their work without making them public figures.
2. The term "Federal Flood" appears to have been coined in the blog, The Wet Bank, which seeks to keep Hurricane Katrina and its impact in the public memory as well as to critique government response to the disaster.

References

Alderman, Derek H., and Heather Ward. Forthcoming. Writing on the plywood: Toward an analysis of hurricane graffiti. *Coastal Management Journal.*

Atkinson, Michael. 2004. Tattooing and civilizing processes: Body modification as self-control. *The Canadian Review of Sociology and Anthropology* 41:125-146.
—. 2003. *Tattooed: The sociogenesis of a body art.* Toronto: University of Toronto Press.
Azaryahu, Maoz. 1996. The spontaneous formation of memorial space: The case of Kikar Rabin, Tel Aviv. *Area* 28:501-513.
Burton, John W. 2001. *Culture and the human body: An anthropological perspective.* Long Grove: Waveland Press, Inc.
DeMello, Margo. 2000. *Bodies of inscription: A cultural history of the modern tattoo.* Durham: Duke University Press.
Fine, Gary A., and Tim Hallet. 2003. Dust: A study in sociological miniaturism. *The Sociological Quarterly* 44:1-15.
Foote, Kenneth E. 2003. *Shadowed ground: America's landscapes of violence and tragedy* (revised and updated). Austin: University of Texas Press.
Kosult, Mary. 2000. Tattoo narratives: The intersection of the body, self-identity, and society. *Visual Sociology* 15:79-100.
MacCash, Doug. 2006. Skin city. *Times-Picayune*, July 16.
Plaisance, Stacey. 2006. Tattoos a tribute to scars left by Katrina. *Houston Chronicle*, July 8.
Reischer, Erica and Kathryn S. Koo. 2004. The body beautiful: Symbolism and agency in the social world. *Annual Review of Anthropology* 33:297-317.
Sarnecki, Judith H. 2001. Trauma and tattoo. *Anthropology of Consciousness* 12:35-42.

A Bricolage of Loss

Donna Maria Bonner
Austin, Texas

Image 14-1: Author returns to her New Orleans home after the floods. October 2005. Photographer: Frank Valls.

If the people of any city in the United States could relate to Emile Durkheim's (2005 [1912]) idea of "collective effervescence" or Turner's (1975) notion of "communitas," it is the people of my city. Life in New Orleans has long been organized around a series of celebrations, with Carnival or Mardi Gras at the apex, which encourage us to leave behind our everyday cares, our material or practical concerns, and come together to celebrate the marvel of life. I'll never forget dancing in a crowd of New Orleanians at a Neville Brothers concert held two days before Mardi Gras, the audience singing along with Cyril Neville (1990), "That's My Blood Out There". I looked around at my fellow New Orleanians, dancing, singing, and celebrating, and felt at one with them, with the city, and with the universe. I remember thinking, "This is what Collective Effervescence feels like." Experiences like this encouraged me to believe that I would always be connected to New Orleans and its people, the only place where I felt this closeness with others, the only place where I could touch the eternal at a music club, and the only place that feels like a true home for my soul as well as my body. I believe that it was this spirit that caused New Orleanians to throw themselves into the celebrations that marked the city's yearly round of activities and to strongly identify themselves as "New Orleanians."

Additionally, we in the city have always been proficient at the use of symbols; those shorthand images and concepts people use to convey complex ideas to one another. The names or "word symbols" for each of the city's neighborhoods, The French Quarter, Lakeview, Gentilly, New Orleans East, and the 9th Ward, for example, are not just geographical locations, but also a local short-hand for different ways of life in the city and types of New Orleanians. Our music, most particularly jazz, brass band music, and New Orleans funk, the dishes that make up our cuisine, and the traditional ways we dance are all symbolic of the city. We mobilize our symbols in our only successful industry, tourism, and in communication with one another, such that the traditional logo for the famous New Orleans Jazz and Heritage Festival is the image of a horn player surrounded by umbrella wielding New Orleanians performing the high stepping dance we call "second-lining" (See Image 14-2). Images of wrought iron balconies, 18th century Creole cottages, and 19th century shotgun homes can bring tears to the eyes of New Orleanians. These images of our distinct architecture represent the history and romance of the city, while images of second-lines, jazz musicians, and heaping plates of red beans and rice represent our traditions. Furthermore, these are not symbols of "dead" traditions. Any New Orleanian knows how to second line; the strains of jazz and funk, with a brass band backbeat, can be heard on our streets any day; and red beans are served every Monday, or "Laundry Day," in restaurants and homes throughout the city because, unlike other dishes, red beans can safely simmer on the stove while you attend to chores.

Image 14-2: A New Orleans Art Car decorated with the image of a "Second-liner" making his way down a city street. May 2005. Photographer: James Thrasher.

Personally, my feelings of connection to the city were also encouraged by my professional experience there. As I approached middle age I was hired by the University of New Orleans, where I had once been an undergraduate. There, I was able to teach alongside professors who had once taught me, my *intellectual ancestors* so to speak, and provide instruction to students I looked on as *the future* of the city. I felt a sense of mission at this university because it provided education to the city's working class, a racially and ethnically diverse group for whom a college degree is an accomplishment rather than a privilege, a group to which I myself belong by heritage. Durkheim notes that knowledge of the human lineage, in other words the understanding people possess that they have descended from those who came before and will in turn hand over the world to those who come after, allows us to touch something "eternal" about the human experience. At the University of New Orleans, I felt part of the city's intellectual lineage and able to contribute to the city not just through my own work but through the future work of my students. Hence, my participation in the life of the city felt to me like something that would extend far beyond my own life span.

I believe that others experienced similar feelings of connection through artistic contribution. Our facility with symbols and the multiplicity of local celebrations allowed us to express ourselves artistically. Music is the obvious example; without music, you can't hold a parade, and New

Orleans hosted many festive street processions during Carnival and throughout the year. New Orleans' musicians, through their connection to long-standing musical traditions and their present-day creative contributions, were connected to the city through its musical lineage. Take for example, the Rebirth Brass Band (1992), which plays traditional New Orleans numbers such as "When the Saints Go Marching In," original songs like "Do Watcha Wanna," and also covers of popular tunes like Michael Jackson's "Shake Your Body Down to the Ground." Many Brass Bands have additionally combined "Bounce," New Orleans' rap music, with the jazz played by their parents, thus further contributing to the inheritance of the next generation.

Outside the realm of music, costuming was another important way people contributed to the city through art (See Image 14-3). We costumed during Carnival, as well as for Halloween, Valentine's Day, Easter, and basically any time we could find an excuse. In truth, there was nothing more unifying than visiting a fabric store during the month before Carnival Day. There, you were surrounded by a diversity of New Orleanians, men and women, Black and white, young and old, purchasing reams of sequins, boxes of feathers, and yards of material. I think every home had a glue gun, although the most creative in our midst sewed their outfits by hand. Our costumes were sometimes sexy, sometimes humorous, and often educational. For example, Mardi Gras Indian Tribes, organizations made up primarily of working class African American men, masked as Native American or West African warriors and royalty. Their costumes encouraged young New Orleanians to honor their ancestors from West Africa, as well as the Native people who helped these ancestors to survive and escape slavery. Once any New Orleanian, including a Mardi Gras Indian, donned his or her *masque*, we took to the streets to second-line, show-off, and make others laugh, cry, scream, and even think.

Image 14-3: Carnival Costume built on to bicycle. May 2007. Photographer: Donna M. Bonner.

My identity as a New Orleanian was developed through participation in traditions such as these. It was developed through the use of symbols and ideology, rather than through the ownership of property or the possession of economic power. Like me, many New Orleanians identified with their city through their participation in local celebrations, their understanding of local symbols, their intellectual and artistic contributions, and their experiences of being a part of the city's heritage. I believe this was even true for those New Orleanians who did own property or hold economic power. In reality, our city's culture encouraged a *carpe diem* approach to life and, when compared with the lives of other U.S. citizens, we were clearly spoiled by the celebratory opportunities we possessed to feel connected to our community.

Symbolic Aspects of Loss

Symbols have similarly played a vital role in New Orleanians' experiences of Hurricane Katrina. Consider, for example, the outrage that so many displaced New Orleanians felt at being labeled "refugees" in their own nation. As one of my former students wrote,

> The media and others calling us refugees was a way to distance us, imply that we are somehow foreign and don't have much in common with the rest of the nation. After the way in which the government bungled the

disaster response, this sort of distancing seems to condone the notion that we did not and do not deserve the help of our government, a government to which we pay taxes and feel allegiance. Like so many other things that happened, this was like kicking us when we were down.

The word or symbol "refugee," with all that it implies of foreignness, alienated many who already felt their city had not been well-served by the U.S. government.

Furthermore, if I attempt to delineate the losses which have hit me the hardest, I return over and over again to the painfulness of seeing places that I knew intimately desecrated by floodwaters, fire, and suffering. I once loved strolling in the historic French Quarter, the streets of which are lined with cafés, boutiques, and antique stores. But today, as I walk down its streets, I never know when I will be haunted by images from the time immediately after the storm when I sheltered in a friend's Quarter property. Walking down a street nearly two years after the disaster, surrounded by waiters heading to work and tourists shopping, I will suddenly picture the look of shock on the face of the bald, shirtless man on Esplanade Avenue who told me there were "bodies" in a nearby neighborhood. Sitting in a restaurant drinking café au lait, I'll find myself wondering what happened to the pretty young woman in the green dress, so scared she carried a two-by-four with nails sticking out of it and yelled to warn me that the floodwaters were heading up Canal Street, filling the city.

When I reflect on the waters that filled the house where I lived in the heavily flooded area of town known as New Orleans East, destroying all of my material possessions, it is the symbolic aspects of this loss that hit me the hardest. Yes, of course, I miss my possessions, but objects can be replaced. What I miss most about my house and belongings is the way in which these items gave me a feeling of safety and comfort. When I returned to the house and saw it filled with damp, dirty water and gossamer webs of mysterious mold, I felt violated, as if there was indeed no safety in the world to which I might ever retreat. As I think about the loss of the many items handed down to me by my now deceased parents and grandparents, I miss the feeling of connection to my ancestors that these objects gave me. Finally, as I consider the loss of so many of the city's residents and iconic businesses, I rue the burden of carrying with me the knowledge that everything you love, everything that gives meaning and structure to your life, may indeed disappear overnight. Finally, even the loss of my job at the University of New Orleans, indeed a practical, material, and economic loss, represented for me a loss of identity and purpose.

As an anthropologist, I've turned to symbolically-oriented research studies to better understand these losses. I look to the geographer Yi-Fu Tuan's book *Space and Place: the Perspective of Experience* (1977) to understand how Austin, Texas, where I now live, seems to me a vast undifferentiated space, while the streets of New Orleans, which I know as intimately as the back of my hand, are to me places endowed with meaning created by my experiences and memories. I look to sociologists Mihaly Csikszentmihalyi and Eugene Rochberg-Halton's pivotal study, *The Meaning of Things: Domestic Symbols and the Self* (1981), to understand how the loss of my possessions has caused me to question who I am and what my life means. I look to the research of disaster studies experts to understand the role of place attachment in people's reactions to destruction (Oliver-Smith and Hoffman 2002). Yet, while these studies help me to understand the viewpoints and struggles of my people and myself, they do not completely explain our experiences of this disaster. As the floods subsided and we entered the period of rebuilding, our ideological connections to the city and our symbolic losses have been largely over-ridden by the economic understanding of the disaster promoted through government aid programs.

The Materialism of Rebuilding and Repatriation

The losses experienced by New Orleanians have been both material and symbolic. Nonetheless, in terms of the institutional structures of our society, only our material losses count. Anyone who has ever sat before a FEMA (Federal Emergency Management Agency) worker to apply for disaster assistance relief knows what I mean. While the disaster victim, often in shock, mourns the destruction of home, neighborhood, or town, she is forced to recite the names and numbers that will elicit help. For individuals, the value of possessions, home, and neighborhood cannot be measured. Nonetheless, institutions like FEMA possess charts and formulas reducing these values to simple monetary amounts. I could spend days discussing the monetary and symbolic value of my lost possessions, but for FEMA the discussion is short, "$10,000."

This reduction of our tragedy to the "bottom line" was made salient by the fact that I rented, rather than owned, my home in New Orleans East. No matter what my contributions to the city, no matter how connected I felt to New Orleans and its people, no matter the fact that I and other members of my family had lived in the same rental property for over 30 years, and no matter how strongly I or other renters might wish to return to help rebuild the city, in the view of FEMA, renters did not own a piece of

New Orleans and hence did not qualify for financial or other assistance to help us return. With the loss of over 70% of the city's housing stock and rental rates, which have doubled and tripled since the floods, this has meant that renters have had few opportunities to return home. For largely materialist reasons, our importance to the city and the city's importance to us were dismissed. In terms of the way in which our government has calculated our loss, Karl Marx (2004 [1847]) was indeed correct that ownership defines privilege and feelings of alienation emerge when individuals are excluded from the profits of ownership.

FEMA and other government aid agencies calculate property loss, while people mourn the loss of tradition, identity, and way of life. One of the everyday traditions I miss most from Pines Village, as my neighborhood in New Orleans East was called, was the way in which my neighbors and I turned yard work into a block party. We'd spend long summer, Saturday afternoons cutting our grass and cleaning up litter. Then, a few of us would head to one of the family-owned seafood markets located along Lake Pontchartrain and buy big bags of spicy boiled crawfish, crabs, turkey necks, corn, and new potatoes. We shared the food in a feast held in the yard of the Haney family who lived next door to me (See Image 14-4). Unfortunately, FEMA will not compensate me for the loss of my neighborhood community, nor will it help me to find the Haneys whose location I've been unable to ascertain since the disaster.

However, despite FEMA's failings, New Orleanians have been forced to turn to this and other aid agencies because of the sheer volume of destruction in the city, the disruption this has caused to our lives, and the lack of funds available locally. In so doing, we have had to push questions of identity and tradition to the background and consider only economic issues in discussions of rebuilding and repatriation. In the Post-Katrina city, place attachment and contributions to the local good play no part in whether a person qualifies as necessary to the community. Similarly, for employers, including educational institutions, the importance of one's work and one's dedication to that work pale in comparison to the need to restructure for economic survival. New Orleanians have been placed in a position in which we can no longer afford the luxury of symbols and the comforts of identity.

Image 14-4. Post-Disaster view of the Haney backyard where the author and her neighbors shared bags of boiled crawfish. April 2007. Photographer: Donna M. Bonner.

As the rebuilding process began, folklore developed to justify the economic nature of reconstruction. In this folklore, the poor, those who did not own property, and those financially unable to return were depicted as "moochers" who were no longer needed in the city. For me, the height of this offensive folklore was the parody poem, "The Night after Katrina," bandied about in various on-line forums by New Orleanians who were able to return to the city. This parody ends with the lines,

> You can call them moochas. You can call them no good. But they ain't comin' back to your neighborhood. To all you evacuees in your plight, hope you like TEXAS and to all a good night.

Much as Marx might have predicted, the realities of U.S. society are economic and material; the reality is the bottom line. As I read the ditty above, sitting in my apartment in Texas reflecting on the fact that I didn't even qualify for a flimsy FEMA trailer because I did not own property, I felt betrayed by my love for the city and kicked for my efforts on her part. I felt as if the meaning-filled relationship I'd had with the city had been a lie. Yet, my "plight" was in no way caused by the city itself, but rather by the economically-oriented nature of government programs. Perhaps what had made New Orleans special prior to Hurricane Katrina, what had originally caused me to turn to idealist rather than materialist social theory to understand my city, was the fact that, while government and bureaucracies encourage people to view the world through the lens of monetary value, New Orleanians valued tradition, meaning, and celebration. Perhaps the greatest tragedy of this disaster is the fact that the economic need created by destruction has caused us to bow to bureaucratic notions of identity.

Conclusion

In November of 2005, only a little over a month after the floodwaters had been pumped from New Orleans' streets, Mayor C. Ray Nagin attempted to call displaced New Orleanians back to the city through the use of a panoply of musical and cuisine-based symbols. He said,

> I'm tired of hearing these helicopters; I want to hear some jazz! You know, I know New Orleans. Once the beignets start cooking up again and the gumbo is in the pots and red beans and rice are served on Monday, in New Orleans and not where they are, they're going to be back (Markels 2005).

When he spoke these words, Mr. Nagin did indeed know New Orleanians; we find comfort in our traditions and we understand symbols of local identity. In the New Orleans I knew and the New Orleans Mr. Nagin referenced, people defined themselves as locals through symbolic means; what counted was whether or not you could cook a good pot of red beans, where you'd gone to high school, whether or not you sucked the heads on crawfish, how well you knew the city streets, whether you'd ever gone for beignets at 3:00am, and how you celebrated Carnival. However, what Mr. Nagin needs to understand is that these symbols can't function properly if the rebuilding context is based explicitly on economics.

In order to understand just what it is that New Orleanians have lost in the Hurricane Katrina disaster, I've employed the method of bricolage, examining both those circumstances in which symbols are significant and those in which material concerns govern occurrences. Durkheim, it seems, explains our joy and our trauma while Marx addresses our relationship to the government and rebuilding. Perhaps materialist theories are best applied to social structure, while idealist theories explain how humans experience their lives.

New Orleanians' losses have been many and varied and we have appreciated every cent of government and charitable aid we've received. We've celebrated every dollar spent on rebuilding, every iconic local business that has reopened, and every job added to the city's devastated economy. However, what I would like to see is more attention paid to the symbolic rebuilding of the lives of New Orleanians, whether they now reside in the city or elsewhere. I'd like to see more mental health programs to deal with the depression and post-traumatic stress we are now experiencing. I'd like to see a national day of mourning commemorating our losses and the loss incurred by our nation as a whole when our government sat back and watched the city suffer during those days following Katrina. Perhaps services such as these might help us to again know that we have a place in the nation, that we are valued for who we are and can again find safety and comfort in our lives. Honoring our symbolic losses might also allow New Orleanians to return to the meaning-filled ways in which we once identified with our city and culture.

Finally, as New Orleanians like me settle in other cities and the local population continues to dwindle due to frustration over the failures of rebuilding and lack of jobs, government officials need to realize that our intellectual and artistic contributions to the city were always as important as our financial worth. Our red beans and second-lines were what made the city the tourism-mecca it has always been. Our mentorship of youth was what gave the city a future. Without the people, even the renters, the poor, and the so-called "moochas," the city may not have a chance at long-term survival. Meanwhile, I can't help but miss the happy time when the lavishness, beauty, or humor of someone's Mardi Gras costume, rather than their possession of property, wealth, or even a job, were how others determined whether or not that person belonged in the city.

Notes

1. In this paper, I employ the method of *bricolage* to understand my experiences as a New Orleanian and a victim of the Hurricane Katrina disaster. Bricolage, inspired by French theorists Claude Lévi-Strauss (1968) and Jacques Derrida (2001 [1978]), consists of employing a diversity of explanatory models or theories dependent on their usefulness in explicating a particular situation, with the idea that different social phenomena require different theories for their exposition. I employ idealist theories, those of Emile Durkheim (2005 [1912]) and others, to explicate my identification with the city and the reactions of New Orleanians to the disaster. Materialist theories come into play as I reflect on our interactions with the government bureaucracies that have provided aid for rebuilding and repatriating the city. In my conclusion, I reflect on the usefulness of idealist and materialist viewpoints in examinations of social phenomena and describe changes in the public discourse concerning New Orleans identity occasioned by New Orleanians' interactions with the government.

References

Csikszentmihalyi, Mihaly, and Eugene Rochberg-Halton. 1981. *The meaning of things: Domestic symbols and the self.* New York: Cambridge University Press.

Derrida, Jacques. 2001 [1978]. Structure, sign, and play in the discourse of the human sciences. In *Writing and Difference*, trans. Alan Bass, 278-94. London: Routledge Press.

Durkheim, Emile. 2005 [1912]. *The elementary forms of the religious life.* Whitefish: Kessinger Publishing.

Lévi-Strauss, Claude. 1968. *The savage mind.* Chicago: the University of Chicago Press.

Markels, Alex. 2005. Beignets back, Nagin wants residents back, too. Morning Edition. Washington D.C.: National Public Radio.

Marx, Karl. 2004 [1847]. *Wage labour and capital.* Whitefish: Kessinger Publishing.

Neville, Cyril. 1990. My blood. On *yellow moon*. Santa Monica, California: A & M Records.

Oliver-Smith, Anthony, and Susanna M. Hoffman. 2002. Introduction: Why anthropologists should study disaster. In *Catastrophe and culture: The anthropology of disaster,* ed. Susanna M. Hoffman and Anthony Oliver-Smith, 1-47. Santa Fe: School of American Research Press.

Ortner, Sherry. 1984. Theory in anthropology since the sixties. *Comparative Studies in Society and History* 26: 126-166.

Rebirth Brass Band. 1992. *Feel like funkin' it up.* Rounder Select Records.

Tuan, Yi-Fu. 1977. Space and place: The perspective of experience. Minneapolis: University of Minnesota Press. Turner, Victor. 1975. *Dramas, fields, and metaphors: Symbolic action in human society.* Ithaca: Cornell University Press.

Turner, Victor. 1975. *Dramas, fields, and metaphors: Symbolic action in human society.* Ithaca, New York: Cornell University Press.

HURRICANE KATRINA:
A TURNING POINT FOR FAMILIES

NICOLE BURAS
UNIVERSITY OF NEW ORLEANS

Image 15-1: Boothville-Venice following Hurricane Katrina. (This photo was taken after the floodwaters had subsided and residents were allowed into the area to assess damage and salvage pieces of their lives. While the trailer behind Brenda belonged to her neighbor, the couch on top of the porch roof was from her living room). September 2005. Photographer: Brenda's Son, Michael.

Located on the west side of the Mississippi River, on a peninsula roughly one and a half hours driving distance south of New Orleans, stand the towns of Boothville and Venice. These two towns are in Plaquemines Parish, the southern-most habitable point of Louisiana known as "the end of the world." According to the 2000 census, the total population of the parish was 26,767; residents of Boothville and Venice make up less than ten percent of this population (Plaquemines Parish Government 2007).

The towns are so small that they are often understood as one area and are referred to jointly as Boothville–Venice. In fact, the two small towns had to be officially combined in order for there to be a school erected.

Traditional means of employment in Boothville–Venice include citrus farming, commercial fishing, offshore work, and small family-owned businesses. The people living in this area are united through interdependence; what Emile Durkheim (1984) would call organic solidarity, where everyone in an area fill their niche and serve their roles so the community functions as a whole. People's livelihoods have long depended on harvesting the rich bounty of water surrounding their homes: fish, shrimp, oysters, crabs, and the like. The fisheries industry and the natural beauty of the moss covered trees attract recreational fishermen who have deemed it a "Sportsman's Paradise" (Plaquemines Parish Government 2007). What I remember most about my childhood are the long hot summers spent on the water. Once the school year ended, I would spend my time deck-handing and driving trawling boats. Now, I live in Chicago—one of the biggest cities in the U.S. The sight I miss the most in this world is the way the sunrise and sunset reflects off the marshland; living near the water and working its depths was wonderfully rewarding.

In the time before Katrina, Boothville–Venice lacked many of the elements that make up larger cities: public transit, large office buildings, a hospital, more than one public school, and major food and clothing chains. The lack of amenities in this small town led families to save their money so that they could visit one of the more exciting northern cities such as Gretna or New Orleans. Many families, including my own, would make a day out of it by eating out, seeing a movie, and stocking up on groceries.

People who live in Boothville–Venice have formed strong community bonds over generations and put family first. It is a small, tight-knit community where extended families live literally right across the street from one another. Like most areas impacted by Hurricane Katrina, Boothville–Venice experienced a complete uprooting of all that was "normal." In an attempt to cope with the great upheaval of their lives, people discussed their experiences of the storm and voiced their concerns for the future. In talking with women I knew in my small hometown, I found that family and community were a constant source of tension for them as they negotiated their post-Katrina lives.

My parents lived through Betsy and Camille. I lived through Hurricanes Katrina and Rita. I cannot imagine my children following in those footsteps. So, for my husband and me, there was no returning to Boothville–Venice. However, as I spoke with women from my hometown, I found that the decision of whether to return or to relocate was sticky, wrought with tension over local meanings of family, of being a good wife, and of being a mother. These women suggest that family ties and marital relationships during and after Hurricane Katrina shifted, shaping their decision-making power when determining whether or not to relocate after the storm.

My Own Story: Family and Hometown Loyalty Versus the Decision to Relocate

I was born and raised in Boothville; generations ago, my family settled in Lower Plaquemines Parish. My father was a commercial fisherman and I was practically raised on a shrimp boat. My husband and I held strong connections to Boothville–Venice; I was raised there and, for a time, he shrimped out of the area. Growing up, I helped my ailing father and mother raise my younger siblings; and in in 2002 I departed to school in Lafayette. I rarely had time for other interests as family was the most important, and my three siblings were like my own children: I made Halloween costumes, helped with homework, attended almost all school functions, went to doctor's visits, and did every other parenting task too numerous to detail here. These tasks were preparing me to be a homemaker, a mother and a functioning member in our small community. As my three friends, whose stories follow, have all pointed out, taking care of the home and family was expected of us as women in this small town; and being a mother and a wife were supposed to be our primary roles within the community.

When I learned of Hurricane Katrina, I was unaware of the threat because I was too busy starting my first week of work and attending graduate school at the University of New Orleans. Knowing the routine for evacuation, I calmly left school to help my parents, siblings, and, at the time, fiancée evacuate. This was not an uncommon occurrence as the social norm for Boothville–Venice residents is to evacuate for every hurricane that entered the Gulf of Mexico. Even while I lived in Lafayette, if my parents and siblings needed to evacuate, my now husband and I would drive to Boothville, assist my parents and siblings, and then return to Lafayette for school. Though I was always calm—I had evacuated a hundred times before—in the back of my mind I knew that each hurricane could be "the one" to devastate our small town.

For Katrina, I followed the same evacuation procedures as I always had; I helped my family get their valuables and necessities packed and loaded and evacuated to Lafayette. Two days later, as I watched the storm ravage my hometown, tensions and emotions in my family began to run high; we knew we could not return to my parents' home as usual. I had spent my entire life preparing for this, and so I went into overdrive and did what I had to do to get through the events ahead of me. I did not start dealing with the emotional consequences of my experience until a year and a half following the storm (and in many ways this piece is part of my grief work).

Like many people, the storm had a direct and long lasting affect on me; and I knew only days after the storm that I could not go through this again. Regardless of our deep connection to Boothville–Venice, my husband and I cannot imagine having our home, vehicles, work, community, and entire life, ripped away from us again. Our ancestors had founded the area and the community has shaped my family's identity. Therefore, my parents never questioned returning; in fact, they were one of the first to start the rebuilding process in Boothville–Venice. Even months after community members were allowed back into the area, I could not bring myself to return; I wanted to remember my home the way it had been while growing up. I am a culmination of my past experiences and many of my memories had been compromised by the physical loss of markers such as photos and home movies (Weigert and Hasting 1977).

My husband echoed my decision to leave Boothville–Venice, which was made easier by the fact that he and I had discussed moving away before Katrina had struck, and returning only to visit. This does not mean that we do not hold dear the life we once had there. My husband and I were perhaps more open to the idea of relocation than my family because we were young and had ties, both personal and professional, to people and places outside of Boothville–Venice. Erving Goffman (1959) suggests that people continue to fit into and function within a group until he or she acts against the agreed upon norms of the group. For my father, acting against these norms included relocating; he saw my decision to relocate as an abandonment of my family and my community. The most difficult aspect of our transition was not having my parents actively involved in our lives as they once were. However, as Peter Berger and Hansfried Kellner (1964) discussed, once two people marry, they collaborate as one unit collectively and socially.Therefore, our decision not to return and to build a life elsewhere was the first step in severing ties with my family, and creating a unit of our own.

With the loss of old roles, new ones emerge. Everyday I wake up and fulfill my roles as a wife, as an urbanite, and as a displaced student, and I grieve for my old roles as a sister, as a daughter, and as a resident of Boothville–Venice. The loss of family I experienced as a result of my perceived abandonment was unique among my friends; therefore, I found that the family and community ties I once believed to be unbreakable had, in fact, been fragile all along. This loss of a defining element of my past lead to a redefinition of my self outside of my immediate family and outside of the community of Boothville–Venice. I never imagined I would have been forced to decide between maintaining family and hometown loyalty or relocating my life after it had been uprooted by a disaster beyond my control. I do not believe I betrayed my family or my hometown; instead I chose education, work, and life in a city far from the threat of hurricanes. However, my life changed drastically once I broke with family tradition and my small town's expectations for women.

Brenda: Good Ol' Hometown Girl

Brenda was a 45 year-old native who had spent her entire life in Venice. She had been brought up, married, and raised her son in Venice. She had hoped and intended to spend her life there. However, after yearly experiences of evacuating, her husband working away two-thirds of the year, and Hurricane Katrina as the final straw, Brenda and her family relocated. She now lives in Houma, Louisiana.

Family was a salient aspect of Brenda's story as she relayed her Katrina experiences to me. She spoke of how her father had dropped out of sixth grade to trawl and live off the land, and how her mother had been a homemaker after graduating high school at sixteen. Similarly, Brenda's own husband, Paul, had dropped out of high school to work with his family's tugboat company; quitting school to earn a living is a common occurrence for young men in Boothville–Venice. Brenda says of herself, "I got married June 23, 1978, right out of high school. I graduated in May, I got married in June, and I turned eighteen in September; and my first child was born February 13th, 1982." Of her work life, she explained, "Paul came and had the tugboat company. I worked there, you know, forty hours a week and made very good money, so I had no desire to go to college or go further." When the tugboat business began to suffer, Brenda worked during the day while her son was in school. In her words, "this was a convenience" since her husband was working fourteen and seven (fourteen days offshore, then seven days home) cycles. This affected his location during Katrina as he was forced to work during the storm.

Brenda was four years-old for Hurricane Betsy and nine years-old for Hurricane Camille; both hurricanes had destroyed her home. Each time, her family had returned because her father's work was in Venice. For Brenda, evacuation was a regular occurrence. She said,

As far back as I can remember, I'm 45 now, I only recall very few seasons where we never had to evacuate. We were always the first ones out because of the area where we lived. It was so vulnerable to the hurricanes; it was a low-lying area.

Brenda pointed out that there was only one way in and out of the area by automobile. With her items already packed from two previous hurricanes, Brenda loaded her car and evacuated for Hurricane Katrina alone. Brenda was separated from her husband during Katrina because he was on a boat in an area affected by the storm. Before losing contact, she begged him to get onto another, larger boat.

> I never cried. Through it all, I never cried. At times it felt like I wanted to cry; [but] I couldn't cry because there were people [family] around me, and I'm not a person to cry in front of others. It's not that I'm ashamed. I don't know what you want to call it. I just, I always felt like I had to be one of the strong ones.

After both Hurricanes Katrina and Rita passed and life began to settle, Brenda's husband and son informed her that neither wanted to return to Venice because of the very real possibility that they may experience another hurricane comparable to Katrina. Her extended family, which pre-Katrina had lived only a few miles away, also told Brenda that they did not plan to return to their hometown. With family anxious to leave Venice, and with the town ravaged, Brenda conceded to relocate,

> I just didn't want to go through that again. You're already in a mental turmoil. It is so hard to concentrate, to try to do anything because sometimes your mind was in such turmoil. You go to work, and every day it helped me. It helped me because when I went to work it took my mind off of everything. But a lot of time, even while I was at work, I had a lot of business to handle: faxing things, receiving phone calls, or having to make phone calls. You find yourself at times thinking, "What else? What do I have to do next?"—because there was so much to do, and I had to do it all. I had to do it all by myself because my husband [was] working on the boats. I raised my child alone because he was off working so much. I'm the one who always took care of all the business.

In many ways, the decision to relocate was not Brenda's, but that of her husband and son. In this way, she conformed to her role as a "good" wife and mother by following and fulfilling the desires of the men in her family. However, her experience of disaster and relocation also reshaped her identity as she lost her home and was uprooted from the community in which she had lived her entire life. Brenda had been the pillar of support and the caretaker in her family for a long time, and as her extended family dispersed throughout the state, she was no longer able to care for her parents and nieces. Her son was older and becoming independent. Therefore, she felt increasingly comfortable with the decision to relocate as she felt she was at an age where she could begin anew in the city.

Mary: The Decision of a Widow

Mary relayed her Katrina story to me through tears of joy and sadness. In 1957, she moved to Venice with her husband who attained a job with the government. They bought property in Venice, her husband built a house, and her children went off to school in Boothville. She and her husband had always wanted a large family; so it was with thirteen children (ten of who survived past their first birthday) that she lived through numerous devastating hurricanes including Betsy and Camille. Each time she and her family returned to Venice, they found that their wooden house had floated away. They would have to search for it, return it to their property, and repair it to a livable state. Hurricane Katrina was no different, once again causing her house to float away. Now 81 years-old, and her husband deceased, Mary chose not to return to Boothville–Venice and now, like Brenda, resides near Houma, Louisiana.

Mary roots her identity in her roles as a mother, a caretaker, and a wife. She has ten children, 28 grandchildren, and eleven great-grandchildren—possibly twelve, she's unsure. She described herself as a homebody, much preferring others to visit her than to go out visiting. Because her husband had often been away from the home for work, she had come to be the "strict" parent in the household. She had never learned to drive, but rather her husband had done all the driving. She had once enrolled in driving school, but shortly after had learned that she was pregnant with her first child, so stopped classes. To this day she relies on her family for transportation to "the store and to church." She explained what her daily life in Boothville had been like years ago,

> We got up in the morning. The children went to school; I had seven children at one time that went to school. We got up, we got dressed, we had breakfast, then the school bus passed. Until the school bus passed I didn't do anything because I always waited for the school bus with them. And then I had work to do; at one time I had a dishwasher but I thought it was just as easy to do the dishes myself. You do your regular housework and if you had a garden, you had to work in it. We did a lot of caning and preserving the food. We always had a great big freezer and it was mostly full all the time. We gardened, we had animals—we always had animals,

all kinds of animals. We had pigs, chickens, we had bantams (a type of the chicken). We had chickens, and ducks, and turkeys, peacocks—you name it, we had it 'cause I always liked animals and we used to feed them. It was expensive, but it was fun; we enjoyed it. We enjoyed making a garden; we had orange trees. Several times we had to replant.

Every time a hurricane moved the house, and the house had to be replaced on its blocks and repaired, her family stayed with her parents in Westwego, Louisiana. On a number of occasions, she mentioned to me that it was always her husband's decision to return the family to Venice,

Well, [when] we went through Betsy my husband redid the house, and we went through Camille and my husband redid the house. But then he wasn't here to do it this time. So I says, if I get enough insurance money I am going to get another house away from home, away from there. Then I decided to buy this house [in Houma], but it wasn't built yet. I always wanted a yellow house. My husband liked white so we had white siding. But then I said, "Well I can make up my own mind this time." So I got the yellow house and the yellow color inside which I am going to be so yellowed out pretty soon. But anyway, I got to choose the two colors of the house; I got yellow in here and grey in the back. I got the stove of my choice. There were several things that I got the choice of. My husband wasn't there any more to do it.

Mary confided to me that it was hard to start over again, so instead of returning, she used her insurance money and bought a new home away from the constant threat of hurricanes. "I decided to take a house and I made a home," she said. Although she moved away from southeast Louisiana, she maintains ownership of the property in Venice, "I do not want to have it bulldozed. I did not want to get rid of it. I am not going to sell it or give permission to get that done because it is there." Mary continues to be attached to the house in which she had raised her kids and had lived her life for so many years. Her connection to the area is strong, but she was glad to finally have the financial and decision-making autonomy to move from Venice, where she had time and time again rebuilt her home under the guidance of her husband.

Mary told me that if her husband had been alive, there would have been no discussion of relocation; she would have returned to Venice with him to again rebuild their lives. Returning was what he did. As a widow, she was allowed, for the first time, the decision-making power to realize her desire to leave the small town of Venice and to build a new home on her own terms—and of her own color choice. I suppose it was easier for me, as a young woman, to break with small town tradition than it was for

Mary. That is, marriage, wifedom, and motherhood mean something different to me as a young woman, and I fully embraced my autonomy while simultaneously being a wife and daughter. Mary, however, is from an older generation more tightly tied to traditional notions of what it means to be a good woman, a wife, and a mother who sacrifices everything for her husband, children, and family. Like many who were uprooted by the events of Hurricane Katrina, Mary lives a life with one foot in her past life, as she still owns land in Venice, and one foot in her new life, in Houma.

Joan: From Wife to Working Woman

Joan was born and raised in Venice, and referred to Boothville–Venice as a town where "everybody knows everybody." She defines herself primarily as a mother, but after finding much-needed work after the storm, also prides herself on being a working woman. Though she took care of the home, she labeled her husband as the decision-maker of the household, "My husband is the type of person who does not speak, he does not talk, he demands." Joan accepted these traditional, socially constructed gender and marital roles, and felt it was her duty to support her husband's decisions and carry out his demands.

Joan remembers evacuating for Hurricanes Betsy and Camille, and taught her children and grandchildren the responsibilities involved in leaving for a storm. She understands evacuating as a routine event in her life that is comparable to a vacation, but noted Hurricane Katrina was different, "You just go on vacation for a few days. You know the only problem was, with this vacation, you are not going home." She and her family evacuated Katrina and stayed at her son's home in Baton Rouge. Soon after the storm struck, she realized that she and her family would not be able to return home for weeks, maybe months.

After Katrina, Joan found work in Belle Chasse for the Plaquemines Parish school board, and found herself commuting for work, ninety miles back and forth, five days a week from Baton Rouge. Her husband, on the other hand, found himself out of work. Conflict between her and her husband arose out of both his discomfort with her new role as a working woman and his attempt to take a patriarchal role within his son's household, in which they stayed for sometime. Joan said that their son knew his father performed his role as a husband and father by taking control and making all the family decisions; as a result, her son, "just got tired of it and decided enough was enough. He didn't want it in his house anymore. So he told him [his father] to leave." While Joan preferred to stay in Belle Chasse, returning to Venice hinged on the ability to rebuild her devastated property. The only benefit she saw in returning to her small town was that she would be closer to work and her younger children would have a yard to play in. However, Belle Chasse offered her and her family easy access to such things as major shopping centers, fast food restaurants, and entertainment. "The children are happier up here," she told me.

Joan's long commute to work was welcome, and she described this time away from her husband as "Peaceful! Very peaceful!" It was during this quiet commute that Joan reconsidered her role as an agreeable wife and redefined herself. She recently noted that, "The return to Venice is still up in the air; I guess it's going to depend on if the family stays together." Her role as a working woman, as a bread-winner for the family, gave her the strength to confront what it was that she liked and disliked about being a wife. She told me that,

> There is a time in my life I dealt with it; I didn't like it, it hurt, but I did it because I am a wife—I am supposed to support him! I am supposed to do what he says! And as the years go by, no I am a human being and I have feelings and I have thoughts, and no, it don't work that way. I am starting to let him know that: "Stop it! I do exist! I do have thoughts! And I will live my life my way!" And that's where our problems are, 'cause I am not supposed to want to do that.

While she wants badly for things in her marriage to change, Joan also suggests that she aligns her beliefs with traditional notions of what it means to be a woman and a good wife; she is supposed to be submissive and supposed to support her husband on each of his decisions—no matter what. However, Joan began to struggle with the meaning of wife as it conflicted with her post-Katrina desire to relocate and build a new life outside of Venice. Taking on the breadwinner role within the house, she challenged both her husband's sense of masculinity and her own idea of what it meant to be a wife; she made the decision to settle in Belle Chase. This was the first major decision Joan made for her family.

Conclusion

During Hurricane Katrina, families were forced to decide whether or not to evacuate, what to evacuate, where to evacuate, and when, if ever, to return home. In this chapter, I explored the role four women played in making these decisions, how their decisions affected their relationships with their husbands and families, and how decision-making power post-disaster is tied-up with traditional and cultural meanings of gender, marriage, and family as well as age, work, and connection to place. These four women of Boothville–Venice suggested that their roles were assigned to them at early ages; roles that were dictated by their families and their larger communities (Berger and Kellner 1964; Ross and Mirowsky 1984). It is important to note that, while Katrina affected the roles these women played in their families (Joan becoming a working-woman in addition to a wife), Katrina also unveiled already existing tensions and desires to leave Boothville–Venice (Mary was finally able to relocate her life outside of Venice). Peter Marris (1975) suggests that following relocation, family and community ties breakdown. This breakdown in relationships played an important role in these women's decision-making abilities and how they came to identify themselves post-hurricane. To the women who generously and patiently shared their Hurricane Katrina stories with me, I thank you.

Notes

1. All names were changed except the author's to protect the privacy of the women.

References

Berger, Peter, and Hansfried Kellner. 1964. Marriage and the construction of reality. *Diogenes* 12:1-24.

Durkheim, Emile. 1997. *The division of labour in society.* In *Classical sociological theory: A reader,* ed. and trans. Lewis Coser. New York: New York University Press.

Emerson, Robert M., Rachel I. Fretz, and Linda L. Shaw. 1995. *Writing ethnographic fieldnotes.* Chicago: The University of Chicago Press.

Goffman, Erving. 1959. *The presentation of self in everyday life.* Garden City: Doubleday Anchor Books.

Marris, Peter. 1975. *Loss and change.* New York: Pantheon Books.

Plaquemines Parish Government. 2007. Residents. http://plaqueminesparish.com/Residents.php.

Ross, Catherine E. and John Mirowsky. 1984. The social construction of reality in marriage: An empirical investigation. *Sociological Perspectives* 27: 281-300.

Weigert, Andrew J., and Ross Hastings. 1977. Identity loss, family, and social change. *The American Journal of Sociology* 82:1171-1185.

ISN'T NEW ORLEANS BACK TO NORMAL? A DRAMATURGICAL ANALYSIS OF POST-KATRINA NEW ORLEANS

CAROLYN CORRADO
UNIVERSITY AT ALBANY, STATE UNIVERSITY OF NEW YORK
AND TAMARA L. SMITH
WESTFIELD STATE COLLEGE

Don't leave the French Quarter. In fact, don't leave Bourbon Street. It's too creepy at night, too scary. Plus, people can tell you are a tourist. The city just doesn't have it together at night, and you just don't want to go down any of the side streets. The food—the food is fabulous. Morton's, The Blue Oyster, Bourbon Street to drink—you have to go to Pat O'Brien's. Just remember, keep your wallet close, and don't wander out of the French Quarter. It's gotten better since my last trip—at least it doesn't smell anymore, but it will never be the same.

That was our first bona fide conversation with someone about New Orleans. The woman giving this advice was not a local New Orleanian; she was a business traveler who frequented the city for work. Our conversation with her took place on the plane en route to New Orleans, where she told us "like it is" after hearing that we had never been to NOLA before.

We disembarked the plane, wondering how much of this conversation to take at face value and how much to assume were ramblings from a conservative woman who gained her information from rumors. This was the first time either of us had ever been to New Orleans. We were there as two graduate students attending a feminist sociology conference, Sociologists for Women in Society. As we made our way to the hotel on Carondelet Street (which turns into Bourbon Street at the French Quarter border), we stared out the taxi window, scouring the landscape for signs of Katrina's historic assault only a year and a half earlier. We didn't know what signs to even look for: A broken window? A demolished home? An abandoned street?

The cab exited the highway and headed onto the city streets. And that's when we saw it: "Look!" We'd seen it inside and out on the news, on PBS, in Spike Lee's film *When the Levees Broke: A Requiem in Four Acts*. It had been a temporary shelter for more than fifteen thousand New Orleanians in late August 2005, when Katrina devastated the city: The Superdome. We snatched up our cameras and took a picture.

We arrived at the hotel, checked in, and found our room. It smelled of cigarette smoke as we'd gotten one of the last rooms available. Opening the curtains, we once again looked for signs of Post-Katrina devastation. A structure a couple of buildings down from our hotel was undergoing demolition. Was this because of the hurricane? The landscape disappeared into the French Quarter and beyond. Was that the infamous Lower 9th Ward?

We decided to wander around near our hotel for lunch. Poised with our cameras, we took pictures of the first glimpses we had of New Orleans: Harrah's Casino, the Riverwalk Marketplace, and the Shops at Canal Place. Along the way, within those few blocks, we saw a few boarded-up businesses and a few broken windows; but our first impression was that the area did not speak of post-hurricane catastrophe. After an hour of searching, we *finally* found an open luncheonette—it seemed like late lunch was not very common in New Orleans. We thought perhaps it was a Southern distinction to not have restaurants serve lunch after two o'clock. At the time, we did not know that the lack of open restaurants was a function of Hurricane Katrina; there were few employees to staff these restaurants at all hours of the day. After a lunch of the New Orleans Sampler—red beans and rice, gumbo, and crawfish étouffée—we popped in and out of several little shops around the French Quarter.

The kitschy shops close to Bourbon Street held the typical tourist fare: T-shirts, shot glasses, and squeaky rotating racks of postcards. Unlike tourist traps in other cities, though, these shops also had beads and feather boas, the hallmarks of Mardi Gras. Walls were covered with them. The variety of beads was endless: Beads small as a pea to clownishly large, beads sporting team logos, cartoon characters, marijuana symbols, brand name beer bottles, and even breasts and erect penises. In one of the shops, there was a narrow doorway whose walls on both sides were covered in beads. The combination of the shiny, colorful plastic beads and the bright florescent lighting was piercing to the eyes. It was understandable from the stores why tourism is such a large venue in New Orleans—the stores were packed with tourists! We walked back to our hotel with the promise that we'd be back in the evening for dinner and to take in a sample of the

Isn't New Orleans Back to Normal? A Dramaturgical Analysis of Post-Katrina New Orleans

New Orleans nightlife. The warnings from our fellow airplane traveler seemed unwarranted.

Later that evening, the French Quarter burst to life. It was the quintessential New Orleans—the scenes that we as New Yorkers see only on "Cops" or other reality shows. Restaurants were packed and overflowing with hungry tourists; hour and hour-and-a-half waiting times were standard at most places. Bourbon Street was packed with people and bars; since cars are prohibited from driving on the street at night, the street was one big sidewalk. Music spilled from bars and clubs onto the street and mingled with people's shouted conversations. Neon signs of the strip clubs and sex shows read "Bewitched Gentleman's Club" and "Larry Flint's Barely Legal." People filled the balconies above.

As we wandered the streets, we witnessed our first "Mardi Gras" bead exchange, which went like one would expect: young woman yells if young men in balcony have any beads; they reply "Hell yeah, show it!;" young woman lifts her top and exposes her breasts; young woman is showered with several strings of beads. We skipped the Kodak moment. Our focus then shifted to the balcony scene across the street: young women and men were dressed in formal wear, drinking and loudly cheering. We wondered out loud whether this had some connection with the pre-Mardi Gras carnival celebrations we've heard about. Then just as we turned to leave Bourbon Street, one last thing caught our eye. Next to one of the bars was a beer keg. Propped up against the keg was a sign that read "It's OK to drink on the streets. Beer: $1.00" (See Image 16-1). This seemed to capture the spirit of Bourbon Street nightlife. We asked the man operating the keg if we could take a picture of him with the sign. He said we'd have to pay for a picture of him because, "Hey, it's New Orleans." We took the snapshot and walked away feeling like we'd gotten a taste of the New Orleans we'd only heard about from other people or read about online.

The French Quarter is a food lover's paradise, and life in the Quarter during the day is a stark contrast to the bustling Bourbon Street nightlife. There are dozens of restaurants, vintage clothing shops, antique stores, and gift shops. The next day, we had coffee and beignets at Café Du Monde, took some photographs of St. Louis Cathedral (See Image 16-2), and both of us bought a small painting from a local artist. We wanted to get a sampling of pralines to bring home to our families and went out in search for the best-of-the-best; this included Southern Candymakers, Aunt Sally's Pralines, Nance's Pralines, and New Orleans Pralines (our personal favorite was found at Southern Candymakers). What we noticed in the daytime were the well-manicured lawns surrounding the St. Louis Cathedral, the iron gates on homes adorned with Mardi Gras ribbons, and the several "open for business" signs throughout the French Quarter. What was absent were the landmarks and signs of Katrina we expected to see: FEMA trailers, graffiti, fallen trees, and disgruntled citizens. The locals were smiling and quick to give tourists recommendations for different restaurants, bars, and attractions. By the end of the day, we had the sense that New Orleans truly had gotten past the worst of the devastation wrought by Katrina's aftermath. If we had left New Orleans after this limited glimpse of the French Quarter, we truly would have returned to New York proclaiming that New Orleans was definitely well into its recovery, and that the worst was behind them. Since those outside of New Orleans define the city as Bourbon Street and the French Quarter, many tourists do return home with this assumption.

Image 16-1: "It's OK to drink on the streets." Sign of New Orleans' nightlife, Bourbon Street. February 2007. Photographer: Carolyn Corrado.

Image 16-2: St. Louis Cathedral. Picturesque New Orleans Landmark, French Quarter. February 2007. Photographer: Carolyn Corrado.

In the Wake of Katrina

The next morning, we attended the sociology conference that had brought us to New Orleans in the first place. The conference theme was "Solidarities across Borders: Gender, Race, and Class in Disaster and Post-Disaster Reconstruction," and New Orleans was chosen specifically by the organizers in an effort to bring business, tourist consumerism, and support to the city. We were welcomed to the conference by Dr. Rose Duchon-Sells, the Vice Chancellor of Southern University at New Orleans. She commented that "The Big Easy" wasn't as big or as easy as before, but that rebuilding had begun. The panels throughout the conference focused on the gender, race, and class inequalities caused by Hurricane Katrina, with a focus on New Orleans.

A number of the speakers at the conference told stories of evacuation and rescue, sorrow and mourning, and rebuilding and hope. They gave a personal voice to the race, class, and gender issues present in Post-Katrina New Orleans. The speakers explained the historical geography of the city and how it was settled along high ground—the French quarter and the garden district. They noted that as people moved in, especially Blacks who were brought in to help build the city and the levees, the (white) settlers pushed these people of color into the undesirable lower-lying areas. Such historic racial inequalities were still in existence when Katrina hit. This context made the current tensions of class and race, and the unequal impact of Katrina, even more understandable. By the end of the conference day, it had become clear to us that there was a disconnect between the everyday reality of residents' lives in New Orleans seventeen months post-Katrina and the "life" in the French Quarter that we had witnessed the day before.

That evening, the conference organizers set aside time for attendees to go to the Town Hall meeting at St. Bernard Church where Mayor Ray Nagin was scheduled to appear. Our cab driver did not know the way to the meeting and could not get clear directions from the police officer he stopped. This cab ride was our first direct look at New Orleans outside of the French Quarter. Although we never found the Town Hall, we witnessed the changing landscape as we rode further away from the French Quarter. Houses had red "X's" on them, and many appeared to be abandoned. It was during this cab ride that we saw our first FEMA trailer. We took a picture, thinking this would be the only sight of FEMA we would witness during our stay. The cab driver told us he had moved to New Orleans just before Katrina; he clearly wasn't too familiar with the roads to the city. This did not prevent him from offering us a tour of Post-Katrina New Orleans "at a good price." We politely took his card, but were skeptical of the quality of the tour he would be able to give, as he clearly didn't have a good feel for the city streets.

After attending the conference and seeing this small glimpse of the city beyond the French Quarter, we decided to take an official "Katrina Aftermath Tour." Since no tour was arranged for conference participants, we made a phone call to a local tour group whose brochure we had found in the hotel lobby. A tour had just left from our hotel and agreed to swing back around to pick us up. We grabbed our cameras, hurried downstairs, and joined the packed van of conference-goers for a tour of Post-Katrina New Orleans. The tour's advertisement read as follows:

> This is a four-hour trip, taking tourists through the French Quarter, virtually untouched by Katrina, giving the history and architecture of this old Creole city: Jackson Square, St. Louis Cathedral, the Pontalba row houses and an overall view of the Mississippi River Port, levees and flood walls. The tour then takes passengers by the French Market, the old U.S. Mint, a number of stately mansions and St. Louis Cemetery #3. It then

takes riders through City Park, the London Avenue Canal Breach, UNO's campus, Lake Pontchartrain's shores, Lakeshore, the 17th Street Canal levee breach, Gentilly, New Orleans East, the Mississippi River Gulf Outlet, Chalmette, St. Bernard Parish and ends with the Industrial Canal, whose levee breach demolished the Ninth Ward.

Our tour guide was a middle-aged white man and native New Orleanian who spoke to us about the history and culture of New Orleans. He had a deep, clear voice with a Southern drawl that made us Northerners cling to his every word. We drove through the French Quarter, stared up at the balconies, and salivated at the smell of fresh beignets. The guide pointed out St. Louis Cathedral and the golden bronze Joan of Arc statue near the entrance to the French Market. We snapped photos of the landmark Jackson Brewery, the Spanish architecture of the French Quarter, and the breathtaking atriums hidden in narrow alleys behind wrought-iron fences. Reflecting on the reason we were on this tour bus, it seemed odd that there were no signs of Katrina in all of the French Quarter. Would a tourist conclude here that New Orleans was "back to normal" after all? Was the intention of the tour company to illustrate the stark disparities between the French Quarter and other areas?

As we left the French Quarter, our guide pointed out the first remnant of Katrina's presence: dark, black water lines that marked many of the houses and businesses we passed on the road. Several of the structures were boarded up and closed for business. He called it the "tub ring" and explained how the topology of New Orleans was like a soup bowl, with the French Quarter on the edge of the bowl and the neighborhoods we'd be driving through in the middle of it. The mark of the "tub ring" looked like someone drew a black line straight across the buildings with a brand new Sharpie. Some lines were only a few feet off the ground, while others were above the windows. Quiet murmurs filled the van as the group tried to imagine water covering the road and sitting there, still that high, for many days. This constant reminder of the flooding seemed to have been branded into these homes and businesses. It was unthinkable that seventeen months after the levee breaks, the "tub rings" were so visible on such a considerable number of buildings. Entire city blocks and neighborhoods had these rings.

We next drove along City Park. It was here that the tour guide explained that Katrina's aftermath left a lot of dead vegetation. He remarked that there were well over a thousand beautiful and ancient trees that had to be removed from City Park alone, decayed or dead because of sitting in salt water, sewage, and chemicals for so many weeks after the hurricane. The dead grass and leafless trees left us gaping. This looked more like the snowless winter scenery of New York State with leafless trees; we never expected to see this in the South. This was in stark contrast to the immaculate lawns, greenery, and shrubs present in the French Quarter and at Harrah's Casino, places to which tourists flocked in New Orleans. It was not until this moment that we realized that the trees in the French Quarter were either spared or recently imported.

The tour continued into devastated parishes. The London Avenue Canal breach was the first levee that we had ever seen. The geography of the levee, in relationship to the lower houses around it, seemed to be very ill-advised engineering; as tourists, we questioned the logistics of positioning the levees so high—having walls that, if broken, would cascade over roofs of houses, seemed to be a recipe for disaster. We commented on how vulnerable the neighborhood looked and saw lawn after lawn of strewn garbage, homemade billboards advertising demolition services, houses with missing windows and doors, and FEMA trailers parked in yards. Several houses had been gutted and seemed to be airing their skeletal remains. The only people to be seen in the neighborhood were individuals working on homes. The homeowners and workers either waved at us or completely ignored us—it seemed obvious that a tour bus coming through the neighborhood was routine for these residents. There were no street-side chats, nobody sitting outside on steps, no children anywhere. The sense of eerie abandonment was all around us. The houses, although damaged, were still standing. The tour driver told us that there was "much worse to come." This was the worst devastation any of us had ever witnessed firsthand; he told us that this was minimal and akin to telling a woman that her labor pains had "barely begun" as she was already screaming in pain. We had no reference point to imagine what "much worse to come" could possibly mean.

We reached Lake Pontchartrain's shores and viewed the remnants of the marina houses, Katrina's footprints clearly visible around us. The houses were mere shells of what was once there. Many of them were boarded up, crushed or abandoned; one was completely gutted out. We all took photographs and videos from our cameras, convinced that nobody would believe us if we didn't have the picture proof. Truthfully, even the pictures and video that we did take don't do justice to the scope of devastation that we saw.

The tour then took us to the parishes and neighborhoods more heavily impacted by Katrina. The tour guide was right—the devastation *was* much worse. In these parishes, we saw a devastation that was astonishing: vans sitting on top of roofs, a boat still in the road, crushed cars. Seeing these vehicles in states of such disarray called to mind the force of the water that created such a scene. We saw house upon house with holes in the top of the roof, where people had desperately axed their way out to survive the onslaught of water, where people had *tried* to ax out, but died in their attics, and where emergency help had axed in to save people, but had found dead bodies floating in the attic waters. Why was this devastation *still* present in New Orleans seventeen months later? (See Image 16-3). What must these constant reminders do to the psyche and well-being of the residents trying to rebuild amid such images?

Image 16-3: Complete destruction seen seventeen months after Katrina. February 2007. Photographer: Carolyn Corrado.

Another disturbing sight as we drove through neighborhoods was the red "X's" spray-painted on almost every house. The tour guide explained that these markings were used to determine what date houses were searched, what organization performed the search, how many people were found alive, and how many people were found dead in the homes. Again, the grim reminder that people died in the aftermath of Katrina was a constant reality for residents who returned to the area to rebuild. As tourists coming to the area, this intricate system of markings was something that we hadn't heard about at all before coming to NOLA. In addition, even though we had seen the red X's painted on houses during our initial cab ride the night before, we did not have a reference to understand what these symbols meant.

We drove across the industrial canal and saw the largest levee breach of all, that which swept away the Ninth Ward and the lives of those who had lived there. The ride through the Lower Ninth Ward was haunting. The silence in the van was deafening. The devastation in this area was farther reaching than in the other areas the tour took us through. There was no grass, the roads were uneven, and there were fewer FEMA trailers in this area. The houses were smaller, and the structural damage to them was greater. Entire house frames were tilted precariously at angles, and sloping rooms were caved in upon themselves. The houses were dilapidated and moldy. Every now and then we saw someone working on a house or a child peeking through the curtains of a trailer. The worst of the destruction was inaccessible via van and so our view of this neighborhood was quite limited. We were told that the streets most publicized through the media in the Lower Ninth Ward had already been demolished and the land was currently being cleared.

In contrast to the Lower Ninth Ward, which had seen minimal rebuilding, the Upper Ninth Ward, the last neighborhood we toured, was undergoing a lot of construction. In contrast to one person coming back to their home to singly try to rebuild, the efforts in the Upper Ninth Ward were the result of mass efforts from organizations and volunteer groups. Particularly visible was "Musician's Village," which was a cluster of brightly colored houses built by volunteers working with Habitat for Humanity. We were struck that the rebuilding volunteer organizations were mainly religious-based organizations, rather than government organizations. What was striking about this effort was that even in homes that were brand new, the residents were still amid a neighborhood that was devastated beyond the few rows of new houses. The disparities between the new, brightly colored houses and the older, dilapidated homes that were literally crumbling next door to new homes were incredible.

When we returned to our hotel, all we could think about was how the sight of those houses, those neighborhoods, would forever be ingrained in our minds. The experience had clear emotional and physical effects on everyone in the van; it was written on our faces. The van riders were quiet on the return trip, silently contemplating the past four hours. This tour provided a different view of New Orleans from that of the French Quarter. What amazed us was that if we had not taken that tour, we would have left New Orleans with only the images of the French Quarter, convinced that the city was in fact in full recovery from Katrina. As tourists, we felt guilty for indulging ourselves in New Orleans in the face of so much suffering. As sociologists, we struggled with how to interpret these contrasting views of the city and our roles as tourists. In taking part in the tourist escapism of the French Quarter, were we contributing to the problem of disconnect between the French Quarter and other parts of New Orleans? Was there a more sociologically informed way that we could have toured the devastated areas, perhaps by requesting a tour as part of the conference? By asking local arrangements to sponsor an alternative tour with local academics and activists who could talk about areas of the city? While it was too late to do any of this, we were compelled to learn a sociological lesson from our trip. Analyzing and contrasting the tourist front-stage of New Orleans with the backstage of the devastated parts of the city was one way to do this.

Dramaturgy and Post-Katrina New Orleans

Is it possible to view the different rates of recovery in varying parts of New Orleans through a sociological lens? If so, what type of theory drives that lens? The conflict approach addresses the race, class, and gender inequalities existing in New Orleans both before and after Katrina (see for example Childs 2007; Dyson 2006; Hartman and Squires 2006; Reed 2006). Issues such as which residents were most devastated by the levee breaks, which residents lacked the possibility of returning home to New Orleans, and even who could afford to buy a private trailer, as opposed to the FEMA rental, all speak to a conflict theory approach. However, after our experiences in New Orleans, we were also struck by the Goffman-esque qualities of our excursion, and how New Orleans serves as a large-scale example of dramaturgy.

Dramaturgy refers to the sociological presentation of self in everyday life, as coined by Erving Goffman (1959). Dramaturgy views the social scene as a stage. The "front-stage" is the formal space where performances reinforce social identity and help manage impressions. These performances are assisted with props, roles, and the delivery of lines to fellow "actors." In contrast, the "backstage" is the informal setting where these same social actors assemble their props, prepare themselves for more formal settings, and are not concerned with impression management. Initially used to examine intimate social interactions, dramaturgy can also be applied to larger social settings. For example, the French Quarter can be understood as the front-stage of New Orleans. The contrasting backstage can be understood as the various parishes and neighborhoods surrounding the French Quarter—the places of New Orleans that are still in states of Post-Katrina ruin.

The props within the French Quarter, which speak to the area being a front-stage, are plenty: an absence of Katrina-wrought catastrophe, fresh plants, green grass, Mardi Gras celebrations, and open businesses. Many tourists who enter New Orleans post-Katrina may only venture into this front-stage area of the French Quarter. In this space, the workers and residents of New Orleans exude a celebratory and triumphant façade. Workers smile, they pose and talk to tourists, and they give the impression that although Katrina was a difficulty to live through, they survived the worst of it and were fortunate in comparison to others. The French Quarter itself is clearly delineated by four perimeter streets, therefore encasing the front-stage completely. Most tourists are scared to wander past this perimeter, which leads to the success of dramaturgy in New Orleans. What purpose does this front-stage serve?

If one left New Orleans only having seen the tourist French Quarter and, thus, the front-stage, the message that they would return home with would be that New Orleans is indeed on the mend, and that it is a fun, energetic city ready to give tourists the samples of the New Orleans they would expect: Mardi Gras celebrations, wonderful architecture, Louisiana food, shopping, and constant reveling on Bourbon Street. The spectacle of New Orleans is structured by consumption and is marketed to tourists through this front-stage (Gotham 2002). In fact, the organization of the front-stage all but eliminates tourists' ability *not* to consume, since the city's economy relies heavily on tourism (Ritzer and Liska 1997, 104). However, despite the importance of tourism for the city, the front-stage also functions to veil both the still devastated state of New Orleans and the desperate outside help the city needs in order to pick itself back up; New Orleans is still suffering.

However, we suggest that once a person leaves the French Quarter, they enter the backstage of New Orleans. As tourists, the bus tour showed a glimpse of backstage, Katrina-ravaged New Orleans. Here, the props that are so meticulously assembled in the front-stage are absent. The trees are not growing greenery, the houses are not bathed in new paint, and the broken windows have not been replaced with smooth shiny glass. Geographically, the backstage is much larger than the front-stage of New Orleans. In this backstage, the scope of devastation is amplified because of the stark contrast to the French Quarter; while the French Quarter overflows with tourist shops, the grocery stores and retail shops in the surrounding parishes and neighborhoods are closed for business. In contrast to the houses that are neatly assembled and painted in the French

Quarter, the neighborhoods in surrounding parishes are in shambles, with entire houses collapsed or demolished.

Taking a tour of the areas still devastated by Katrina opened our eyes to the disparities between the tourist front-stage and the backstage of New Orleans. A chance meeting with a cabbie on our last day suggested that even the backstage that we were allowed to glimpse as tourists may have been a more upbeat and, therefore, front-stage portrayal of the city.

On our last day in New Orleans, we decided to go to places in which we had not yet ventured. After walking for a couple of hours, we wandered into the Praline Connection, a soul food restaurant, for lunch. This was our last chance at "authentic" Creole cuisine before returning to New York. After eating a fried clam po' boy sandwich, chicken, and rice with gravy, we called a cab to pick us up. The cabby seemed surprised that he was picking up two white women from the restaurant. He said, "Do you have any idea where you just ate?" After responding that no, we didn't, he said, "Girls, that's a taste of home, is what that is." We were amused with his affection for the restaurant, amplified by his yearnings to run in to get some gumbo "to go." Upon returning to the cab, he wanted to know how two white women had found their way to that part of town and how we knew what soul food was. We explained to him that we were sociologists attending a conference, and we were in New Orleans as conference participants trying to learn about how things really were after Katrina; and, oh yeah, we happened to like soul food. He laughed, telling us we would never hear the whole story of how things really were because: 1) we were tourists, and 2) we were white.

The cabdriver explained that race and class are important factors in New Orleans. He first wanted to know how we came to see the different areas of New Orleans. Upon learning that we took a tour to visit the devastation, he wanted to know whether the tour guide was a white man or a black man. Further, the cabby wanted to know whether we were led into any houses that had to be gutted, or if we viewed them from the street. Also, he wanted to know where the tour guide lived, and whether *his* house had been ruined in the wake of the storm. We had to admit that our tour guide was white, we hadn't seen the inside of any houses, and our guide's house was not completely destroyed from the aftermath of Katrina. Point taken. Our cabdriver proclaimed that it was too bad that we were on the way to the airport, because he'd give us a tour of some of the predominantly African American neighborhoods, including his own family's home. This, he said, would give us an idea of what was really occurring in New Orleans, devastation that we could not even fathom.

This conversation led us to postulate that there are backstages upon backstages; the extent that any tourist will understand the scope of the devastation really relies on how willing (and knowledgeable) the person introducing them to New Orleans is to display the backstage realities of the city. In addition, Ritzer (2004) states that performances meant for tourists are "...often watered down, if not eviscerated, with esoteric or possibly offensive elements removed" (176). As tourists, we are aware that we were exposed to the backstage from a tourist position. Our tour was informed by the stories of a tour-guide and experienced from the air-conditioned comfort and safety of a van. Each resident of New Orleans has a different backstage. They have experienced this backstage as homelessness, in the process of rebuilding their homes, or from entirely different locales. Certainly as tourists, we didn't have to live there, we didn't experience the destruction firsthand, and we don't live with the aftermath of Katrina on a personal level.

As sociologists, we hope to convey that the tourist perception of New Orleans—that New Orleans is essentially the French Quarter—is problematic. The representations of the French Quarter, as seen both in-person and in the mass media, are very narrow windows into what is really going on in Post-Katrina New Orleans. The French Quarter shows outsiders only the front-stage and, therefore, encourages them to forget and marginalize the continuing devastation of this historic city. At the same time, it is problematic not to resume tourism, especially in a city such as New Orleans that relies so heavily on it for economic continuance. While New Orleans residents may never become accustomed to tours through their neighborhoods, tours of "the closed-off spaces or 'back regions' of everyday life" may "demystify our notions of 'the other' in all of its manifold forms" (Rojek and Urry 1997, 19). Being aware of the concepts of dramaturgy empowers tourists to walk away from their post-Katrina trips to New Orleans with a broader and more critical appraisal of the city and its state of (dis)repair.

Notes

1. We wrote this narrative after our first trip to New Orleans, February 2007. It is important for the reader to understand that our interpretation of the city is filtered through our eyes as tourists. Our references to restaurants, nightlife, and activities to do in New Orleans should be read as tourist-based references. We consulted other travelers and tourist guides to construct an agenda of where to go while in New Orleans. The French Quarter is often seen as the "real" New Orleans by travelers and "tourist" New Orleans by residents. Our experiences are grounded within this tourist perspective. We do not claim to have knowledge of the daily life

of residents of the city; rather, we wrote this narrative to specifically reflect on the experiences and perspectives of tourists in New Orleans seventeen months post-Katrina.

References

Childs, John Brown, ed. 2007. *Hurricane Katrina: Response and responsibilities*. Santa Cruz: New Pacific Press.
Dyson, Michael Eric. 2006. *Come hell or high water: Hurricane Katrina and the color of disaster*. Cambridge: Basic Civitas Books.
Goffman, Erving. 1959. *The presentation of self in everyday life*. New York: Anchor Books.
Gotham, Kevin Fox. 2002. Marketing Mardi Gras: Commodification, spectacle, and the political economy of tourism in New Orleans. *Urban Studies* 39: 1735-1756.
Hartman, Chester, and Gregory D. Squires, eds. 2006. *There is no such thing as a natural disaster: Race, class, and Hurricane Katrina*. New York: Routledge.
Reed, Betsy, ed. 2006. *Unnatural disaster: The nation on Hurricane Katrina*. New York: Nation Books.
Ritzer, George. 2004. *The McDonalization of society*. (revised New Century edition). Thousand Oaks: Pine Forge Press.
Ritzer, George, and Allan Liska. 1997. "McDisneyization" and "post-tourism": Complementary perspectives on contemporary tourism. In *Touring cultures: Transformations of travel and theory*, ed. Chris Rojek, 96-109. New York: Routledge.
Rojek, Chris, and John Urry. 1997. Transformations of travel and theory. In *Touring cultures: transformations of travel and theory*, ed. Chris Rojek, 1-19. New York: Routledge.

CONTRIBUTORS

Derek H. Alderman is a Professor of Geography and a Research Fellow at the Center of Sustainable Tourism at East Carolina University. He received a PhD from the University of Georgia in 1998. Alderman is a cultural geographer specializing in public commemoration and symbolic representation. He has a general interest in popular culture, having written about the geography of NASCAR, Internet as regional electronic folklore, Graceland as a pilgrimage landscape, the politics of Wal-Mart's expansion, the cultural history of kudzu, the naming of streets after Martin Luther King Jr., and hurricane graffiti as a social indicator. Alderman is the author or co-author of 70 journal articles, book chapters, book reviews, commentaries, and encyclopedia entries. He has published in respected journals such as *Annals of the Association of American Geographers*, *Urban Geography*, *Area*, *Southern Cultures*, *Journal of Geography*, and *Geographical Review*. In 2008, he co0authored (with Owen Dwyer) *Civil Rights Memorials and The Geography of Memory*, published by the Center for American Places and University of Georgia Press.

Carl L. Bankston III is Professor and Chair of Sociology, and Co-Director and Coordinator of the Asian Studies Program at Tulane University in New Orleans. He is author or editor of fifteen books and over 100 journal articles and book chapters. His books have received a variety of awards, including the Thomas and Znaniecki Award for outstanding book in international migration, the Louisiana Library Association Literary Award, the Mid-South Sociological Association Distinguished Book Award, and the Stanford M. Lyman Distinguished Book Award. His areas of research and publication include international migration, ethnic studies, Asian American studies, sociology of religion, and sociology of education. Bankston is past president-elect and program chair of the Mid-South Sociological Association.

Kristen Barber is an Assistant Professor of Sociology at Southern Illinois University, Carbondale. Her areas of interests include gender inequality, work & occupations, sociology of the body, and qualitative research methods. She is currently studying the effects men's increasing participation in the beauty industry has on the organization and experience of labor amongst women beauty works. Other projects include the impact virtual spaces have on ethnographic research and the subjective experiences of sociologists who experienced Hurricane Katrina (forthcoming in *Critical Sociology*). She is author or co-author of several journal articles, book chapters, and encyclopedia entries, and she has received paper awards from the Mid-South Sociological Association and the Pacific Sociological Society. Barber earned her Masters in Sociology from Tulane University in New Orleans, where she lived before, during, and after Hurricane Katrina.

Pamela Behan is an Assistant Professor of Sociology at Our Lady of the Lake College. Her teaching focuses on medical sociology, research methods, social problems, and women in developing nations while her research focuses on health inequality and the comparative politics of health care policy. Behan received her Bachelors in Nursing from the University of Kansas in 1971 and her Doctorate in Sociology from the University of Colorado at Boulder in 2000. She is author of *Solving the Health Care Problem: How Other Nations Succeeded and Why the United States Has Not* (SUNY Press 2007). Behan is most recently interested in how health care decisions are affected by health insurance arrangements and finances.

Donna Maria Bonner is a native New Orleanian who holds a PhD in Cultural Anthropology from the State University of New York at Buffalo. Since that time, Bonner has worked as an oral historian and conducted research on inter-ethnic relations in Belize, Central America. At the time of Hurricane Katrina, Bonner was an instructor at the University of New Orleans and held a post-doctoral position in African Diaspora Studies at Tulane University. She now lives in Austin, Texas, where she is writing a memoir with ethnographic reflection concerning her experiences of Hurricane Katrina.

Nicole Buras was born and raised in Boothville-Venice, Louisiana, "at the end of the world." As a child and young woman she was a commercial-shrimper, as were most of the men in the area—and almost none of the women. Nicole received her Associates Degree from Nunez Community College and her Bachelors Degree from the University of Louisiana at Lafayette. In 2007, Nicole earned her Masters degree in Sociology at the University of New Orleans.

Carolyn Corrado is a Doctoral candidate in Sociology at the University at Albany, State University of New York, and teaches in the Humanities and Social Sciences department at The Hotchkiss School. Her specialties include gender, racial identities, and youth cultures. She has published on the topic of Gender Identities & Socialization and of Toys in the *Encyclopedia of Gender and Society* (forthcoming in 2008). She is frequently sought as a presenter on sociological pedagogical issues, and has developed teaching workshops for the University at Albany, the Eastern Sociological Society, and Sociologists for Women in Society. Her teaching activities have been included in the *ASA Syllabi and Teaching Materials* collections. Corrado is a member of the Career Development Committee of Sociologists for Women in Society and the Committee on the Status of Women of the Eastern Sociological Society.

Kirsten A. Dellinger is an Associate Professor of Sociology and Chair of the Department of Sociology and Anthropology at the University of Mississippi. She has published articles on workplace culture and sexual harassment, workplace dress norms, the construction of masculinities in organizations in *Gender & Society*, *Gender Issues*, and *Social Problems*. In 2010, she published an edited book "Gender and Sexuality in the Workplace' with Christine L. Williams. Current ongoing projects include a study of gender dynamics at work in the catfish industry and an in-depth interview study of members of an NSF-funded survey research team working on the Mississippi Gulf Coast after Hurricane Katrina. The latter study explores the methodological implications of disaster research and the subjective experiences of disaster researchers.

Glenn W. Gentry is a currently teaching at The State University of New York College at Cortland. In 1996, he received his Bachelors from Texas A&M University in Geography with a specialization in Environmental Policy and Management. In 2004, he earned his Masters from East Carolina University with a certificate in Rural Development. His research at East Carolina focused on the representation and commodification of dissonant histories and memories through ghost walk tourism. Glenn is continuing his study of the connections between memory and landscape through the surge of body art, namely tattoos, that memorialize the trauma and survival of the city of New Orleans and its citizens following Hurricane Katrina. This research does not treat tattoos as passive memories, but as active representations of once and continued traumas hidden and evident in the landscape and memories of New Orleans. This is part of a larger interest in how places are represented through geographical images in often overlooked and undervalued places.

Timothy J. Haney is an Assistant Professor of Sociology at Mount Royal University in Calgary, Alberta, Canada. His research spans several subfields of sociology including urban sociology, workplace inequalities, environmental justice, and the sociology of disaster. He was a resident of New Orleans before, during, and after Hurricane Katrina. Since 2005, his research has increasingly focused on the inequalities exposed and created by the storm.

Andrea Wilbon Hartman is a Doctoral Student in Sociology and McNair Fellow at the University of Illinois at Urbana-Champaign. She earned her Masters Degree from Tulane University with a thesis entitled "Casinos and Crime: A Sociological Investigation of the Relationship Between Gambling and Crime Rates in Louisiana." Her current research endeavors focus on the intersectionality of race, gender, and class, and urban redevelopment. Hartman was living in New Orleans during Hurricane Katrina, and was forced to temporarily relocate to New York City where she was a teaching assistant at Columbia University. Upon her return to New Orleans, she engaged in studies such as the Neighborhood Change Survey, which is dedicated to understanding the social impacts Hurricane Katrina has had on the New Orleans area.

Danielle Antoinette Hidalgo received her Ph.D. from University of California, Santa Barbara. She completed three years of graduate study at Tulane University in New Orleans. Working for the Southern Sociological Society's Annual Conference in New Orleans, she co-organized a Silent Auction for the SSS Katrina Fund, Gulf Coast Historically Black Colleges and Universities, and the ASA Minority Scholarship Fund. Additionally, she organized a panel session that directly led to this book project. Her areas of interest include gender, sexuality, the sociology of the body, immigration, Asian and Asian American studies, the sociology of development, and Southeast Asia with a particular emphasis in Thailand. She is co-editor, with Carl L. Bankston III, of *Immigration in U.S. History: An Encyclopedia survey of U.S. Immigration* (Salem Press 2006) and has authored or co-authored numerous journal articles and book chapters.

Ruth S. Idakula is a native Nigerian who has lived in the United States for twenty years. She is a mother of three whose passions lie in justice and human rights. She has lived in New Orleans for the past eleven years and has since returned after Hurricane Katrina. With a background in psychology and sociology, she has worked as an advocate for children, domestic abuse survivors, and the homeless. Idakula currently works for the City of New Orleans.

Jeffrey T. Jackson is an Associate Professor in the Department of Sociology and Anthropology at the University of Mississippi. His research focuses on the processes of globalization in the developing world. His recently published book, *The Globalizers: Development Workers in Action* (The Johns Hopkins University Press 2005), explores how the international development profession actively promotes various globalization agendas in the country of Honduras. This analysis includes a discussion of the relief assistance and rebuilding efforts following Hurricane Mitch in 1998. A resident of Oxford, Mississippi, Jackson, like many throughout the region, became involved in the post-Katrina relief efforts on the Mississippi Gulf Coast. He has visited the Mississippi Gulf Coast and New Orleans several times since the Hurricane and has become interested in the similarities and differences between the Hurricane Mitch and the Hurricane Katrina disasters.

Deanna Meyler is a Research Scientist with Higher Ed Holdings in Dallas, Texas where she is collecting data that address education as an inequality issue among teachers and students in disadvantaged schools. She holds a PhD in Sociology from the University of Nebraska-Lincoln. Her research interests include race, class and gender inequalities, environmental sociology, and qualitative research methods. Her recent research examines the role of enculturation in determining mental health and substance use outcomes among Latino youth, empowerment among Latinas along the United States/Mexico border, and social inequalities in the radical environmental movement. She has published studies on the health impact of acculturation among Latinos and health concordance among married couples.

Jessica W. Pardee is an Assistant Professor of Sociology at the Rochester Institute of Technology who came to New Orleans as an undergraduate at Tulane University. Interested in issues of poverty, housing policy and urban development, she remained in New Orleans for graduate school. At the time of the storm, Jessica had lived in New Orleans for ten years and was preparing to study the relocation experiences of women from two public housing sites for her doctoral dissertation. However, due to the massive flooding of the city and one of her research communities, Pardee reorganized her work to examine the post-disaster survival of these same women. Her interests centered on how women with limited incomes rebuilt their lives and re-established housing and survival security following the storm. While she returned to New Orleans to live in early October 2006, after nine months, she found an instructor position at the University of Central Florida, where she remained until July 2010. Jessica graduated with a Ph.D. from Tulane University in May 2009.

Tamara L. Smith is an Assistant Professor of Sociology at Westfield State College. Her specialties include families and aging. She has published papers in *The Gerontologist*, the *Journal of Gerontological Social Work*, and *Research on Social Work Practice*. She has given numerous talks and workshops on professional development and teaching at the local, regional, and national levels, and several of her teaching activities have been included in the ASA Syllabi and Teaching Materials collections. She received the Paul Meadows Excellence in Teaching Award, the University at Albany Outstanding Leadership Award, and was the recipient of the Initiatives for Women Presidential Fellowship at the University at Albany. Smith was the 2005-2007 co-chair of the Committee on the Status of Women for the Eastern Sociological Society and is currently on the Steering Committee for the Carework Network and the 2007-2009 chair of the Career Development Committee of Sociologists for Women in Society.

Russell Stockard Jr. is an Associate Professor of Communication at California Lutheran University with research interests in globalization, cultural studies, disaster studies, diaspora studies, information, communication technologies (ICTs) and social movements, environmental communication, and Latin American/Caribbean Studies. He served on the International Advisory Board of Radio for Peace International, Colón, Costa Rica, where he did broadcast journalism. His publications include the *African American Consumer Handbook*, "The Social Impact of Gender and Games" in Eileen Trauth, (ed.), *Encyclopedia of Gender and Information Technology* (2006), "Dimensions of Sustainable Diversity in Information Technology: Applications to the IT College Major and Career Aspirations among Underrepresented High School Students of Color," Goran Trajkovski, (ed.), *Diversity in Information Technology Education: Issues and Controversies* (2006), and *AfroGEEKS* (2006). Following the

Haitian earthquake, he spent a month in the capital, Port-au-Prince, where he blogged on conditions there in his blog *Three Suns, Thick Culture* and *HaitiRewired*. He is currently working on book chapters on environmental justice, Katrina and the BP oil spill and ecocriticism, digital diasporas and postcoloniality in Katrina and 9/11 literature, music, and other texts.

Russell L. (R.L.) Stockard taught History and Geography, and was a professional journalist for more than fifty years. He taught at Florida A&M University, Southern University Baton Rouge, and Southern University New Orleans. His journalism career began in the 1950s. While at Southern University Baton Rouge, he observed that sports activities at historically black colleges and high schools were systematically overlooked. To address this shortcoming, he became the first African American staff sportswriter on a non-black daily in the United States, serving on both the States-Times (Baton Rouge) and the States-Item (New Orleans) newspapers. Stockard helped found the original Southwestern Athletic Conference (SWAC) Commissioner's Office in 1974, occupying posts as public relations director, sports information director, and compliance officer. He also belonged to the committee that established the Bayou Classic football game between Grambling State University and Southern University. He successfully combined the professions of college teaching and sports writing. His former students continue to serve their cities, states, and nation.

Sarah Stohlman studied in the Department of Sociology at the University of Southern California. Her research focused on Central American immigrant Pentecostalism in Los Angeles and in New Orleans. Her article, "At Yesenia's House... Central American Immigrant Pentecostalism, Congregational Homophily, and Religious Innovation in Los Angeles," published in *Qualitative Sociology,* received both the Distinguished Graduate Student Paper Award from the Pacific Sociological Association and an honorable mention for the Graduate Student Paper Award from the Society for the Scientific Study of Religion. Stohlman lives in New Orleans where she teaches pre-school.

M. Belinda Tucker is a Professor of Psychiatry and Biobehavioral Sciences at UCLA. Tucker has participated in the direction of several landmark studies, including the National Survey of Black Americans and a national survey of Jamaica that examined psychosocial risks for HIV infection and AIDS. She is currently directing a NICHD-funded seven-year re-interview of residents of 21 U.S. cities (including New Orleans) that examines the social context, as well as social and psychological correlates, of family formation behaviors and attitudes. She is co-director of an ethnographic examination of transition to adulthood in three culturally distinct groups of African-descended adolescents in Los Angeles (also NICHD). Tucker serves on a number of national panels and directs the Family Research Consortium IV, which is a national network of family mental health scholars. She also directs the FRC IV postdoctoral training program. Her writings have centered on family, marriage, and personal relationships.

Stan C. Weeber (Ph.D., University of North Texas, 2000) is an Associate Professor of Sociology and Criminal Justice at McNeese State University in Lake Charles, Louisiana. His interests in sociology include storytelling sociology, political sociology, social movements, and sociological theory. The author or editor of 18 books, his work has appeared in *The American Sociologist*, *The Sociological Quarterly*, the *Journal of Public Management and Social Policy*, *Journal of Sociology*, *Social Work and Social Welfare*, *International Review of Modern Sociology*, the *Canadian Review of Sociology and Anthropology*, the *Contemporary Law and Justice Journal*, the *Journal of Popular Culture*, the *Journal of Law, Politics, and Societies*, the *Journal of Global Analysis*, and several other journals. In addition, Weeber serves on the editorial boards of four international sociology journals. In 2010, he participated in the Oxford Roundtable on Social Justice, a social issues think tank at Oxford University.

INDEX

Alienation, 207
American Red Cross, 86, 109, 112, 115, 119, 122, 123, 164, 196
Anomie, 113
Armstrong, Louis, 162
Astrodome, 43, 57-59, 121
Bateman, J. M., 66
Berger, P., 215, 222
Berger, R. J., 1, 5, 89
Blaikie, P., 51, 63
Blasé, 6, 80, 82, 87, 90, 153-155, 157-158, 162-168
Bourdieu, P., 15-16, 138
Bricolage, 209-210
Bureaucracy, 6, 27, 44, 75, 132-137, 139-140, 210
Coleman, J. S., 29
Collective
    Consciousness, 63
    Effervescence, 108, 200
    Memory, 144-145, 197
    Trauma, 160
Collins, P., 42
Collins, R., 110
Communitas, 200
Convention Center, 17, 29, 40, 64, 72
Csikszentmihalyi, M., 206
Culture of Fear, 144
Cutter, S., 68
Department of Agriculture, 134
Department of Education, 32
Department of Family Service (DFS), 131, 134
Department of Housing and Urban Development, 44
Department of Transportation, 112, 116

De Waal, A., 73
Dramaturgy, 100, 233-234, 236
Du Bois, W. E. B., 13
Durkheim, E., 108, 113, 200, 202, 209-210, 213
Dyson, M. E., 69, 233, 237
Eckstein, S., 108
Edwards, B., 66
Emotional Labor, 89, 109
Erikson, K., 156, 160
Farm Bureau, 116
Federal Emergency Management Agency (FEMA), 27, 31, 39, 44, 86, 112, 116-117, 138-139, 159-161, 165, 186, 192, 206-208, 226, 228, 230, 232-233
Fleur-de-lis, 189, 194-195
Folklore, 208, 238
Foote, K. E., 187, 238
Foucault, M., 132
Frame
    Gown, 94, 96-97, 99, 102-103
    Primary, 93-94, 99, 114, 214,
    Town, 94-100, 102, 104,
Fuchs, J., 107, 108, 111, 115, 124, 125
Giddens, A., 3
Glassner, B., 143
Goffman, E., 15, 83, 89, 90, 93-100, 215, 233, 237,
Gottdiener, M., 30
Habitus, 15-16, 137-139
Halbwachs, M., 143-145
Harding, S., 50
Hochschild, A., 6, 83, 87, 90
hooks, b., 13
Houston Food Bank, 53

Hurricane
    Betsy, 36, 65, 68, 73, 141, 143-144, 147, 149, 213, 216, 218, 220
    Camille, 213, 216, 218, 220
    Mitch, 114
    Rita, 5-6, 49-50, 59-60, 70, 100-103, 172-174, 177-178, 180-182, 213, 217
Hutchinson, R., 30
Iles, C., 94
Intersectionality, 63, 74
Jesse Tree, The, 51-57
Jones, R., 75
Kellner, H., 215, 222
Klinenberg, E., 74
Lareau, A., 28
Lee, Spike, 69, 224
Lowe, S., 107, 110, 113, 126
Marx, K., 82, 207-209
Meritocracy, 45, 53
Micro Relief, 114
Mid-South Sociological Society (MSSA), 27
Miller, P. J., 70
Mills, C. Wright, 3, 28
Molotch, H., 134-135
Morial, Mayor, 145
Musick, M. A., 109
Nagin, C. Ray, 136, 209, 228
National Guard, 39, 40, 42, 112, 117, 119, 167, 186, 188
Neville, C., 200
New Normal, 5, 103
Oliver, M., 69
Panopticon, 132
Positioning Theory, 75
Quinney, R., 1, 5, 89
Rationality, 5-6, 63, 67-68, 73-74, 84, 88, 133, 140, 145, 154-155, 157, 168
Rebirth Brass Band, 203
Refugee, 22, 26, 72, 96-97, 104, 159-160, 204-205
Ritzer, G., 133, 234, 236
Rochberg-Halton, E., 206

Role Conflict, 83, 90
Salvation Army, 119, 123, 164
Second-lining, 201, 203, 210
Sensationalism, 145
Shapiro, T. M., 44, 69
Simmel, G., 6, 81, 87-88, 90, 154
Simulacra, 166, 169
Social Capital, 29, 60, 97, 109
Social Disaster, 5, 62, 140
Sociological Imagination, 2-3, 28
Sociologist for Women in Society (SWS), 223
Solidarity
    Organic, 213
    Rituals of, 110
    Symbolic, 110
Southern Sociological Society (SSS), 2, 89
Spoiled Identity, 95, 96, 104
Stage
    Front-stage, 89, 233-236
    Backstage, 96, 233-236
Standpoint, 50, 60, 104
St. John, C., 107-108, 111, 115, 124-125
Storytelling Sociology, 1, 2, 4-5, 89, 90
Stranger, The, 87-90, 102
Superdome, 5, 17, 24, 29, 35-41, 43-45, 52, 59-60, 67, 72, 145-146, 224
Sweeney, K. A., 45
Tourism, 7, 32, 48, 50, 63, 201, 205, 210, 224-236
Tuan, Y., 206
Turner, V., 200
United Way, 112
Volunteerism
    Collective-Based, 108
    Spontaneous, 107, 108, 110-111, 113, 125-126
Voyeurism, 30, 117, 167
Weber, M., 73, 132-134, 149, 155
Wilson, J., 107-109, 111
Worker, Ideal Masculine, 83-84, 90

World Bank, (2007) "Budgeting and Budgeting Processes-Participatory Budgeting."

Zimbabwe Christian Alliance (2007) "Background - the Zimbabwe Christian Alliance. Available on http://www.tearfund.org/News/Zimbabwe/Background+the+Zimbabwe an+Christian+Alliance.htm